Hélène Smith

OXFORD STUDIES IN WESTERN ESOTERICISM

Hélène Smith

*Occultism and the Discovery
of the Unconscious*

CLAUDIE MASSICOTTE

OXFORD
UNIVERSITY PRESS

OXFORD
UNIVERSITY PRESS

Oxford University Press is a department of the University of Oxford. It furthers
the University's objective of excellence in research, scholarship, and education
by publishing worldwide. Oxford is a registered trade mark of Oxford University
Press in the UK and certain other countries.

Published in the United States of America by Oxford University Press
198 Madison Avenue, New York, NY 10016, United States of America.

Library of Congress Cataloging-in-Publication Data
Names: Massicotte, Claudie, 1984– author.
Title: Hélène Smith: occultism and the discovery of the unconscious/ Claudie Massicotte.
Description: New York, NY : Oxford University Press, [2023] |
Series: Oxford studies in Western esotericism | Includes bibliographical references and index.
Identifiers: LCCN 2023004894 (print) | LCCN 2023004895 (ebook) | ISBN 9780197680025 (paperback) |
ISBN 9780197680018 (hardback) | ISBN 9780197680032 (epub)
Subjects: LCSH: Smith, Hélène, –1929. | Mediums—France—Biography. | Spiritualism.
Classification: LCC BF1283.S618 M37 2023 (print) | LCC BF1283.S618 (ebook) |
DDC 133.8092 [B]—dc23/eng/20230405
LC record available at https://lccn.loc.gov/2023004894
LC ebook record available at https://lccn.loc.gov/2023004895

DOI: 10.1093/oso/9780197680018.001.0001

Paperback printed by Marquis Book Printing, Canada
Hardback printed by Bridgeport National Bindery, Inc., United States of America

There are more things in heaven and earth, Horatio, than are dreamt of in your philosophy.

Hamlet (1.5.167–68)

Contents

Figures

Acknowledgments

While researching Hélène Smith, I was repeatedly made aware of the fact that authorship, like all intellectual pursuits, is never the fruit of singular endeavors. It is, rather, the product of various dialogues, influences, and encounters—be they with like-minded scholars or long-lost loved ones. This work is no different and would have never come to be without the help and contributions of various colleagues and friends, along with the internalization of mentor's voices and encouragements.

I would first like to thank Professor Laure Murat for her invaluable insights through the early phases of writing and her continued support ever since. Her influence is a constant presence in the following pages, as our discussions and my reading of her various works shaped my understanding of gender, medicine, and madness. Throughout the writing, I also collaborated and shared ideas with various scholars whose research has done much to advance the fields of psychoanalysis, Western esotericism, and spiritualism. I am thankful to Evrard Renaud, Thomas Rabeyron, Philippe Baudouin, Janine de Peyer, Daniel Zamani, Philip Dickinson, Júlia Gyimesi, Christopher Keep, Marlene Tromp, and many others who welcomed my work, shared their scholarship with me, or provided helpful insights on my ideas. I am also grateful to Professor Alain Cohen for his generosity, both in his conversations and in his work. His contributions were invaluable throughout the final stages of this work.

Hélène Smith originated in research conducted while I joined UCLA's Department of French and Francophone Studies as a postdoctoral candidate, thanks to the financial assistance of the Social Sciences and Humanities Research Council of Canada. It was developed through the help of librarians, archivists, and curators from the Université de Genève, the Bibliothèque de Genève, and the Musée Victor Hugo, who offered suggestions, answered questions, and directed me to appropriate resources along the way. I am thankful to these institutions, and the many individuals who opened their doors and helped me navigate within them, for their support.

Lastly, I owe all my gratitude to my husband for accompanying me through the joys and pains of writing and to my family for their unrelenting encouragement.

Introduction

Hélène, or the Ghosts of Depth Psychology

> The phenomenon of the speaking tables does not diminish the nine-
> teenth century, it enlarges it.
>
> —Victor Hugo, *Le livre des tables*[1]

In the very last days of the nineteenth century, two major works were published that effectively transformed the future of psychology. The *Traumdeutung* by Sigmund Freud (1856–1939), first went relatively unnoticed, selling little and reaching only a few interested specialists. In the six years following its publication, the book sold only 351 copies, and its first English translation, *The Interpretation of Dreams*, would have to wait more than a decade.[2] However, as the author's popularity grew in the following years, the book began to circulate widely and is largely known, today, as a cornerstone in the development of theories of the unconscious. Simultaneously, *Des Indes à la planète Mars*, by Théodore Flournoy (1854–1920), initially created a stir in both the popular and scientific press, appeared in three editions and an English translation (*From India to the Planet Mars*) within less than a year, and brought much attention to its author's claims.[3] Having since fallen into oblivion, however, it is today rarely cited, almost always by historians of psychology—most often as a bizarre but fascinating text reminding readers of the historical relations between depth psychology and occultism. In this sense, historian of psychoanalysis Elisabeth Roudinesco considers the work "a nice book that should one day be the object of a film," for instance, by François Truffaut, who might find in its protagonist, Hélène Smith, "a replica of Adèle Hugo."[4] Yet, for this historian, *From India to the Planet Mars* and *The Interpretation of Dreams* offer highly unequal contributions to the history of psychology. Indeed, she writes: "Freud tells the same stories as Flournoy, but in a different language, a language coming from the crepuscule, a new language." As for

Hélène Smith. Claudie Massicotte, Oxford University Press. © Oxford University Press 2023.
DOI: 10.1093/oso/9780197680018.003.0001

Flournoy, he "seems to be sitting between two centuries, one buttock on the epistemological and Romanesque tradition of the nineteenth century, and the other on the moving ground of the twentieth century, toward which he looks desperately, . . . At the opposite of Freud, Flournoy . . . is not an innovator, but a magnetizer *à l'ancienne*."[5]

Such remarks certainly understate the similarities (much more than chronological) between the two works. Flournoy was highly interested in the psychological functions of dreams and spent five years attending the séances of Geneva medium Hélène Smith in order to understand the unconscious origins of her somnambulism and dreamlike visions. Unlike the famous magnetizers of the preceding century, he critically investigated the modalities of the unconscious mind.[6] As in Freud's magnum opus, Flournoy also employed a narrative "I," highly involved in the process of scientific discovery, slowly unfolding a plethora of repressed or unacknowledged ideas, desires, and memories that he found to be the source of Smith's trance creations. Transference and suggestion were also constant problems in Flournoy's reflections, and his work—although imperfectly—incessantly questions his role in the formation of Smith's visions.

Why, then, has *From India to the Planet Mars* escaped scientific and popular memory? In a postface to the 1983 French re-edition of this work, Mireille Cifali reviewed the distinction between Freud and Flournoy's legacies in a different light than Roudinesco. "Freud," she wrote, "uncovered an unconscious marked more by the effects of censure, of disguise, and of its link to the symptom; Flournoy is for his part more sensitive to the intricacies that link the unconscious to artistic creation."[7] In this major psychological work, Flournoy indeed formulated important and original discoveries on the unconscious and the workings of imagination. Yet their systematic integration under a theory of the subject has been forgotten. Their occult history— for it was from an extraordinarily gifted medium that Flournoy conceived them—is perhaps responsible for this forgetting.

In this book, I position Flournoy's work alongside those of many other colleagues of Freud, including Jean-Martin Charcot (1825–1893), Pierre Janet (1859–1947), William James (1842–1910), and Frederic Myers (1843– 1901), whose contributions to the history of psychology have recently been reexamined by historians. Some of these authors paved the way for Freud's discoveries, and others continued to explore the unconscious alongside— or in opposition to—the father of psychoanalysis. But the thread I follow does not weave specifically between these authors' works nor between their varying conceptions of the subject. Rather, it primarily follows Flournoy's medium, whose productions fascinated various investigators of the mind. Among the many authors who were drawn to write on the medium were the linguist Ferdinand de Saussure (1857–1913), the poet André Breton (1896–1966), the art historian and archaeologist Waldemar Deonna (1880–1959), and the psychoanalyst Jacques Lacan (1901–1981). In retrieving and analyzing the lost story of Hélène Smith and those she enchanted, I bring to light the history of a differently schematized unconscious. This unconscious, formulated through the analysis of mediums' somnambulistic and automatic activities, as opposed to hysterical manifestations, constituted a complex machinery, where the dangers and revelations of creativity were constantly threatening the subject with disintegration.

This story is one of occult explorations, a field of study that has, until recently, been largely banished from the history of psychology.[8] However, studies of paranormal experiences were crucial in the formulation of modern understandings of the subject. Philosophers, psychiatrists, and psychopathologists of the late nineteenth century were confronted with a plethora of diseases they could not understand, and their works are filled with references to occult forces, mesmeric cures, and spiritual apparitions. Taking Smith as its main exemplar, this book thus focuses on mediums as a particular category of experimental subjects at the origins of depth psychology.

In his foundational work, *The Discovery of the Unconscious*, Henri Ellenberger remarked: "The role of patients in the elaboration of dynamic psychiatry has been all too neglected and would also be worthy of intensive investigation."[9] Indeed, most pioneers of depth psychology formulated their ideas through only a few cases, a methodology that opens questions concerning the role of patients at the origins of psychological theories. For instance, Pierre Janet pointed out that Charcot's descriptions of hysteria were based on a very limited number of cases. Among them, Blanche (Marie) Wittmann (1859–1913), then referred to as "the Queen of the hysterics," was presented in countless photographs of the *Iconographie de la Salpêtrière* (*The Salpêtrière's Iconography*) and rapidly became a model for the master's definition of hysteria.[10] Histories of psychoanalysis generally begin with Josef Breuer's (1842–1925) patient Anna O., or Bertha Pappenheim (1859–1936), whose story inspired Freud to define the "talking cure" as the primary analytic means to understand and relieve symptoms of hysteria. Dora, or Ida Bauer (1882–1945), a patient whom Freud analyzed while writing *The*

Interpretation of Dreams, also appears as a fundamental character framing the origins of the discipline.

More than fifty years after the publication of Ellenberger's work, historians, psychoanalysts, and feminist scholars have retrieved many details of these patients' lives and their participation in the formulation of psychological concepts. Blanche Wittmann, Anna O., and Dora have now been the objects of innumerable books and articles detailing their impacts on—among others—Charcot's visual understanding of hysterical symptoms,[11] Freud's sexual etiology of hysteria,[12] and his interpretation of transference and countertransference.[13] Such studies have further enlightened the roles of women in intellectual history and the medical constructions of femininity at the turn of the century. However, in neglecting the occult history of modern psychology, contemporary historians have yet to recognize the different contributions of mediums in the field. As with hysterics, these medical subjects were most often women, but their claim to spiritual wisdom transformed their positioning in scientific investigations. In retracing the story of Hélène Smith, the medium who fascinated Théodore Flournoy through her somnambulistic creations of mythologies, images, and languages, this book asks: What lineage can be traced for depth psychology if we find at its origins, not only the symptoms of (female) hysterics, but also the creative productions of (female) mediums? What notions of the body and mind surfaced from performances of mediumship? How did mediums' performances enact, question, or challenge prevalent notions of the mind? And to what extent did their responses to social and cultural norms reveal a different version of women's modes of resistance? Along these lines of inquiry, this book brings forth a different perspective on the history of the unconscious, the role of women in its formulation, and a now-forgotten vision of its creative modalities. This chapter sets the stage for such a story by presenting its protagonists and the context in which they met.

Hélène Smith and Her Scholars

Élise Catherine Müller (1861–1929), yet to become the renowned medium Hélène Smith, was generally described as a healthy-looking, intelligent, and determined woman. Born in Martigny (Valais, Switzerland), on December 9, 1861, she had a younger sister, who died at the age of three, and two older brothers, who pursued successful business careers abroad. Smith, for her part, left school at the age of fifteen to begin working as a clerk in a silk store and remained in the same enterprise, gaining higher status and responsibility in the following years. Théodore Flournoy, who retrieved the records of her school years, noted that she had not distinguished herself "either for good or ill from the point of view of deportment, but she certainly did not reveal the full measure of her intelligence, since she failed to pass her examinations at the end of [her intermediate school] year, a fact which decided her entrance upon apprenticeship."[14] In 1892, when she was in her early thirties, Smith discovered her abilities as a medium and began to hold séances in her home in Plainpalais, a district of Geneva. Her séance room was described as bearing "a certain stamp of elegance." As Flournoy later explained:

> She arranged for herself a small *salon*, coquettish and comfortable in its simplicity. She took lessons in music, and bought herself a piano. She hung some old engravings on her walls, secured some Japanese vases, a jardinière filled with plants, cut flowers in pretty vases, a hanging lamp with a beautiful shade of her own make, a table-cover which she had put together and embroidered herself, some photographs curiously framed according to her own design; and out of this harmonious whole, always beautifully kept, she evolved something original, bizarre, and delightful, conforming well to the general character of her fantastic subconsciousness.[15]

In 1894, Flournoy joined her circle, and he observed her trance experiences until 1900. A professor of psychology at the University of Geneva, he had been in search of a powerful medium to study psychologically for some years in the hope of discovering unknown psychological processes. It is in his work *From India to the Planet Mars* that Müller acquired the pseudonym that made her famous across the ocean. She soon gained the interest of a rich American woman who gave her a monthly rent. Although Smith never accepted payment for her séances, the rent allowed her to quit her previous employment and spend the rest of her days independently while pursuing her spiritualist activities.

Smith's mother, with whom she lived at the time of Flournoy's investigations, was born in Switzerland and spoke only French. Her father, whom she had lost to a sudden death, had lived in Italy and Algeria before moving to Geneva. He spoke Hungarian, German, Italian, Spanish, English, and French, in addition to knowing Greek and Latin. Smith, for her part, had tried to learn German between the ages of twelve and fifteen, but had found herself untalented for languages. Yet, this "beautiful woman about thirty years of age, tall, vigorous, of a fresh, healthy complexion,"[16] as Flournoy described her, invented while in trance some wonderfully complex poems and stories in unknown languages that greatly impressed the artistic and scientific community of Geneva.

Smith's very first spiritual séances began with the visitation and address of the great literary genius Victor Hugo. Hugo, who had cultivated a profound interest in spiritualism during his lifetime, appeared to Smith for the first time in April 1892. He was soon followed by Léopold, or Joseph Balsamo, an alias for Alessandro di Cagliostro, another well-known figure of the spiritualist movement. Cagliostro had been immortalized in a novel by Alexandre Dumas (himself a strong believer in the benefits of mesmerism) as a great magician and magnetizer. Under the latter's influence, Smith described in trance the recollected memories of her past lives, in which she was incarnated as a fifteenth-century "Hindoo" princess and as Queen Marie-Antoinette, on whom Léopold had bestowed his eternal love and devotion. Smith also believed that her soul could travel, while she was entranced, to the planet Mars, from where she brought foreign visions and conversations.

From India to Mars, Smith created stories and drawings of the scenes she witnessed. She also spoke in what she believed were Sanskrit and Martian and even created an alphabet and translations of the later language. Flournoy, who was deeply impressed by her creations, brought experts such as Ferdinand de Saussure to analyze the languages.[17] The writer, philosopher, and semiotician Tzvetan Todorov wrote on the medium many years later and remarked with surprise the passion the linguist displayed for the case: "The analysis of the 'Hindoo' language seems to have fascinated Saussure to a degree that is difficult to fathom. He took the greatest care in commenting upon Mlle Smith's linguistic productions; he attended séances and suggested possible interpretations of her case. As a result, fully half the chapter in which Flournoy deals with the Hindu language is composed of excerpts from Saussure's letters."[18]

When Flournoy began to attend Smith's séances in 1894, he was chair of experimental psychology (a post created for him by the University of Geneva in 1891) but found little interest in his daily work. On December 30, 1892, he wrote to his friend the psychologist and psychical researcher William James: "I do not speak to you of my laboratory, which bores me more and more and in which I accomplish nothing worth while."[19] Again, he spoke of his disappointment on December 18, 1893, remarking that few students were inclined to pursue research in experimental psychology: "This year, I only have three hard-working students (two of them women!) in the laboratory. . . . My theoretical course brings together, as a rule, about 35 regular visitors. The fact that scarcely one-tenth frequent the laboratory (which costs nothing) proves to me that experimental psychology is not yet in demand here."[20] Perhaps in part to relieve his boredom, he continued: "I try to penetrate into the spiritualistic world of our city, but it is rather difficult. At the present time they do not have very outstanding mediums; I should be very content, indeed, if I were only able to observe closely those who experience the phenomena about which I hear, but they surround themselves with solitude and darkness."[21]

Over the following months, Flournoy presented various lectures on the occult, but believed he displeased both the medical and the spiritual communities by not adopting a firm position on the reality of occult phenomena. He regretted that the séances he attended did not present the remarkable manifestations that could lead to a decisive conclusion concerning the objective existence of occult experiences. However, his approach began to change shortly after he joined Smith's circle. He wrote to James, in a letter of August 13, 1895:

> I was forgetting to tell you what has interested me most during the last six months; it is a certain medium (nonprofessional, unpaid) of a spiritualist group into which they agreed to accept me in spite of my neutral position. I have attended about twenty of the séances, of which a third were here at my home; psychologically, it is very interesting, because this woman is a veritable museum of all possible phenomena and has a repertoire of illimitable variety: she makes the table talk,—she hears voices,—she has visions, hallucinations, tactile and olfactory,—automatic writing—sometimes complete somnambulism, catalepsy, trances, etc.

Flournoy interpreted the medium's trance discourses as manifestations of the unconscious. He considered her past lives and Martian travels as "romances of the subliminal imagination" and demonstrated that many of her claims originated from a book she had read in childhood. While the reading had long been forgotten by her conscious self, it had remained imprinted in other layers of her psyche and had been revived during her trance sessions. Thus, Flournoy interpreted Smith's trance discourses as cryptomnesia—the expression of long forgotten memories that occurred without the subject's conscious recognition. He traced Smith's mediumship to "the influence, so often verified, of emotional shocks and often certain traumatisms upon mental dissociation."[22] His examination further demonstrated that Smith experienced in trance "a large and varied assortment of sensory and motor disturbances which . . . are thoroughly identical with those that may be observed in cases of hysteria (where they are more permanent)."[23] A year following the publication of his work, Flournoy also published *Nouvelles observations sur un cas de somnambulisme avec glossolalie* (*New Observations on a Case of Somnambulism with Glossolalia*), in which he reviewed and responded to the criticism of his work and deepened his understanding of the unconscious.

Flournoy's interpretation, unsurprisingly, did not please the spiritualist circles in which Hélène Smith began acquiring increasing fame. In a text entitled *Autour "Des Indes à la planète Mars"* (*Surrounding "From India to the Planet Mars"*), published by the Société d'Études Psychiques de Genève in 1901, one spiritualist remarked:

> I would be curious to know in what way the subliminal explanation is more normal than the spiritual explanation, how our view is more occult than his. For indeed, a subliminal . . . that has promptness, finesse, a surprisingly delicate and exquisite flair . . . a remarkably calm and pondered imagination, attached to the real and the probable, a wonderfully talented and prodigiously fertile subconscious . . . , a subliminal that makes the medium write in a different hand, that changes a soft female voice into the deep, low, and slow voice of a man, . . . such a subliminal seems to me, at the very least, as much an occult, implausible explanation as the one advocated and accepted by spiritualists.[24]

Although she had read *From India* before publication, Smith also rejected Flournoy's theories. In the years following his publication, their divergent views, along with a dispute over the monetary revenues of Flournoy's study, brought an end to their collaboration.

Between 1903 and 1915, Smith's beliefs developed into a new form of creativity. She took lessons in painting shortly after the publication of Flournoy's work and began to form large tableaux representing the visions she received during her intercourse with her spiritual guide—now Jesus Christ himself. These large panel paintings depicted life-size figures from the New Testament. After long consideration, she decided to sign them under her birth name, Élise Müller, thereby distancing herself once more from the identity Flournoy had attributed to her. Yet, not considering herself the author—nor the owner—of the paintings, she never brought herself to sell them and was even advised by her spirit guide to wait before attaching *any* name to the paintings. At her death in June 1929, at the age of sixty-eight, Smith willed her works to the Musée d'Art et d'Histoire de Genève, where they were exhibited for some weeks in November 1929. The museum received "a large influx of visitors," and the exhibition moved to Paris in 1932.[25] That same year, the paintings became the object of a book by Waldemar Deonna, art historian, professor at the University of Geneva, and director of the Musée d'Art et d'Histoire de Genève between 1920 and 1951. Deonna's *De la planète Mars en Terre Sainte* (*From Mars to the Holy Land*) reproduced many of Smith's creations along with manuscript excerpts documenting the realization of her paintings. After residing in the museum and spending some time in the psychological laboratory founded by Flournoy, they were acquired by members of the Hungarian branch of her paternal filiation who had contested her will. With the exception of the reproductions included in Deonna's work, most have since disappeared.[26]

After her death, Smith's works enjoyed a revival of interest through authors of the surrealist movement. André Breton considered her "by far the richest" of all mediums and he reproduced a number of her creations in his work "The Automatic Message" for his magazine *Le Minotaure* (*The Minotaur*). Breton had learned of the medium through the Paris exhibition and Deonna's study of her works.[27] Referring to Smith as the "muse of automatic writing," he found profound artistic inspiration in her séances. Breton's experiments through the surrealists' "period of sleeping fits" revealed powerful mediumistic power in Robert Desnos, whose productions successfully reproduced the material of séances. Secularizing the practice of trance, these authors retrieved, through Smith, powerful modes of unconscious creativity.

As for Flournoy, his translator and historian of psychology Sonu Shamdasani explains: "*From India to the Planet Mars* was [his] masterpiece. Never again would he find such a subject, though he went to great lengths attempting to do just that."[28] In 1911, he published a work called *Esprits et mediums* (*Spirits and Mediums*), which compiled the results of a survey he had distributed among spiritualist circles during the time of his investigations with Hélène Smith. The documents included seventy-two responses, varying from a few lines to thirty pages. Flournoy had further visited "almost all [his] correspondents to better record their observations and additional clarifications" and reviewed their "notes, minutes, automatic writings and drawings, etc.," even attending a few séances.[29] Yet he regretted its results, having found "in all nothing that went beyond the ordinary, nothing, for instance, that approaches the beautiful subliminal imagination, creator of languages and myths, that at the same period I saw unfold in the somnambulisms of Mlle Smith."[30] A second section of this work included a compilation of Flournoy's writings on spiritualism's psychological mechanisms and was translated by Hereward Carrington as *Spiritism and Psychology*. Here Flournoy iterated his wish that, one day, "the subliminal psychology of Myers and his followers and the abnormal psychology of Freud and his school [will] succeed in meeting, and will supplement and complete each other."[31] The book paved the way for such encounters, including sections on the subliminal psychology of psychical researcher Frederic Myers, studies of the psychological roles of benevolent and deceiving "spirits," and observations on the mediumship of Eusapia Paladino (1854–1918). The same year, he also published a volume on the philosophy of William James, a work originating from a course he had developed for Switzerland's Christian Association of Students. The course had been the result of a moral obligation he felt following his friend's death, a death that occurred only two weeks after the passing of his own wife in August 1909.[32] An avid reader of Freud, Flournoy also taught psychoanalysis for a number of years at the University of Geneva before his own death in 1920.

Spiritualism and the (Dis)enchantment of Modernity

When Smith discovered her mediumistic powers, the conjunction of technological developments and the advancement of a new scientific materialism had already led to the formation of spiritualism as a central movement in modern understandings of the occult.[33] Encompassing a plethora of exceptional experiences from telepathy and clairvoyance to spiritual possession and automatic writing, the spiritualist movement provided an alternative to the era's growing secularization, or to what Max Weber defined as disenchantment, by claiming to demonstrate empirically the existence of supernatural phenomena.

The spiritualist movement originated on March 31, 1848, when two young American sisters, Kate (1837–1892) and Margaret (1833–1893) Fox, began communicating with a spirit through a simple code of knockings in their house in Hydesville, New York.[34] Friends and neighbors rapidly shared the peculiar incident they had witnessed, and infatuation with spiritual communications rapidly spread across the country. Soon, the expressions "turning tables" and "spirit-rapping" entered the popular press to describe the mysterious phenomena emanating from the Fox sisters' séances. Now famous across America, touring in both family homes and public amphitheaters to reveal the words of the dead, the Fox sisters founded the Spiritualist Church in 1852. The new religious movement grew rapidly on an international scale, reaching England and Germany in 1852 and France in 1853. As a French commentator wrote the same year: "The whole of Europe—what am I saying, Europe, at this moment the world—has its head turned by an experience that consists of making a table turn. We hear from all sides that tables can turn: Galileo himself made less noise on the day he effectively demonstrated that it was in fact the Earth that revolved around the Sun."[35] Carl Gustav Jung confirmed this claim in a 1905 lecture, noting: "In Europe, spiritualism took the form chiefly of an epidemic of table-turning. There was hardly an evening party or dance where the guests did not steal away at a late hour to question the table."[36]

How can the movement's exponential popularity throughout the last half of the nineteenth century be explained within the scientific and intellectual context in Europe and North America? Historians of Western esoteric traditions—and modern occultism more specifically—have remarked upon the apparent paradox of disenchantment. In the words of Egil Asprem, the "very period of disenchantment—the nineteenth and early twentieth centuries—is characterised by a tremendous interest in precisely the sort of ideas that blend religion and science, facts and values. This is the period when spiritualism and modern occultism take shape, and spread rapidly around the globe."[37] While recognizing the increasing "disappearance of 'mysterious and incalculable' forces from the natural world," such scholars have convincingly detailed the rise of modern occultist movements as consequences of (and responses to) the rise of "science and natural philosophy [as] the dominant framework of interpretation in all domains of thought."[38] In an era of positivism, spiritualism proposed to rationally explore invisible forces, thus formulating an apparent compromise between blind adherence to doctrinal faith and entirely materialist world views.

Indeed, from the early days of the movement, spiritualists opened the séance doors to scientists, and well-known academics brought experimental methodologies and instruments to investigate spiritual phenomena. Among

many others, these scientists included Nobel Prize laureate and physicist
Charles Richet (1850–1935), astronomer Camille Flammarion (1842–1925),
physicist and inventor Oliver Lodge (1851–1940), and naturalist and first recipient of the Charles Darwin Medal, Alfred Russel Wallace (1823–1913).
Akin to many adherents of the movement, these authors believed mediums'
abilities, spiritual photography, and materializations could empirically demonstrate the existence of another world, and they saw little contradiction
between their orthodox scientific pursuits and supernatural explorations.[39]
They gathered through international societies for psychical research to
share their discoveries. The very first of these societies, the British Society
for Psychical Research, established in London in 1882, explained that its aim
was to "investigate that large group of debatable phenomena designated by
such terms as mesmeric, psychical, and spiritualistic."[40] Such alliance between mediums, spiritualists, and scientists—though not always without
tensions—provided validation for beliefs in a celestial realm.

Similarly, technological advancements gave credibility to the movement's
imagination: when the Fox sisters introduced spiritual rappings in Hydesville,
the general public was still marveling at the telegraph, invented by Samuel
Morse in 1844. The spiritualist movement reimagined the possibilities
opened by such new technologies of communication that allowed for invisible transmissions across vast distances. Centered on mediums' transmission
of spiritual messages, the movement used the scientific terminology of waves,
radiations, electromagnetic fields, and telegraph lines in order to conceptu-
alize other realms of communication.[41] Such conceptualizations were not
unusual: as Anthony Enns writes, even some of the most renowned inventors
of the century were infatuated with the occult possibilities arising from their
discoveries: "The notion of the brain as an electric battery . . . seemed to provide a plausible scientific explanation for the transmission of thoughts using
electricity, and both Alexander Graham Bell and Thomas Edison conducted
experiments in electrical thought transference around the turn of the century."[42] When the Fox sisters and their followers began touring in America
to demonstrate their mediumistic powers, the comparison of séance communications to the workings of "celestial telegraphs" was common. The term
"medium" itself referenced this new communication technology.[43]

Thus, under the impact of secularization and modernity, spiritualism
presented what Wouter J. Hanegraaff defines "as a direct outcome of the
disenchantment process as formulated by Weber."[44] On the one hand,
"It contained everything now seen as incompatible with a disenchanted

worldview"; on the other hand, it defined "a positive counter-tradition of en-chantment (or, eventually, re-enchantment) by those who felt that the evapo-ration of mystery emptied the world of any deeper meaning."[45] Spiritualism, akin to the larger traditions of Western esotericism to which in pertains, can therefore be viewed, in the words of Henrik Bogdan, as "a third pillar of Western culture, a form of thought that took a middle position between doctrinal faith and rationality."[46] This position was not left unchallenged, as "To the adherents of doctrinal faith . . . this type of knowledge or gnosis smacked of heresy," while, for many established or mainstream scientists, its concerns were irrational and without foundations. Yet, Bogdan continues, "These three forms of knowledge were not watertight compartments, but on the contrary highly complex and inter-connected currents."[47] Smith's story illustrates such complex interconnections, as she worked to reconcile her spiritualist practices with her Christian faith, while inviting scientists to in-vestigate and help her define her experiences. The encounters, conversations, rejections, and recognitions that emerge through the following pages exem-plify how modern occult movements could come to play a significant part in European intellectual history and the development of modern sciences.

Hysteria, Spiritualism, and the Ghosts of Psychoanalysis

Spiritualism came to play a particularly significant role in the formation of modern psychology, as medical authorities began to formulate their own materialist explanations of the spiritual craze. By the turn of the century, to quote Ellenberger, spiritualism "indirectly provided psychologists and psychopathologists with new approaches to the mind" as "a new subject, the medium, became available for experimental psychological investigations, out of which evolved a model of the human mind."[48]

The intricate relations between spiritualism and psychology can largely be traced back to mesmerism and its momentary integration in orthodox med-ical practice through studies in hypnosis. Popularized in Western Europe through the eighteenth and nineteenth centuries, mesmerism was the crea-tion of German physician Franz Anton Mesmer (1734–1815), who suggested that a magnetic force called animal magnetism could be manipulated for the treatment of illnesses. Mesmer believed that such a force permeated the world and that diseases resulted from its disharmony. The magnetizer, a strong-willed individual who was said to control the magnetic force, could redistribute it properly in the ill body by using passes of hands to entrance the patient. In later life Mesmer moved from Germany to Paris, where his technique became highly fashionable. In the words of Patricia Jensen: "When Franz Anton Mesmer introduced to pre-revolutionary Europe his vision of an invisible, universal, superfine, magnetic fluid that surrounded and penetrated all bodies, he did so in an atmosphere already imbued with a host of ideas about vitalistic forces, agents and fluids."[49] During the enactment of trance, the mesmeric cure rapidly became marked by a series of repeated behaviors. These included patients' convulsions, amnesia, and mystical experiences. Many magnetizers also remarked that their patients possessed extraordinary gifts under trance, such as an ability to capture thought, to see at a great distance, and to detect diseases in themselves and others. In 1784, a royal commission, whose members included Benjamin Franklin (1706–1790) and Joseph-Ignace Guillotin (1738–1814), set up to investigate mesmerism. The commission's experts agreed that magnetizers could indeed entrance their subjects and that the latter often claimed feeling better afterward. However, the commission rejected the influence of magnetism and attributed the trance and its effects to individuals' imagination. Both nineteenth-century spiritualists and medical authorities were thus indebted to mesmerism, whose experiments provided a first opportunity to investigate trance and hypnotic states.[50]

In the late nineteenth century, a medical interest for somnambulistic states arose, particularly through studies of hysteria by the head of the Salpêtrière, Jean-Martin Charcot. Charcot, who had noted the similarity between Mesmer's patients and his own, introduced hypnosis at the institution in order to open new experiments on the state of trance. While rejecting the occult elements of magnetism, he used trance to demonstrate and relieve the symptoms of hysteria. Charcot himself linked the states of hypnosis among his patients to the trance states experienced in séance circles. One of his *Lectures sur les maladies du système nerveux* (*Lectures on the Diseases of the Nervous System*) entitled "Spiritisme et hystérie" (Spiritualism and Hysteria) associated these two conditions and identified the weakness of the (prevalently female) nervous system as their cause.[51] Charcot believed hysteria could explain such phenomena of possession, and he retrospectively diagnosed earlier demoniacs, such as Jeanne des Anges and the possessed of Loudun, as hysterics. With colleague Paul Richer (1849–1933), he published *Les démoniaques dans l'art* (*Demoniacs in the Arts*), a work aiming to demonstrate that hysteria was not a product of the nineteenth century, but could be found among many earlier demoniacs, epileptics, and possessed individuals.[52]

After Charcot, many other psychiatrists, psychologists, and psychopathologists studied the manifestations of trance among mesmerists and spiritualists. What they discovered through their studies of trance, however, were different manifestations of the unconscious. In France, Pierre Janet's psychological studies began with experiments on a French peasant woman named Léonie who could apparently carry certain hypnotic commands without the means of direct communications. Janet described his experiments with Léonie in a paper he presented before the Société de Psychologie Physiologique in 1885.[53] He confirmed hypnotizing Léonie from a distance and mentally giving her posthypnotic instructions while she remained under the observation of invited witnesses. At a distance of several kilometers, for instance, Janet would hypnotize his patient and command her to turn on a light at a specific moment of the day.[54]

Carl Gustav Jung (1875–1961), whose work was deeply influenced by Flournoy, wrote a similar psychological study of a medium in his 1902 doctoral dissertation.[55] Acknowledging the importance of Flournoy's mentorship in his *Dreams, Memories, Reflections*, Jung further noted that *From India* had made such an impression on him that he had contacted Flournoy to tell him of his interest in translating the work into German. While he regretted that Flournoy had appointed someone else for the task, Jung visited him in Geneva and came to see him as an important figure during his break with Freudian psychoanalysis. He noted: "As I gradually recognized where Freud's limits lay, I went up to him from time to time, and I talked with him. . . . He put his finger on Freud's rationalism, which made much of him understandable, as well as explaining his onesidedness."[56] The medium under observation through Jung's dissertation was his younger cousin S. W. (Hélène Preiswerk), who impersonated a plethora of spirits during séances. Jung interpreted these spiritual incarnations as unconscious creations of S. W. through which she was shaping different aspects of her own personality.[57]

In Freud's circle, Sándor Ferenczi (1873–1933) also studied mediums. His first psychological publication, which appeared in a Hungarian medical journal in 1899, was devoted to the topic of spiritualism.[58] The very choice of the journal had been suggested to him during an episode of automatic writing. Ferenczi's interest in occultism continued long after this publication, and, along with Jung, he often discussed with Freud the possibility of telepathy and even accompanied the latter to a séance with a Berlin psychic named Frau Seidler.[59] In a letter to Ferenczi from 1911, Freud stated: "Jung writes that we must also conquer occultism and requests permission to undertake a campaign in the realm of mysticism. I see that the both of you can't be restrained. You should at least proceed in harmony with each other; these are dangerous expeditions, and I can't go along there."[60]

Despite Roudinesco's claim that Freud invented "a different language, a language coming from the crepuscule, a new language,"[61] it should be noted that the father of psychoanalysis was not immune to the great epidemics of séances. Propelled by the fascination of his two disciples with the occult, Freud even developed his own investigations into the telepathic abilities proclaimed by many mediums. His 1925 article "The Occult Significance of Dreams," for instance, revealed a cautious belief in the possibility of telepathy by stating: "If reports of telepathic occurrences are submitted to the same criticism as stories of other occult events, there remains a considerable amount of material which cannot be so easily neglected. . . . I believe I have found a class of material which is exempt from the doubts which are otherwise justified."[62] Referring to "experiments" he would have conducted "in [his] private circle," Freud even attempted to explain the process and functioning of telepathy by adding: "I am inclined to draw the conclusion that thought-transference . . . comes about particularly easy at the moment at which an idea emerges from the unconscious, or, in theoretical terms, as it passes over from 'the primary process' to the 'secondary process.'"[63] The experiments mentioned by Freud were those of February 15, 1925, in which—like the magnetizers à l'ancienne—he himself became a medium, analyzing the captured thoughts of his daughter Anna and his disciple Ferenczi. After these experiments, Freud wrote to his colleague and biographer Ernest Jones: "Ferenczi was here recently on Sunday. The three of us carried out experiments in thought-transference. They were remarkably good, particularly those in which I played the medium and then analyzed my associations. The matter is becoming urgent for us."[64]

The Society for Psychical Research also gathered many members whose contributions greatly influenced the development of psychology, including William James and Frederic Myers. Notably, James identified the subconscious self as the source of religious experience. As Júlia Gyimesi explains: "The subconscious self depicted by him lacked the reductive emphasis on human sexuality. Instead, it opened the way towards transcendence."[65] Flournoy was directly influenced by James, and their correspondence demonstrates profound intellectual and personal affinities. Myers, for his part, participated in the propagation of psychoanalysis in Europe, as he was among the first authors to introduce Freud's works in England. His reflections on the subliminal personality also shaped Flournoy's understanding of mediumship. To quote Shamdasani: "Without Myers's concept of the subliminal consciousness—which was informed by James's notions of consciousness— and Myers's psychologization of mediumistic experience, *From India to the Planet Mars* simply could not have been written."[66]

Whether or not these authors endorsed the spiritual origins of trance communications, they were deeply intrigued and preoccupied by séances' manifestations. Through their investigations, the state of trance became a central stage for their formulation of new theories of the unconscious. To quote William James, spiritual séances provided them "instruments in research, reagents like litmus paper or the galvanometer, for revealing what would otherwise be hidden."[67] For these modern investigators, mediums could reveal the secrets of the mind, from its potential powers of telepathy to its distorted expression of long-forgotten memories. Séances thus made way for new discoveries concerning subjectivity that transformed the definition and treatment of madness.

In the twentieth century, as increasing discoveries of frauds and scandals tainted the fields of mesmerism and spiritualism, the credibility of psychologists' and psychical researchers' experiments on séances largely suffered. Official psychological knowledge separated itself from research in occult phenomena and relegated its questions to the now autonomous discipline of parapsychology or psychical research. As Le Maléfan suggests: "From parallel, these questions became unacceptable."[68] Illustrating a step in this process of demarcation, Flournoy remarked, in a letter to James on August 27, 1900, that much controversy arose regarding the administration of the newly founded Institut Psychique International, because members could not agree on its purpose and objects of study. According to Flournoy, Janet, who had by now rejected the study of occultism, "consented to devote himself to it only with the very fixed idea that it would not be concerned with occultism, spiritism, etc." Others, however, saw these fields of research as important for the advancement of sciences of the mind. This conflict was also apparent in debates regarding the very name of the Institut,

> some members wishing Institut PSYCHIQUE, this word alone being capable of interesting the general public and adding money to the treasury of the Institut—other members demanding the name Institut PSYCHOLOGIQUE,

in order to stress a concern with psychological studies in general, to the exclusion of the occult field. But the general public will never bring its offerings to an institution whose aim is not to satisfy the public curiosity on psychic, occult facts.[69]

The institute indeed saw its name, Institut Psychique International, change to Institut Général Psychologique two months after its creation at the Fourth International Congress of Psychology in 1900, but it kept in its ranks a Groupe d'Étude des Phénomènes Psychiques (or Group for the Study of Psychical Phenomena).[70]

Despite his interest in thought-transference, Freud also wished to distinguish psychoanalysis from psychical research. As T. W. Mitchell writes: "Freud's Unconscious is in truth not very different from Myers' Subliminal, but it seems to be more acceptable to the scientific world, in so far as it has been invoked to account for normal and abnormal phenomena only, and does not lay its supporters open to the implication of belief in supernormal happenings."[71] Although Freud had been a member of the Society for Psychical Research between 1911 and 1938, he wished to demarcate his science from the unscientific reputation of psychical research. Therefore, when the society asked him to write for its 1912 *Proceedings*, he wrote an article entitled "A Note on the Unconscious in Psychoanalysis" to emphasize the distinction between his notion of the unconscious and that of the subliminal consciousness. Freud here stated: "I wish to expound in a few words and as plainly as possible what the term 'unconscious' has come to mean in psychoanalysis and psychoanalysis alone."[72] Freud thus distinguished his science by excluding the transcendental hypothesis from his understanding of the unconscious, and by replacing it with his theory of sexuality. In time, "The psychoanalytic theory of the unconscious gained the victory over other theories of the unconscious. . . . It was fruitless to speak about the subconscious in psychology if its theory remained unelaborated or referred to spirituality and transcendence. The key to the scientific reception of such theories seemed to be their materialistic, biological orientation."[73]

Chasing Ghosts

In this book, I focus on studies of mediumship in modern formulations of the mind at a time when psychology and paranormal research were not yet clearly separated. In doing so, I distinguish between mediumship and hysteria, a distinction that many nineteenth-century authors would have considered negligible. Indeed, mediums and hysterics presented many similarities, and observers of the late nineteenth century often interpreted the complex discourses and feelings of dissociation experienced by mediums as symptoms of the disease. Professor of psychological medicine and medical jurisprudence in New York R. Frederic Marvin, for instance, viewed mediumship as one of "these forms of insanity which are associated with derangements of [the reproductive] system."[74] In *The Philosophy of Spiritualism and the Pathology and Treatment of Mediomania*, published in 1874, he described "the insanity of mediums" as one of the most common female disorders and concluded that "the word mediomania, though not actually synonymous with the word utromania, is very closely allied with it in meaning."[75] Likewise, American neurologist William Alexander Hammond claimed in his 1876 work *Spiritualism and Allied Causes of Nervous Derangement* that "at most of the Spiritualist meetings which I have attended . . . there have been hysterical phenomena manifested."[76] In France, a doctor named Philibert Burlet published a volume in 1863 arguing that spiritualism was about to become the main cause of mental alienation in the country.[77] Flournoy himself noted, in a letter to James, that in Smith's séances "all the classical hysterical phenomena . . . present themselves in turn, in any order and in the most unexpected fashion, varying from one time to another."[78]

For contemporary historians, hysteria and mediumship also resemble one another, as both notions were culturally determined constructions framing ill-understood bodily performances and linguistic productions. In his history of demonic possession, Brian Levack notably writes: "The word [hysteria] is after all a cultural construct, just like possession itself, and as such it has been applied to a wide variety of psychoneurotic disorders, especially those classified as dissociative, which involve a loss of identity, and those classified as the product of a conversion syndrome, such as amnesia, paralysis, blindness, and deafness."[79] Janet Beizer similarly remarks, in her study of nineteenth-century hysteria, that "there has never been a time when hysteria existed as an entity outside a web of contexts (misogyny, pathology, death, religion, and the supernatural, among others)."[80] Both hysteria and spiritualism surged in the nineteenth century, forming cultural events that questioned the connections between the body and the mind. Both phenomena also elicited reflections on their agents' manifestations, from intentional acts of dissimulation to proofs of real suffering. And, like hysterics, mediums seemed to follow "cultural scripts" informing their performances or "symptoms."[81]

Yet, as this book argues, while both spiritualism and hysteria produced phenomena similarly addressed within emerging European psychology, mediums effectively disturbed and challenged the authority of medical and psychological experts by performing their own autonomous discourse of knowledge. Unlike hysterics, mediums and believers formulated their own interpretations of diseases, producing a vocabulary of normalcy and pathology that directly confronted medical orthodoxies. Further, experiences of spiritual possession often presented heightened sensitivity, creativity, and linguistic abilities that were not easily explained in strictly pathological terms, as they appeared highly beneficial to mediums. Eluding psychiatric and psychological classifications, mediums thus presented, unlike hysterics, an important threat to the establishment of knowledge by giving rise to a form of discourse legitimizing their claims to truth.

As an exemplar of the relations between mediumship and nascent psychology, Hélène Smith reveals how mediums offered a complex, unclassifiable, form of agency that defied contemporaneous epistemologies of the mind. In the following chapters, I retrace the fascinating story of this gifted medium and the authors, scientists, and artists she inspired in order to bring to light a forgotten chapter in the history of the unconscious. Smith's mediumship, I argue, sheds a different light on the role of women in the construction of psychological discourses, one that challenges traditional representations of female patients as powerless victims and passive objects. The medium also illuminates the many valuable concepts and discoveries concerning the unconscious and its relations to the workings of creativity that emerged through studies of mediumship. While such concepts and discoveries were certainly shaped according to specific cultural constructions of the late nineteenth century, they also illuminated now forgotten but striking aspects of human personality.

To begin this investigation, Chapter 1, "Bodies," explores the parallel and often connected developments of spiritualism and depth psychology in modern Europe, as well as the roles played by women in both discourses. In order to set the stage, I first turn to Paris and Charcot's understanding of hysteria at the Salpêtrière hospital, then the largest medical institution in Europe. Particularly, this chapter retraces the construction of the female body in the "golden age of hysteria" in the late nineteenth century. It addresses perceptions of female embodiment within spiritualist doctrine and suggests that, while both fields developed from similar understandings of the entranced female body as passive recipient for the voice of the other, female mediums reshaped stereotypes of femininity to access a discursive authority in séances. This chapter establishes the context for further explorations of Smith's séances and interpretations of her embodiment of exotic, powerful, and creative voices.

Chapter 2, "Desire," addresses the relationship between Flournoy and Smith and introduces the psychologist's theorizations of the unconscious in his two studies of the medium, *From India to the Planet Mars* (1900) and *Nouvelles observations* (1901). In so doing, this chapter focuses on the notion of suggestibility in trance and hypnosis, which later transformed, in Freudian psychoanalysis, into the more complex dynamic of transference and countertransference. One of the most frequently cited stories in the history of Freudian discoveries is that of Anna O., whose relationship with Breuer helped Freud conceive of the sexual nature of transference and countertransference. An inadvertent consequence of the unexplored seduction in Breuer's relationship with his patient, according to Freud, was the development of a hysterical pregnancy in Anna O. following a separation with her doctor. In retracing a similar event shaping the dynamic between Smith and Flournoy, I suggest that the vocabulary of labor and bearing (which ironically rendered both relationships unbearable to the doctors) illuminates the excesses of an unacknowledged desire. While aware of Freudian theories regarding the sexual motivations behind hypnotic productions, Flournoy appeared blind to Smith's yearning for closeness, expressed through occult experiences. But the parallels between Anna O. and Hélène Smith's pregnancies more importantly illuminate—as I argue through an analysis of Smith and Flournoy's correspondence following the publication of his two studies—an alternative expression of both women's unrecognized labor toward the production of scientific discourse.

Chapter 3, "Languages," examines the involvement of Ferdinand de Saussure and other linguists in the study of Smith's séances as it introduces her glossolalic inventions, from her Martian and Sanskrit to her Ultra-Martian and Uranian. I suggest that the medium's linguistic creations influenced Saussure's later theorizations of signification and shaped some of the first encounters between psychoanalytic and linguistic concepts—encounters that would later define Jacques Lacan's conception of the unconscious. In retracing the glossolalic episodes in Smith's mediumship, which gave rise to the first modern studies of glossolalia, this chapter demonstrates how Smith defied her savants by creating forms of symbolization that undermined their knowledge and methodologies. Here again, Smith's productions offer evident parallels with hysteric symptoms: since the 1980s, feminist theorists have indeed noted that hysteria expressed a radical but silent rejection of the patriarchal order through the hysteric's disarticulation of grammar and syntax. In *The Knotted Subject: Hysteria and Its Discontents*, Elisabeth Bronfen explains: "What the hysterical broadcasts is a message about vulnerability—the vulnerability of the symbolic (the fallibility of the paternal law and social bonds)."[82] But while the hysterical loss of language can be interpreted as a rejection of the social order that could only express itself through paralyzing symptoms, Smith's glossolalia illustrates that spiritual possession could, following this rejection, provide an avenue to reconstruct a new structure to legitimize the manifestations of women's voices.

Chapter 4, "Creativity," explores the artistic aspects of Smith's séances, which ranged from theatrical performances and musical compositions to poetry and painting. Smith's visual creativity notably developed after Flournoy's study, as she began to paint large tableaux representing her visions of major Christian figures. The latter were the object of a 1932 study by Waldemar Deonna, then director of the Musée d'Art et d'Histoire de Genève, who attempted to retrace the unconscious modalities behind her creativity. Through her trance imagination, Smith challenged contemporaneous notions of unconscious acts (or automatisms) as purely symptomatic, monotonous, and echolalic. This, at least, appears to be what the surrealist artist and poet André Breton recognized in Smith's séances. Well aware of the scientific discourses on the medium, Breton indeed drew on her trance performances as a model to unveil the limits and risks of a radical form of creativity as he conducted with his group a series of experiments in "psychic automatism" aimed at creating art without "any control exercised by reason [and] exempt from any aesthetic or moral concern."[83] After discussing Smith's artistic corpus, this chapter retraces the surrealists' experiments in trance writing—experiments that ended after the group was found in a closet attempting to commit collective suicide[84]—to further interrogate how the performances of the automatic body could bring the subject to its limit. I demonstrate how the loss of conscious control during séances was a simultaneously dangerous and powerful tool that dramatically transformed the meaning of artistic and authorial agency. In his study of Smith's imagination, Flournoy conceived the medium's experiences as subliminal romances of the "mythopoetic unconscious." Through this notion, he portrayed the unconscious as continuously concerned with creating fictions and myths based on forgotten memories. Accordingly, Ellenberger explains that what psychoanalysts now call fantasies, derived largely from earlier studies of hysteria, "represents a minute part of mythopoetic manifestations . . . a power that fathered epidemics of demonism, collective psychoses among witches, revelations of spiritualists."[85]

In all, Smith's extraordinary life presents her as caught up in several important movements and debates of her time. Even before the medium could discover her own extraordinary abilities, as the next pages reveal, strange articulations of femininity, enchantment, and sciences were emerging in the mid-nineteenth century: within the first explorations of trance in neuropsychology and spiritualism, a similar imagination of the female body as a mysterious entity demanding scientific mastering began to make way for the apprehension of transcendence through the materiality of female embodiment. When Smith entered the scene, she engaged with such prior movements and debates, thereby offering an important perspective on various aspects of European modernity, from the often-forgotten enchantment of modern sciences to the yet-obscure role of women mediums at the birth of psychology. Forgetting Smith's imagination, I suggest, has meant burying some of the ways women could exploit their marginalized positions by establishing their discourses from liminal spaces. It has also meant forgetting crucial and fascinating discoveries concerning the unconscious: for many psychologists, mediums indeed illuminated highly complex modalities of the unconscious mind that extended far beyond the productions of symptoms and revealed different mechanisms of a prodigious creativity, an inexhaustible imagination, and the extraordinary powers of these forces upon the body.

1

Bodies

Ventriloquizing Agency, Magic Dolls, and Spiritualist Authorship

Flournoy's hypothesis
Confuses and perplexes me:
Man would have a second self
Of a very complex nature.
Of the natural self this underlying self
Would take control . . .
And, it's astounding!
Would transvest itself, change its sex . . .
Certainly, for a self, this is not trivial.
This original self
Was given the name of Subliminal.

—Popular song created in Geneva[1]

Wind-Up Dolls and Speaking Machines

Completed by André Brouillet (1857–1914) in 1887, *A Clinical Lesson at the Salpêtrière* pictures the master of the institution, Jean Martin Charcot, as he provides instruction to a white, male, and upper-class audience, the latter observing his famous patient Blanche Wittmann.[2] Perhaps only surpassed by Tony Robert-Fleury's 1876 *Pinel Freeing the Insane*, Brouillet's painting is one of the best known in the history of medicine. Wittmann, who was dubbed "the queen of hysterics," is held by Joseph Babinsky (1857–1933), chief house officer at the institution, while two female nurses stand by, their gazes fixed on the hypnotized patient, ready to obey the master's commands. Among audience members are Albert Londe (1858–1917), the Salpêtrière medical photographer, Charles Féré (1852–1907), author of multiple works on hypnotism, animal magnetism, and criminality, Georges Gilles de la Tourette (1857–1904), discoverer of the syndrome bearing his name,

Hélène Smith. Claudie Massicotte, Oxford University Press. © Oxford University Press 2023.
DOI: 10.1093/oso/9780197680018.003.0002

and Désiré-Magloire Bourneville (1840–1909), author of *La bibliothèque diabolique* (*The Diabolical Library*), a famous historical reinterpretation of possession and witchcraft cases as ill-interpreted episodes of hysteria. In the background stands another portrait, that of a woman, breasts aloft and exposed, back arched, illustrating a posture of "grande hystérie." The woman offers symmetry to Brouillet's composition, reflecting the contorted body of Wittmann, whose breasts also stand prominently, illuminated by the daylight shining from the nearby windows. Like the *Pinel* painting, *A Clinical Lesson* therefore presents a stunning portrayal of nineteenth-century medical understandings of gender, agency, and madness. The entranced Wittmann, like the figure in the portrait she faces, is at once convulsive and voluptuous. Both bodies are exposed but unseeing, their eyes closed or hidden. Both are subjects of discourse, yet they remain silent. While Charcot appears to methodically explain their bodies' strange contortions and articulations, the patients themselves remain outside his medical gloss, for which they figure simply as silent models (see figure 1.1).

In her analysis of *Pinel Freeing the Insane*, a work representing the unchaining of female patients in the Salpêtrière courtyard, feminist critic Elaine Showalter wrote that the Robert-Fleury painting "depicts 'the insane' as madwomen of different ages, from youth to senility. . . . The representatives

Figure 1.1 André Brouillet, *Clinical Lesson at the Salpêtrière*, 1887
Université de Paris Descartes. Public domain.

of sanity in the painting are all men, and this division between feminine madness and masculine rationality is further emphasized by the three figures at the center. In the foreground is a lovely, passive, disheveled young woman, her eyes modestly cast down. . . . The keeper who holds up her arm while he unlocks her chains seems less to be releasing her than winding her up, like some huge doll; her nominal freedom, the composition suggests, exists in a complex tension with male control."[3] Although Robert-Fleury represented events occurring almost a century before, his work was contemporaneous to Brouillet's, and their codifications of gender and madness echo one another. Indeed, *A Clinical Lesson* similarly offers a dichotomy between male authority, discourse, and rationality on the one hand, and female submissiveness, silence, and madness on the other. One can easily see Blanche as another of the institution's dolls, an inarticulate marionette producing only the scripts for her ventriloquist's medical knowledge.

In sharp contrast with Brouillet's Blanche Wittmann, the woman at the center of a famous séance scene from Fritz Lang's *Dr. Mabuse the Gambler* (1922) embodies another dimension of trance states. Like Blanche's posture, her body works to situate her as frail and delicate (she is the smallest member of the sitters). She also shares with the hysteric a marked class distinction easily visualized through the comparison of her and her audience's clothing. Yet the woman's expression alerts the viewer to a mysterious power: while the well-dressed male and female sitters in the audience look at the table in anticipation of some production, she looks elsewhere, perceiving what they cannot see. Although she shares Blanche's beauty, our gaze rests differently on her. When she speaks, we know others will listen. It is this power, defying all material, sexual, and social circumstances, that draws our attention (see figure 1.2).

Behind this contrast, however, Blanche Wittmann and Lang's medium share similar codifications of femininity shaping their bodily performances. From the second half of the nineteenth century to the early years of the twentieth century, both mediums and hysterics were important sites for scientific speculation, for the discovery of otherworldly or physical mysteries. In such discourses, both were conceived as passive vehicles for the transmission of other voices, other meanings. If the medium's body moved, spoke, and acted, spiritualist authors understood that *she* was not the originator of this symbolization. Just like Charcot's hysteric, who ventriloquized her male doctor's discourse, the medium was conceived, within spiritualist understandings of trance, as agentless machinery predisposed to be taken over, possessed, by forces stronger than her own subjectivity.

Figure 1.2 Still from Fritz Lang's *Dr. Mabuse the Gambler*, 1922
Public domain.

As this book argues, both the hysteric and the medium were female figures at the origin of significant modern developments on subjectivity. Both figures shaped discoveries about the mind through their adoption of trance states that challenged Cartesian understandings of the self as transparent master of its own thoughts and discourses. Their trance experiences also rested on similar understandings of female embodiment, as medical science and spiritualist doctrine shared an interpretation of women's bodies as more propitious sites for trance through their passivity, nervousness, and general imbalance. In the present chapter, I address the parallel and often connected developments of mediumship and hysteria in modern Europe, as well as the roles played by women in both discourses. Particularly, I wish to interrogate the construction of the female body and agency in medical orthodoxies— especially at the Salpêtrière—and in spiritualist discourse at the turn of the century. Although spiritualist and medical authors similarly codified the entranced female body, the medium and the hysteric, I argue, subverted such codifications in different ways. This chapter will therefore provide important context for further explorations of Smith's séances and her enactment of exotic, powerful, and creative voices that baffled scientific authorities of her time.

Hysteria and the Female Body at the Salpêtrière

An important point of departure in the history of modern psychology emerged under Charcot's reign at the Salpêtrière, which lasted from 1872 to 1893. As the head of the largest medical institution in Europe, Charcot held considerable influence over interpretations of trance in European sciences, particularly through his understanding of the growing and ill-understood epidemics of hysteria seemingly affecting European women.[4] As Brouillet's painting illustrates, his demonstrations on hysteria brought many distinguished visitors, and several of his students—among them Sigmund Freud and Pierre Janet—went on to define the new field of depth psychology through their own experiments with trance and hypnosis. In shaping this history, Charcot importantly framed the female body as passive object of the scientific gaze. By the twentieth century, many of Charcot's theories would be rejected by pioneers of psychology. However, a focus on the pathological aspects of trance states continued to prevail. His construction of female embodiment as mechanical, passive vehicle for the transmission of mysterious meanings would also continue to inform understandings of trance states well into the following decades. Among the various symptoms of hysteria Charcot presented, none better illustrated the mechanical nature of femininity than his patients' hysterogenic zones, propensity for dermographism, and hypnotic suggestibility, each of which presented themselves in turn in Blanche Wittmann's case.

The Salpêtrière master notably discovered "hysterogenic zones," found principally in the ovaries and the breasts, which could, when touched, either trigger or prevent attacks of hysteria. As historian Asti Hustvedt notes, "The female body, that 'dark continent' of the nineteenth century, was presented to doctors as uncharted territory in need of scientific exploration. Charcot confronted the chaos of the hysterical female body and created a new topography, one that included a map of 'hysterogenic zones,' mechanical buttons of sorts."[5] To reach these buttons, doctors would notably use their fist, a baton, or a belt-like device compressing the patients' ovaries when hoping to trigger or delay an attack. As Michel Foucault explained in his *History of Sexuality*, "Charcot suspends an attack by placing first his hand, then the end of a baton, on the woman's ovaries. He withdraws the baton, and there is a fresh attack."[6] Wittmann herself chose to use the ovary-compressing belt on various occasions: one day, she wished to exercise in the hospital gymnasium but felt that an attack was imminent. She requested the ovary compressor and completed her exercise routine with the heavy device before returning to her room, removing it, and succumbing to her delayed crisis. Although Charcot is well known for rejecting the uterine theory of hysteria and relocating the disease in the nervous system, he nonetheless saw the topography of the female reproductive organs as a more fertile ground for the spread of the disease. Like a moving fuse box, the female body appeared to him unpredictable yet largely controllable through various switches activating different mechanisms.

Another symptom of particular interest for Charcot and the Salpêtrière specialists was a bizarre condition associated with hysteria, a form of urticaria called dermographism. Charles Féré and Henri Lamy, who discussed the condition in the *Nouvelle iconographie photographique de la Salpêtrière* (*New Photographic Iconography of the Salpêtrière*), defined it as "a singular phenomenon caused by a particular excitability of the skin, which consists in the appearance of edematous protrusions surrounded by redness, similar to urticarial plaques, which can form various figures at will, under the influence of excitations of the integument."[7] In other words, doctors could inscribe words and images on their patients' skin through different manipulations. In 1881, the journalist and novelist Jules Claretie (1840–1913), who had attended many of Charcot's lessons, published a fictionalized account of hysteria in his novel *Les amours d'un interne* (*The Loves of an Intern*), an account that further described the skin condition and the language through which it was interpreted. In the novel, a group of interns gather in the hysteria ward of the institution around the beautiful Mathilde, whose silent body produces a demonstration for the doctor's explanation of dermographism. The narrator remarks: "Mathilde was completely anesthetized, and it was enough to trace on her white skin, as soft as a child's, the characters we wanted so that immediately, at the place touched by the doctor's nail or pencil, appeared a red protrusion of such a prominence that, by feeling these characters, one could recognize the letter that had just been written there."[8] Mathilde's fictionalized case resembled that of "Julie," a twenty-nine-year-old hysterical patient entering the Saint-Antoine Hospital in Paris two years before Claretie's publication. George Dujardin-Beaumetz (1833–1895) reported on the jarring experiments he conducted on the patient to identify her anesthetic symptoms and dermographism: "We can pierce from one side to the other the skin of her limbs, belly, breasts, face, without her feeling the slightest pain. . . . Sensitivity to cold, heat, and tickling is not encountered either." On her skin, he added, the doctor could "execute . . . the most varied drawings [and] write names of ten to fifteen letters."[9]

Demonstrating the doctors' penchant for using female bodies as canvasses reproducing their own signifiers, the hysteric's skin could be—and was—repeatedly inscribed with her medical condition, her doctors' names, or the latter's creative ornaments. In one particular experiment in August 1878, Wittmann again confirmed the bizarre symptom, as she saw her own body stamped with her new medical identity. Her doctors explained: "We used the point of a stylus to trace the name of the patient on her chest, and on her abdomen, we traced the word 'Salpêtrière.' This produced a red stripe that was several centimeters high, and on this band the letters appeared in relief, about two millimeters wide. Little by little, the redness disappeared, but the letters persisted."[10] The letters remained on her skin for the following days, and they reappeared when a second experiment was set to repeat the first trial: the doctors imprinted once again upon her skin her name and that of the institution in which she would spend the rest of her days.

Experiments with dermographism thus permitted the Salpêtrière authorities to relocate, so they believed, symptoms and afflictions from the domain of religions and superstitions to the empirical field of modern medicine. In various experiments, the doctors inscribed signs of the Devil, or the name "Satan," on the hysteric's body to indicate that previous sightings of this mark had been ill-understood manifestations of hysteria. In so doing, they also relocated the production of meaning away from the agency of their female patients, making themselves the authors of their bodies' strange manifestations. While men and women could be affected by dermographism, doctors' recurrent use of terms such as *femme-cliché* and *femme-autographe* indicated an understanding of the female body as akin to an empty vessel, a ventriloquist's dummy awaiting the inscription of male discourse.[11]

Somnambulism also fascinated Charcot, who highlighted the strange mechanisms of female embodiment by examining the degrees of suggestibility encountered in hysterical patients. Considering trance states a mark of hysteria, he experimented with hypnosis to reproduce and understand symptoms of the illness. While hypnosis had previously been shunned by many medical authorities as a hoax produced by ill-intentioned magnetizers, Charcot legitimized this practice by attaching it to a coherent theory of hysteria. He defined three stages of hypnosis—catalepsy, lethargy, and somnambulism—and reproduced them in various experiments. In all stages, the patients' bodies were markedly suggestible to the doctors' commands, though their responses indicated different physical conditions. In the state of catalepsy, the hysterics' bodies were quite rigid, their eyes were opened, and their limbs could be positioned into various figures and postures. The docility of this hypnotized state permitted doctors to become sculptors, molding and shaping hysterics as perfect statues (see figure 1.3). In the words of Claretie, when the hysteric was in this state, the doctor could become "master of the thoughts and feelings of this mass of flesh, which has become easier to mold between his fingers than the block of clay under the sculptor's thumb."[12] According to Charcot, this stage could be transformed into lethargy by

Figure 1.3 Hypnotized and sculpted subject at Salpêtrière

Nouvelle iconographie photographique de la Salpêtrière. Vol. 2. Paris: Progrès Médical, Lecrosnier et Babé, 1889, Plate 10.

Public domain.

closing the patient's eyes. Her body then became limp, suggesting the appearance of a very deep sleep. In somnambulism, the third and last stage, the patient's suggestibility expressed itself through her acceptance of every one of her doctors' assertions. In this stage, the doctors' words became veritable performatives: when they described the presence of a snake, the patient recoiled in terror at sights only her eyes could see; when they suggested a skunk, she described her nauseating olfactory hallucinations; and when they screamed "Enemy!" she asked for her imaginary shield and sword, ready for battle. Charcot and his assistants found particular interest in role reversals, transforming working-class women into aristocrats and prude patients into immodest seductresses. In his treatise on hypnotism and criminality, Gilles de la Tourette thus noted how easily unscrupulous hypnotizers could take advantage of entranced women. He conveyed the case of a girl who had been sent to a magnetizer to treat symptoms of an illness. When a pregnancy was later discovered, a report concluded that she may have been "deflowered" by the man, though she retained no recollection of the event.[13] While somnambulism could certainly lead to sexual compliance, however, Gilles de la Tourette added that such a degree of control could require time. Therefore, he added the bizarre warning: "As a general thesis, the one who, during a first hypnotization, will want to rape a woman, should rather take advantage of the lethargic state, in which she is inert."[14] Over time, however, Charcot asserted that the somnambulist phase was entirely controllable. "In this domain," he wrote, "our power knows no bounds; for, in reality, we can vary our action almost infinitely."[15]

For nineteenth-century authorities at the Salpêtrière, hysteria provided new understandings of the self and its relation to transcendence by portraying the female body as a blank canvas for others to inscribe with their own meanings, or a passive wax figure for doctors to mold, move, and control. The Salpêtrière became Charcot's doll house, with hysterics quite literally embodying their doctors' signifiers. As de la Tourette and Richer summarized, the hysteric was like "an actual automaton."[16] Charcot's understandings of hysteria therefore produced images of femininity as a silent signifier, a container for others' meanings.[17] As Janet Beizer remarks in *Ventriloquized Bodies: Narratives of Hysteria in Nineteenth-Century France*, "ventriloquy" serves as an appropriate "metaphor to evoke the narrative process whereby woman's speech is repressed in order to be expressed as inarticulate body language, which must then be dubbed by a male narrator."[18] If hysteria was conceived to epitomize femininity (women's nervousness, sensitivity, and uncontrollable feelings), theorizations of the disease at the Salpêtrière thus also confirmed the essence of female embodiment as a vehicle for male discourse and desire.

Mediumship and Female Embodiment
in Spiritualist Discourse

The hysteric's body, with its tendency to create and archive meanings and images determined by her doctors, finds a parallel in the mediumistic productions of the nineteenth century. While Salpêtrière doctors framed the female skin as a white canvas upon which new layers of meaning could perpetually be inscribed, spiritualist authors imagined female mediums as passive vehicles for the voices of other, more authoritative (and often male) agents. As Rhodri Hayward explains in his history of English psychical research, "The inspired words of the speaking mouth or the moving hand could only be distinguished from the medium's subjective responses through a rhetorical performance which severed the familiar relationship between mortality and the body."[19] Through this performance, the medium became "like the ventriloquist's dummy, a body spoken through rather than a speaking body."[20]

Like hysteria, mediumship did not require womanhood, but the female body seemed more propitious for the emergence of its peculiar productions. Thus, many mediums were women, and male mediums were often described as possessing feminine characteristics. In France, for instance, Lyon doctor Philibert Burlet's 1863 work on spiritualism equated femininity—and its characteristic irrationality—with mediumship. Burlet wrote: "Let us also say that the enlightened part of the population has been able, with a few rare exceptions, to see in spiritism only a crude deception practiced on a large scale. And indeed, women, especially young girls, together with a good number of more or less ignorant or lazy workers, make up the vast majority of the faithful."[21] In such writing, women's and girls' participation did not require particular qualifications, but men interested in spiritualism were specifically defined through their ignorance or intellectual laziness. Both in Europe and across the Atlantic, historians of the spiritualist movement have therefore remarked upon the frequent nineteenth-century characterization of mediumship as an essentially feminine practice. Citing a spiritualist writer of the period, Ann Braude summarized, in her work on women mediums in

America: "The medium may be a man or woman—woman or man—but in either case, the characteristics will be feminine—negative and passive."[22]

Spiritualist authors generally explained the large proportion of women mediums through dominant framings of the female body as a passive container, an empty vessel likely to be taken over by stronger wills. Such conceptualizations rested on the semantic field of new technologies permitting apparently invisible communications to travel across vast distances—the telegraph, after all, had emerged in 1844, just four years before the Fox sisters began hearing the spirits' Morse-like codes. The language of electricity and magnetic waves provided spiritualists, so they believed, with a scientific foundation on which to rest their fate, and the mysteries of the female body suited it for such theorizations. Media historian Jeffrey Sconce thus explained that "the majority of 'mediums' were women, and mediumship itself was thought to be a function of the unique 'electrical' constitution of women."[23] Therefore, "Many believed that . . . Kate Fox had opened a 'telegraph line' to another world," and spiritualist authors deployed "decidedly technological terms" to explain the rapid development of spiritual communications across the globe.[24] Even the scientists and members of psychical research societies who hoped to determine the spiritual or mundane origins of mediumistic powers embraced this vocabulary. As Marina Warner writes in *Phantasmagoria*, in 1882, the year of the founding of the Society for Psychical Research in England, Frederic Myers

> coined the word "telepathy," to characterize thought-transmission, as posited by Crookes, Charles Richet, and others. With this Hellenic neologism, the psychic researchers hoped to elevate "second-sight" from the disparaged domain of folk belief into a scientific concept. The prefix tele- was being used to form any number of new compounds to describe new discoveries—some established today as incontrovertibly physical, but others challenged by doubt and worse: telegraph, telephone, telekinesis, teleportation, and, later, television.[25]

Allan Kardec (1804–1869), a prominent spiritualist leader, also integrated electricity to his theorization of mediumship, further illustrating the confluence of modern technological developments and the mysteries of female embodiment. Kardec, born Hippolyte-Léon-Denizard Rivail in Lyon, had been raised Catholic, but later attended a Protestant school in Switzerland. Like Hélène Smith, he therefore found himself between two faiths before he discovered spiritualism as a truer, more universal version of Christianity. Since he did not himself possess the gift of mediumship, women mediums were behind many of his doctrines, as they transmitted his inquiries beyond the veil and provided him with the spirits' answers. Kardec's monthly journal, *La revue spirite* (*The Spiritualist Magazine*), which he founded in 1858 and directed until his death, along with his two major works, the 1857 *The Book of Spirits* and the 1861 *The Book of Mediums*, propagated his teachings on reincarnation and codified spiritualist rituals into coherent practices in Francophone Europe. Immediately following its first publication, *The Book of Spirits* sold extremely well, with over forty-eight thousand copies printed and translations produced in English, German, and Spanish by 1874.[26] In such works, Kardec framed electricity as the generating force behind what he considered to be a lower form of mediumistic abilities. He defined through the term "electrical persons" a special category of individuals who were "endowed with a certain amount of natural electricity, true human torpedoes, producing by simple contact all the effects of attraction and repulsion."[27] This "strange faculty," he added, could be productive of certain forms of mediumship, notably among spirit rappers and those whose séances produced spectacular physical effects, such as musical instruments playing by themselves and furniture dancing around the sitters. Kardec concluded: "The question is whether electrical persons would have a greater ability to become physical mediums; we think so."[28]

In this sense, nineteenth-century spiritualist and medical authorities agreed. Although their interpretations of possession opposed one another, both discourses conceived women as "communicating vessels" controllable by strong minds, whether incarnated or ethereal.[29] Women were conceived as sites of electrical imbalance, nervousness, and passivity, thereby allowing them to transmit mysterious symptoms or spiritual discourses. Kardec again illustrated such parallels as he distinguished between somnambulists and mediums. While he conceived the somnambulists, like Charcot, as inclined to develop heightened sensitivity and greater awareness while entranced, he believed this unusual faculty resulted from the liberation of their spirit. "In a word," he wrote, "they live in anticipation of the life of spirits."[30] For him, the somnambulists' abilities were distinct from, but not incompatible with, mediumship: "The mediums, on the contrary, are the instruments of a foreign intelligence; they are passive, and what they say does not come from them."[31] Thus "passive mediums," whom Kardec also called "mechanical mediums," had "not the slightest awareness of what they write," and this "absolute unawareness . . . is valuable in that it leaves no doubt as to the independence of thought of the writer."[32] In Kardec's and others' writings, spiritualism could therefore be hailed as an essential evolution of Christian doctrines facilitating the reconciliation of science and religion in an era otherwise marked by positivism and the decline of faith. Here, joining medical and spiritualist discourses was their construction of female embodiment as conduit for the scientific apprehension of the marvelous. The female body, this "dark continent" of nineteenth-century science, could reframe and contain other occult mysteries, and provide either empirical proof of spiritual life or incontrovertible demonstrations of the secular nature of alleged possession.

Enchanted Bodies and the Construction of Modern Sciences

Recounting an episode during which a doctor traced his name on a hysteric patient's arms, then instructed her to bleed where the letters had been traced at precisely four o'clock in the afternoon, Asti Hustvedt explains how Charcot and colleagues relocated transcendence within the hysteric's body.

> The idea of "possession" could hardly be dramatized better than this: of course this "possession" is that of a patient by her doctor. To emphasize his ownership, the man signed her. And, like a member of some Satanic cult, the physician inscribed himself on the body with the victim's own blood. Such grotesque examples prompt the critique that here is sadism masquerading as science. At the very least, the science of hysteria articulated a desire to possess and immobilize women.[33]

Extraordinarily, the doctor claimed, several drops of blood emerged from the patient's body at the determined hour, and the name they traced on her skin remained visible for several months. Empty vehicles for the production of symptoms, hysterics thus brought the marvelous under the realm of science through its inscription on their body. Since doctors could empirically reproduce the stigmata and signs of evil possession, Charcot argued, the possessed was always only haunted by the symptoms of a disease no one had been able to recognize. Charcot therefore viewed his endeavors as part of a process of disenchantment in the modern world.

To provide another example, before Charcot began studying hypnotism, the scientific establishment had largely shunned the phenomenon as the province of charlatans, mesmerists, and quack "doctors" who deployed their extraordinary demonstrations by abusing the many hysterics who—unaware of their illnesses—naively believed in the marvelous nature of their trance. Paul Brouardel (1837–1906) expressed such a view in his preface to Gilles de la Tourette's work on hypnotism, noting that before Charcot's discoveries, mesmerists could abuse the public's fascination with the enchanted: "[The mesmerists] entranced, convulsed a whole generation, and exploited for their own benefit hysterical sufferers and the public's credulity."[34] Thankfully, he added, "We are nowhere near that date. Thanks to [Charcot], thanks to the work of his students, we are now in possession of a truly scientific field."[35] For Brouardel, scientific disenchantment defined a mature European understanding surpassing its childish imagination. While "the love of the marvelous and the fear of the supernatural are innate in all of us," he claimed, "these feelings are more or less manifest and may, depending on the case, characterize a people, an epoch, or an age, but, whether in the case of peoples or of men, they . . . are more profound in those who are at the beginning of their intellectual development. The child's imagination draws its most vivid joys and terrors from them."[36] Charcot agreed with such assertions and therefore worried about the negative effects of spiritualism, whose practices would rekindle belief in the marvelous and overcharge individuals' imagination. In a lesson on the topic of "spiritism and hysteria," the master indeed noted that "anything that vividly strikes the mind, anything that strongly impresses the imagination, singularly favors, in predisposed subjects, the onset of hysteria. Among all these traumatisms to cerebral functions, there is perhaps none more effective, and whose action has been more often reported, than this belief in the marvelous, in the supernatural, which is maintained and exaggerated either by excessive religious practices or, in a related order of ideas, by spiritism and its practices."[37]

Spiritualist authors, however, did not see their practices as outside the scientific realm. And spiritual circles, like that of Hélène Smith, frequently welcomed scientific inquirers among their members. Akin to Charcot, they interpreted their practices as part of a scientific endeavor bringing the marvelous under the realm of science, by offering physical proofs or experimental demonstrations of the afterlife. Logie Barrow explains that, in England, the spiritualist movement formed a "democratic epistemology" whereby all participants could investigate the manifestations, from physical ectoplasms to visual apparitions to automatic writings. In France, Lynn Sharp adds, "The spread of rudimentary scientific knowledge among the masses of spiritists, combined with the increasing importance of institutional specialization for acceptance as an orthodox science, led spiritist leaders to work towards co-operation with the scientific establishment."[38] Spiritualists "could thus feel integrated into a [scientific] world which they had made their own and familiar rather than separated and excluded."[39]

Spiritualists also agreed that an inflamed imagination could produce dangerous results in "fragile" mediums, but they framed the careless-ness of medical experimenters as the greater danger occurring in séances. Kardec thus noted: "Reason revolts at the idea of the moral and bodily tortures to which science has sometimes subjected weak and delicate beings in order to make sure that there was no deception on their part; these experiments, most often carried out maliciously, are always harmful to sentient organisms; serious disorders could result from them."[40] Much later, in a response to Flournoy's publication of From India to the Planet Mars, the Société d'Études Psychiques de Genève published a 220-page volume refuting the psychologist's major claims concerning the secular nature of Smith's productions. While accepting Flournoy's assertions that mediums were suggestible and that their unconscious or subliminal self might play a role in determining the séance scripts, the volume also argued that there remained events, in both Smith's and other mediums' séances, that could not be explained without adoption of the "spiritual hypothesis." The work, entitled Autour "Des Indes à la planète Mars" (Surrounding "From India to the Planet Mars"), framed such a hypothesis within the empirical scope of scientific inquiry. Indeed, the author asserted, "We certainly have facts and manifestations that are scientifically sound" and "The Myers, the Hodgsons, the Wollaces, the Aksakofs of this world, along with many others . . . , after long hesitations and patient research, come to the same conclusion as we do."[41] By focusing too much on the medium's unconscious suggestibility, Flournoy had thus been the one lacking scientific rigor:

We know what a considerable role suggestion plays in psychic experiences, how far the suggestibility of mediums goes. This fact duly noted, what is the duty of the observer? To strive to remain neutral, to do whatever pos-sible in order to observe the phenomenon with all its sincerity and sponta-neity. Instead, what do we see? Active interventions that disturb it at every turn, either by attempting physiological experiments on the subject or by interrupting communication with questions and observations that hinder its free flow or divert it. This may have its advantages; it certainly has very serious disadvantages. Such a delicate study requires great delicacy.[42]

Thus, spiritualists did not perceive their beliefs as remnants of an infantile or primitive attraction for the marvelous and the magical. Instead, they generally considered themselves engaged in a great scientific project to demonstrate the soul's survival after death. For Kardec, the best evidence emerged through the intelligent discourses of mediums, so distinct from their daily lives, that they could only demonstrate the existence of other agencies. For other spiritualists, the physical manifestations of séances, like spirit photography and ectoplasms, offered more irrefutable proof of life after death. Again, however, it was the otherness of the female or feminine body of the medium that permitted these explorers to bridge the marvelous and the scientific.

In other words, both medical sciences and spiritualist doctrines pertained and responded to the modern process of disenchantment, as they brought the marvelous under the realm of science. While medical authorities did so by secularizing the occult and reframing its manifestations as ill-understood physical symptoms, spiritualists attempted to demonstrate its existence through empirical experiments. Thus, the Société d'Études Psychiques de Genève could add,

Our world was going adrift, without a helm to guide its course, without a lighthouse to illuminate the port. . . . Matter triumphed through materialism. Hopes for the future faded one after the other. Death had to be the end of everything. We now know—and we know from sound science—that death is only the passage from one life to another. What we [spiritualists] used to say in the face of public mockery and contempt, the scientists, the most positivistic scientists, the most adverse to vain dreams and disappointing mirages, now confirm more and more every day.[43]

For many spiritualist adherents, modern fate should derive from experimental knowledge rather than blind faith. Both spiritualist responses to and medical forms of disenchantment, however, rested on a paradoxical enchantment of female embodiment: the female body, it seemed, came to acquire a variety of magical properties, from bleeding letters at elected hours to capturing spirits in séance rituals.

The Powers of Automated Discourse

Although the discourses on spiritual mediumship and hysteria resembled one another in their codification of female embodiment, an important difference rested in the relative powers of mediums and hysterics. A largely democratic and individualist practice, spiritualism—in suggesting that any individual could receive and transmit spiritual wisdom through trance—indeed offered an original response to sociopolitical conditions regulating sexual and gendered expectations. Contemporary research on the movement suggests that practices of mediumship opened new possibilities for the latter's participation in religious, political, professional, and artistic spheres.[44] For many women, mediumship offered a privileged speaking position and, under the identity of spirits, young daughters and modest wives were often found revealing words of wisdom to their fathers, husbands, and communities. By attributing their words to the dead—and often to the spirits of distinguished men of science, politics, and the arts—mediums gained a certain authority that allowed them to be taken more seriously by believers. These factors had important implications for the development of feminism in the Western world during the nineteenth century as they permitted mediums to question the social conditions regulating women's lives. As Alex Owen explains in her study of spiritualism in Victorian England: "The years which saw the development of spiritualist societies . . . also witnessed the developing controversy over sexual inequality and agitation for women's rights. Spiritualism emerged contemporaneously with the consideration of women's proper role and sphere."[45] In this context, nineteenth-century séances played an important—if paradoxical—part in the movement for the emancipation of women through their mediums' addresses. Mediumship provided many women a tool for individual empowerment, as it transformed as valuable qualities for the exercise of their profession the very stereotypes that portrayed their bodies as fragile and passive technological instruments. But more importantly, reinscribed in the phenomenon of "trance speaking" during which the mediums' bodies were said to host the dead's messages, these stereotypes produced a safe space in which reflections and ideas for the collective advancement of women could be heard. Lynn Sharp similarly argues that, in France, "the nineteenth-century view of women as subordinate to men and generally occupying the private sphere did not make it easy to use their own voice in the public sphere. Women mediums used the strength of authority lent by the spirits to publish their expressions of women's needs."[46]

Trance states allowed mediums to more easily disseminate feminist concerns and opinions for the paradoxical reason that they temporarily seemed to annihilate their own voices and subjectivities. First, by attributing their discourses to spirits—and most often to the spirits of distinguished men of sciences—mediums gained a certain authority which allowed their words to be taken more seriously by believers. Hence, whereas an illiterate and poorly educated woman's opinions about her unequal access to economic independence would have been rebuffed by many, the opinions of a previously well-educated and recognized dead man was more likely to be considered. Second, because their bodies were conceived as mere vehicles for the transmission of meanings, mediums did not have to endorse the possible controversies resulting from their discourses. For instance, in 1871 Andrew Jackson Davis, a well-known American clairvoyant and spiritualist author, stated that mediums should not be held responsible if their words produced scandals or indignation, and he explained the sometimes seemingly confused, foolish, or offensive discourses of mediums in the following way: "*The positive will* controls *the passive mind*, causing it to reason erroneously from correct impressions, and compelling the weaker will to assume another character, to the temporary exclusion and forgetfulness of its own, and thus personify that which is *pro tempore* paramount in the imagination."[47] This alleged control over mediums' subjectivities thus granted the possessed a certain freedom of speech that others did not have when approaching divisive social and political topics.

Therefore, the phenomenon of trance speaking played a prominent role in the diffusion of feminist ideas; whether the sitters met among family members and friends or in large assemblies composed of hundreds of men and women from different social strata, the phenomenon of trance speaking gave mediums access to a public platform. Hence, for Ann Braude: "Spiritualism became a major—if not *the* major—vehicle for the spread of woman's rights ideas" in the United States.[48] For Lynn Sharp, French "women and workers found their voices in spiritist circles as mediums and translators of the spirits. They frequently interpreted spirit messages in ways that challenged contemporary society. These visions not only endorsed socialist politics but also included challenges to gender roles and sometimes promoted an androgynous gender ideal."[49] Nicole Edelman similarly remarks that, beginning in the 1850s, the first French spiritualists, "and the first mediums in particular, relied on this new religion to speak out, often critically.... The modified state of consciousness in which they really are (or say they are) gives them a protective mask conducive to speaking or writing, which was otherwise difficult for women in the nineteenth century, as we know. Spiritism would therefore be for these women an original and diverted means of embracing political and social positions."[50]

Through the highly democratic practice of séances, spiritualism crossed class boundaries, joining both the worker and the elite in circles of communications with the dead. It also promoted greater equality between genders, permitting both men and women to speak, write, and participate in the proceedings at the séance table and encouraging gifted women to develop their powers as mediums. Under the authority and armor of the spirits, the mediums thus occupied a strategic position from which to verbalize in circles of believers new and sometimes radical ideas relating to feminist concerns. It was, paradoxically, the very discourses on the annihilation of feminine subjectivity and objectification of the female body during trance that allowed mediums to play an important role in the feminist movement and to defend the rights of women to control their own possessions, body, and self.

Historians have now demonstrated how spiritualism produced a subversive form of authorship, an enactment of agency that participated in the transformation of women's roles, particularly in England and the United States, through the erasure of the speaking body. In France and Switzerland, where nineteenth-century spiritualism evolved in conjunction with Kardec's ideas of reincarnation, this erasure proceeded differently: as Kardec and his followers believed in the soul's incarnation in multiple existences, the medium's agency was not always completely detached from the words she carried. As the Société d'Études Psychiques de Genève put it: "When a child is born, it does not simply come to earth, it comes back to earth. We know ourselves and we know our surroundings. We have already lived here, we will probably live here again. Some have stayed here more often, others less often."[51] In trance, the medium's reenactment of past lives could provide her with a discursive position of authority that was not entirely distinct from her individuality outside the séance. Thus, the entranced Smith not only carried the voices of important male spirits, such as Victor Hugo and Cagliostro; she also performed the identity of Queen Marie Antoinette as her very own previous incarnation. Ideas of reincarnation therefore provided a certain authority to mediums beyond the séance. They also promoted equality through their very performance, for, if the soul could incarnate in any human body— female or male, rich or poor, black or white—adherents were inclined to accept progressive reforms ideas as they considered their future lives. Consequently, many promoted educational and marriage reforms.[52]

Conclusion: Ghost in the Machine

In Fritz Lang's famous séance scene, the unnamed medium and her illustrious sitters—including the beautiful and apathetic Countess Told (played by Gertrude Welcker)—await the arrival of Dr. Mabuse. Performed by Friedrich Rudolf Klein, the latter is indeed "our most renowned psychoanalyst" and one taking "a keen interest in the occult sciences." Almost as soon as the séance begins, however, its medium appears disturbed and declares, seemingly frightened, that "there is a foreign entity among us!" She then abruptly awakens, as her sitters stand, turn on the lights, and look at one another in confusion. Already losing interest in this common spectacle, the Countess breaks the silence and claims to be the troublemaker as she retires to another room. After her, the great Dr. Mabuse also excuses himself and promises to keep her company, in order for the séance to resume without them (see figure 1.4). In many ways, Lang's portrayal of spiritualist practices encapsulates this book's approach to Smith's mediumship. On the one hand, the medium appears to share important knowledge, as Lang's viewers will immediately associate her words with the evil nature of the film's eponymous protagonist—an important truth that has yet eluded all of its cast. Although her powerful discourse moves all members of her circle, the latter fail to read

Figure 1.4 Still from Fritz Lang's *Dr. Mabuse the Gambler*, 1922
Public domain.

this modern Cassandra's truth. Upon her immediate awakening, she herself does not appear to remember her utterance, and her sitters are left to formulate their own interpretation. When the séance begins again, Lang's viewers must imagine its proceedings, for they now follow the psychoanalyst's discourse outside her circle.

Historical investigations of nineteenth-century mediumship are inevitably marked by similar complexities. If tasked to determine the authorship of séance productions, one must admit that no personality, no intentionality or agency, can be retrieved as originary producer of the séance knowledge. Similarly vain is the hope of unveiling a truth or knowledge hidden behind the medium's enunciation. While the parameters and encodings of mediumship provided a rare opportunity for women to overcome material, social, and gender expectations, even for "their" words to be given near-sacred status, this form of authorship was never received transparently or directly. Thus, for instance, an elaborate dynamic of legitimation generally took place around the séance table, whereby male and upper-class sitters began the rituals by introducing and explaining their proceedings, thus making themselves representative of the séance's rational organization and shaping its interpretation. Following this framing, the medium spoke words she often could not remember, while other sitters wrote, translated, and decoded her productions. Like the viewers of Lang's silent film, historians thus find themselves locked out of the séance room, able only to follow the writings of psychoanalysts, investigators, and upper-class members of the séance, whose records and interpretations largely framed mediums' discourses.

At the beginning of this writing, I had hoped to retrieve a coherent picture of Hélène Smith, whose creativity fascinated me. Naively, I had hoped that archival and historical research could have permitted me to trace the contours of an extraordinary woman whose life and thought remained a mystery. I viewed mediumship, in all its distinction from hysteria, as an important frame to retrieve the experiences of nineteenth-century women, whose access to public discourse was otherwise so limited. What I found, instead, was a palimpsest of interpretations by the male savants who, like me, had found themselves entranced by the medium. The séance notes now available at the Archives of Geneva were compiled by Auguste Lemaitre (1857–1922), a professor of psychology at the Collège de Genève. Her story was introduced to the public by her principal investigator, Théodore Flournoy, whose own relationship with the medium was decoded by his grandson, a psychoanalyst and student of Jacques Lacan, Olivier Flournoy (1925–2008). Letters from Ferdinand de Saussure and renowned French and Swiss academics embellished this archive, before the publication of art historian and archaeologist Waldemar Deonna. Deonna's *De la planète Mars en Terre Sainte* (*From Mars to the Holy Land*), published in 1932, perhaps came closest to revealing Smith's agency, for it reproduced some of her collected journals and correspondence, which it deployed to frame its interpretation of Smith's religious paintings. But Deonna soon had to give these writings away in a dispute over Smith's will, and they have since been lost to us. The interpretations of Breton, who investigated the medium and reproduced many of her paintings before they, too, became lost, complete this palimpsest. Like Lang's viewers, therefore, I found myself outside the séance room, catching only glimpses of words and manifestations I tried to understand.

Despite the marked differences between hysteria and mediumship, despite the momentary power attributed to mediums, the possessed body was thus already inscribed with layers of male writings and interpretations.[53] Behind these, of course, no pure remnant, no original author or intentionality, can be retraced. And yet this is perhaps why Smith's story fascinates so many to this day. The medium illuminates, perhaps better than any other figure, the complex nature of all discourse, for one's enunciation never emerges outside of a context that permits it, legitimizes it, allows it to be received, or transforms it. Thus, my questioning soon moved away from the rediscovery of Smith's authorship to an interrogation of *what happened* to the idea of authorship—its relation to desire, language, and creativity—in Smith's séances. Within this palimpsest of interpretations, if no originary truth could be discovered, at least the confluences of an era's conceptions of mystery, femininity, embodiment, and agency began to take shape. Around Smith, indeed, a battleground emerged between different visions of the gendered self and its relation to speech. And yet, within this field of knowledge, Smith never allowed herself to become completely docile, erased under others' theorizations. In the few documents retrieved and reproduced by Deonna, Smith wrote, discussing the spiritualist societies with which she broke contact, "I did not want to be their thing, their machine." Elsewhere, she added,

I have always believed that my work, and the admirable and unforgettable visions that accompany it, had no need of men's control; that I was accountable to no one for my actions. That even to want to put human direction into my work would be like a desecration, a sacrifice. So I remained firm, energetic, prudent, especially in the presence of the mission entrusted to me from the Other Side, feeling at all times the need for the control of God alone.[54]

Far from subservient tools for scientific inquiry, Smith and her spirits emerged in constant tension with her surrounding scholars. It is within this tension, I suggest, that the medium forced them to reconceive dominant ideas of subjectivity, thus participating in important transformations of modern thought. The following chapters address these transformations, beginning with the fertile origins of psychoanalysis.

2

Desire

Bearing, Authoring, and the Symbolizations of Excess in Psychoanalysis

From Anna to Hélène

If histories of modern hysteria generally take Charcot's Salpêtrière as their starting point, the story of psychoanalysis often begins with the case of Josef Breuer's (1842–1925) patient Anna O. As the first medical case reported in Freud and Breuer's 1895 *Studies in Hysteria*, Anna O. indeed established the foundations of psychoanalysis as a method for listening to the manifestations of the unconscious.[1] The case related, under its now famous pseudonym, the story of Bertha Pappenheim (1859–1936), a young woman who fell victim to hysterical symptoms while she was nursing her dying father in the early 1880s. During this period, Pappenheim experienced physical paralysis, loss of appetite, and mood swings. Akin to many nineteenth-century mediums, she also developed a secondary personality. At first, she appeared to be divided into "two selves, a real one and an evil one which forced her to behave badly."[2] Later on, she developed a different alter ego, one who appeared to be experiencing events that had occurred precisely a year earlier. Day after day, Breuer would confirm, through his readings of her mother's diaries, that Anna's feelings, visions, and vexations corresponded precisely to events that had occurred on the same date a year earlier—an example of extraordinary remembrance that Flournoy would have certainly understood as cryptomnesia. Like Smith, who remained ignorant of the details of her séances, Anna O. also appeared incapable of remembering the events experienced by her other selves. Breuer explained that, in the middle of a sentence, she would enter in a secondary state, run off, climb up a tree, and, if awakened, would continue the sentence as if uninterrupted.

Anna O.'s most damaging symptoms, however, were those affecting her speech. Breuer explained how she gradually lost her ability to communicate: "It first became noticeable that she was at a loss to find words, and

Hélène Smith. Claudie Massicotte, Oxford University Press. © Oxford University Press 2023.
DOI: 10.1093/oso/9780197680018.003.0003

this difficulty gradually increased. Later, she lost her command of grammar and syntax; she no longer conjugated verbs, and eventually she used only infinitives. . . . In the process of time she became almost completely deprived of words."[3] Despite these paralyzing symptoms, Breuer made continuous efforts to listen: when she could not hear him, he began to write to her; when she could no longer understand her German tongue, he spoke to her in English; and on the occasions when she could speak, he let her "talk herself out" of crises. When "for two weeks she became completely dumb" and, despite great efforts to speak, was unable to utter a single syllable, Breuer began to recognize the mechanisms of her disorder: "She had felt very much offended over something and had determined not to speak about it."[4] When he suggested this hypothesis to his patient, her linguistic disability disappeared, although she could only express herself in English. For months, her family, doctors, and nurses were able to communicate with her, though she would respond only in that language.

While these symptoms incapacitated her, others could have made her a renowned medium. Her sentences, though unintelligible, were sometimes put together out of four or five languages. During her English-speaking period, Breuer was astounded by her multilingual abilities: if she had to read French or Italian aloud, "what she produced, with extraordinary fluency, was an admirable extempore English translation."[5] Her writing, interrupted for some time, also came back with extraordinary changes. She not only began to write with her left hand, but also used the "Roman printed letters, copying the alphabet from her edition of Shakespeare."[6]

Through her extraordinary cure, Anna O. came to be discussed as the "inventor of the talking cure" and as an essential part of the legend of the origins of psychoanalysis. Departing from Charcot's methodology, Breuer and Freud's treatment of hysteria shifted from physiological considerations of the body toward an understanding of the symptom as its own signifier. Under the preceding reign of Charcot, the body was never made to signify for itself. The hysterical subject was both silent and silenced, the doctor speaking for her and objectifying her under his medical gaze. By contrast, as Anne Golomb Hoffman remarks in her history of the body in psychoanalysis, "Freud was drawn early in his career to study the hysterical symptom as the bodily locus for meanings that have been lost to consciousness."[7] Already with the case of Anna O., psychoanalysis appeared not to be dealing with objectified bodies, but with symptoms that could reveal secret meanings. Illustrating this shift, Breuer remarked that his patient's symptoms could be removed "after she had described the experiences that had given rise to them,"[8] and Freud later added that "we (Breuer and I) had often compared the symptomatology of hysteria with a pictographic script which has become intelligible after the discovery of a few bilingual inscriptions."[9] Freud thus conceived the body as a text or an "alphabet" that required translation; the symptom expressed what had not been consciously verbalized or linguistically acknowledged.[10] Hysteria, in other words, was a disease of language, the body expressing what the patient could not put into words.

Yet, as various historians have remarked, the transition to this new understanding was not exempt of obstacles, and Pappenheim's cure was far from decisive. Breuer's new method of analysis had required many hours dedicated to his "markedly intelligent" and "astonishingly quick" patient.[11] For approximately two years, he visited her almost every day, sometimes more than once, and remained with her for hours. At one point, when her disease led to sleeping disorders, he hypnotized her, preventing her from waking until she heard his command to open her eyes. Thus, he became the last and first person to see her every day. The neglected Mrs. Breuer allegedly became jealous of the patient, and, after her analysis was terminated, Breuer traveled with his wife to Venice. According to Freud's English editor, James Strachey, accompanying this episode was another event, unacknowledged in Breuer's account, which "made manifest . . . the presence of a strong unanalyzed positive transference of an unmistakably sexual nature."[12] Indeed, when he thought his patient had been successfully cured, Breuer was surprised to receive news of her renewed hysterical attacks. He then visited her house and found her with abdominal cramps, in the midst of a hysterical pregnancy, announcing that "Dr. B.'s child is coming!" In "Hysteria, Psychoanalysis, and Feminism: The Case of Anna O.," Diane Hunter explains that Breuer never successfully analyzed this transference: "He calmed her with hypnosis and then fled the house, abandoning her to a colleague. He never saw her again, and later when he heard that she was ill, he wished she would die and so cease to be miserable. Breuer . . . never acknowledged the erotic element in their attachment."[13]

Flournoy, who refused to consider Hélène Smith a hysteric, nonetheless remarked upon the parallels between her mediumship and the hypnoid states of Anna O. After noticing that Smith's daily communications would occasionally be impaired by her glossolalia (as Martian words or phrases would slip into her normal conversations, rendering them unintelligible), he wrote: "Compare the case of Mlle. Anna O. understanding her German entourage, but only speaking English without suspecting it."[14]

Though a reader of Freud and Breuer's *Studies in Hysteria,* Flournoy could not have known about the hysterical pregnancy of Pappenheim. Nonetheless, his own connection with the medium fatefully reproduced the motifs deriving from the unacknowledged dynamics of transference and counter-transference in Breuer's case. *From India to the Planet Mars* itself presents many traces of the desire that linked its two protagonists, from the displays of love by Smith's secondary personality toward Flournoy to the spirits' repeated commands that the psychologist "kiss her arm" so that she could produce automatic writings.[15] The present chapter critically addresses the works *From India to the Planet Mars* (1900) and *Nouvelles observations* (*New Observations*) (1901) by Théodore Flournoy, which constitute the most comprehensive publications on Smith's séances. While recounting the narrative of the protagonists' complex relationship, this chapter explores the concepts of transference and countertransference in depth psychology. From Anna O.'s hysterical pregnancy of "B.'s baby" to Smith's spiritual communications with Flournoy's "love rival," I retrace the complexity of a desire for closeness, expressed through the vocabulary and experience of the occult.

Introducing the Case of Hélène Smith: From Marie Antoinette to Mars and Beyond

Performing her store clerk duties for nearly eleven hours each working day and assisting her mother in housekeeping tasks during the mornings and evenings, Smith had little time left for the spirits. Her séances were therefore limited to Sundays, with the occasional workweek evening sitting. On those days, her circle would most often convene in the room she had herself designed to hold her séances. On rare occasions, her performances would also occur at the houses of Théodore Flournoy and another sitter (Auguste Lemaitre, a professor of psychology at the Collège de Genève). While the former examined, studied, and questioned the medium, the latter took dutiful notes of the proceedings, copying down everything from her performances to her linguistic inventions and musical compositions.

Lasting from 1892 to 1901, the séances analyzed by Flournoy led Smith to travel to various places and meet a plethora of characters. Flournoy called the most significant themes of the séances *romans,* a term that may be translated as novels or romances. Through each of these successive *romans,* Smith appeared to travel further and further beyond known (or conscious) worlds as she revealed the languages and stories of hidden lands. She traveled to eighteenth-century France, where her relationship with her spirit guide Léopold was explained through the secret love story between his previous incarnation as Cagliostro and hers as Queen Marie Antoinette. She also moved to fifteenth-century India, where she was incarnated as Princess Simandini, the eleventh wife of Sivrouka, himself a prior incarnation of Théodore Flournoy, and to Mars, where her astral body encountered interplanetary travelers and inhabitants.

Flournoy was cautious to note that, while revealing their connection to literature, the *romans* in Smith's séances did not follow traditional literary conventions, where series of events lead to a final denouement. Rather, her somnambulism presented "only a succession of detached scenes, . . . without order or intimate connection, and showing no other common trait beyond the language spoken in it, the quite frequent presence of the same personages, and a certain fashion of originality . . . in the landscapes, the edifices, the costumes, etc."[16] The *romans* were "somewhat like the panorama of a magic lantern, unfolding . . . in successive tableaux."[17] Yet, in selecting the term *roman*, Flournoy also highlighted the clear influence of the epoch's literary imagination on the medium's performances.

In 1892, Smith's very first experience of mediumship notably involved the presence of Romantic author and spiritualist enthusiast Victor Hugo. In life, Hugo had held séances almost daily for more than two years after the poet Delphine de Girardin had introduced him to "table turning" during his exile in Jersey. From 1853 to his move to Guernsey in 1855, he had received messages from more than one hundred spirits, with his son Charles often acting as medium and himself as transcriber. Although some spirits had advised Hugo never to divulge their secrets, he had compiled the séance proceedings for posthumous publication. The manuscripts were later retrieved and published, revealing a series of communications between Hugo and various entities, from Shakespeare and Dante to Death and Drama.[18]

In a séance of April 1, 1892, Hugo announced himself in Smith's voice, claiming to be her "guide and protector."[19] Over the next year, he continued to appear frequently, but was soon dislodged by the presence of another spirit named Léopold. The latter, who had first appeared five months after Hugo's introduction, rapidly became so strongly felt as to completely eradicate the Romantic author's presence. As Flournoy noted, Léopold also originated from nineteenth-century literature, as he claimed to bear the identity of the famous occultist and healer Count Alessandro di Cagliostro, or Joseph Balsamo, who had been immortalized in Alexandre Dumas's four-volume novel *The Memoirs of a Physician.* For some weeks, Smith had herself briefly considered that she may be the reincarnation of Lorenza Feliciani, Cagliostro's wife, before determining that she had, in fact, previously been living as Marie Antoinette.[20] While Léopold never explained the motivations behind his alias, Flournoy remarked that, in Dumas's novel, Cagliostro wore on his chest the letters L.P.D., the initials of the motto *Lilia perdibus destrue*, which might have inspired Smith's unconscious creation of this name. Unbeknownst to Flournoy, Léopold might also have been formed through conscious or unconscious associations with Victor Hugo, whose interest in spiritualism had emerged from a desire to communicate with his daughter, Léopoldine, whom he had lost to a tragic death (Léopoldine had drowned with her husband on the Seine at the age of nineteen) and to whom he had dedicated various poems.[21]

First *Roman*: Léopold and Marie Antoinette

In Smith's somnambulism, Léopold emerged not as a lost daughter, but as a dual figure of paternal protection and amorous passion. As a lover, he declared his love for Marie Antoinette when she emerged from Smith's trance and, as a fatherly figure, he protected or guided the medium as an inner voice during her daily activities. At the séance table, Léopold conversed with the audience in a variety of ways, occasionally giving commands and explanations through knockings of the little finger, taking the pen to write letters and prescriptions to sitters, or directly possessing Smith's voice and body. On the latter occasions, her constitution changed so greatly that her onlookers were left in awe and amazement. Flournoy wrote:

> Her throat swells into a sort of double chin, which gives her a likeness of some sort to the well-known figure of Cagliostro. All at once she rises, then, turning slowly towards the sitter whom Léopold is about to address, draws herself up proudly, turns her back quickly, sometimes with her arms crossed on her breast with a magisterial air, sometimes with one of them hanging down while the other is pointed solemnly towards heaven . . . the words come forth slowly but strong; the deep bass voice of a man . . . with a pronunciation and accent markedly foreign, certainly more like Italian than anything else.[22]

After his years of observation, Flournoy concluded that the spirit guide was a hypnoid formation "of a psycho-sexual nature and origin," a secondary personality whose seeds had emerged as a defense mechanism protecting the young Smith against the unwanted advances and the desiring gaze of strange *Monsieurs*.[23] Now fully formed as a spiritual entity through the development of her autohypnosis, he became a jealous protector, thus personifying the sexual prohibition. When she was courted (which, according to Flournoy, occurred rather frequently), Léopold encouraged her to decline, promising that her true soulmate was yet awaiting.[24] Léopold also came to crystallize her higher ambitions, offering medicinal remedies to sitters, writing devotional poems, and becoming "a wise friend, a rational mentor, and as one seeing things from a higher plane, [giving] her advice, counsel, orders, even sometimes directly opposite to her wishes."[25]

Differing from the countenance of Léopold, Smith's Marie Antoinette was feminine, majestic, and superb. Flournoy explained: "When the royal trance is complete no one can fail to note the grace, elegance, distinction, majesty sometimes, which shine forth in Hélène's every attitude and gesture. She has verily the bearing of a queen." The psychologist even noted the "movement, full of grace and ease, by which she never forgets at each turning around, to throw back her imaginary train."[26] Flournoy originated Smith's identification with the Dauphiness from an engraving in Dumas's novel representing a scene between her and Cagliostro. The young queen first emerged in a séance of January 30, 1894, and reappeared through various séances over the coming years as Smith reenacted defining scenes of her life as well as episodes of her existence beyond the veil. These performances showed the queen still living in some spiritual version of her gardens or apartments and meeting with old acquaintances, discussing philosophical subjects, singing and dancing with the sitters, or gossiping about the latest festivities at Versailles. Flournoy, who considered this romance the "result of subconscious megalomaniac reveries,"[27] classified it within the comedic genre of plays and literature.[28] Yet, clearly impressed by Smith's inventive performance, he added: "In her role as queen, Mlle. Smith gives evidence of a great deal of ingenuity. She is full of witty repartees, which disconcert her interlocuters, the style of which is sometimes perfectly after the manner of the epoch."[29]

Second *Roman*: Simandini and Sivrouka

By contrast, the "Hindoo romance" was defined by its tragic themes, presenting in multiple performances the enactment of Princess Simandini's sati following the death of her husband, Sivrouka. Through these performances, it soon emerged that, at the end of the fourteenth century, Simandini had been the daughter of an Arab sheikh whom she left in order to become the eleventh wife of Prince Sivrouka. Of the latter, Flournoy explained, "I have the honor to be the actual reincarnation."[30] Simandini had been his favorite wife, and his death was followed by her burning alive on his grave "after the fashion of Malabar."[31] Flournoy described thus the emotional scene on the funeral pile:

> [Smith] goes slowly around the room, as if resisting and carried away in spite of herself, by turns supplicating and struggling fiercely with the fictitious men who are bearing her to her death. All at once, standing on tiptoe, she seems to ascend the pile, hides with affright, her face in her hands, recoils in terror, then advances anew as though pushed from behind. Finally she falls on her knees before a soft couch, in which she buries her face covered by her clasped hands. She sobs violently. By means of the little finger, visible between her cheek and the cushion of the couch, Léopold continues to reply very clearly by yes and no to my questions. It is the moment at which she again passes through her agony on the funeral pile; her cries cease little by little, her respiration becomes more and more panting, then suddenly stops and remains suspended during some seconds which seem interminable. It is the end! Her pulse is fortunately strong, though a little irregular. While I am feeling it, her breathing is re-established. . . . This scene of fatal denouement lasted eight minutes.[32]

Clearly moved by Smith's enactment of this tragic death, Flournoy added that she showed "a perfection of play to which the best actress, without doubt, could only attain at the price of prolonged studies."[33]

Other tableaux of this tragic romance included remembrances of the construction of a royal palace—which, as Léopold explained through rappings of the finger, occurred in Tchandraguiri, Kanara, in 1401—and tender declarations of love by Simandini/Smith to Sivrouka/Flournoy. Smith also sang in a beautiful voice chants that appeared "Hindoo," as she moved with a "languishing grace, an abandon, a melancholy sweetness, a something of languor and charm, which corresponds wonderfully to the character of the Orient."[34] Akin to her declarations of love, which she frequently made while resting her head gently on Flournoy's knees, these songs were uttered in a language that Flournoy could not recognize but that sounded similar to what he knew of Sanskrit. Attempting to decipher the origins of this romance, Flournoy consulted various specialists of Indian history. This research, he hoped, would either corroborate, debunk, or explain, the historical accuracy of her romance. When none of the scholars he consulted could confirm the existence of Sivrouka and Simandini, he persisted, visiting many libraries and consulting various historical volumes. There, he encountered "an old history of India, in six volumes, by a man named Marlès" that contained the passage " 'Tchandraguiri,' which signifies *Mountain of the Moon*, is a vast fortress constructed, in 1401, by the rajah Sivrouka Nayaka."[35] Later learning that Marlès's scholarship had long been disputed and that the historical accuracy of his discoveries was highly questionable, Flournoy suggested that the volume, or some other text having inspired it, must have been encountered by Hélène, who, though forgetting it consciously, would have retrieved it under trance and formulated her fabulous romance around this initial episode of cryptomnesia.

Third *Roman*: Mars and Its Inhabitants

Flournoy's last *roman* related Smith's voyages to the planet Mars, which began in November 1894 and continued until the publication of *Des Indes*. The initial travel to Mars, as Flournoy remembered it, must have once again enchanted her audience. In a delightfully detailed description of the séance, the psychologist explained the lively performances that accompanied her first utterances:

> Hélène thereupon mimics the voyage to Mars in three phases, the meaning of which is indicated by Léopold: a regular rocking motion of the upper part of the body (passing through the terrestrial atmosphere), absolute immobility and rigidity (interplanetary space), again oscillations of the shoulders and the bust (atmosphere of Mars). Arrived upon Mars, she descends from the car, and performs a complicated pantomime expressing manners of Martian politeness: uncouth gestures with the hands and fingers, slapping of the hands, taps of the fingers upon the nose, the lips, the chin, etc., twisted courtesies, glidings, and rotation on the floor, etc.[36]

Following these comedic forms of salutation, Smith described hearing words that she could not understand. Soon came Esenale, the interpreter of the language, who declared himself to be the discarnate spirit form of Alexis Mirbel, the lost son of a circle member and a pupil of Auguste Lemaitre. Alexis had died at the age of seventeen, leaving his mother, Mme Mirbel, both widowed and childless.

As the royal romance before it, the creation of Smith's Martian universe reflected literary and scientific concerns frequently encountered in late nineteenth-century spiritualist circles. Following the reports of canals on the planet's surface by Giovanni Schiaparelli, one of Europe's most distinguished astronomers, in 1877, Mars indeed came to infatuate the popular and scientific imagination. Various psychical researchers were themselves astronomers and had linked their interest in interplanetary discoveries with spiritual communications. Thus, in his history of the Martian imagination, Robert Crossley remarks that "one of the most peculiar instances of symbiosis in the cultural history of Mars is the one that developed in the late nineteenth century between astronomy and psychical research."[37] Most famously, the astronomer Camille Flammarion, who would become president of the International Society for Psychical Research in 1923, shaped his observations of Mars through his understanding of life after death. Akin to many of his contemporaries, he saw the Red Planet as home to a civilization more spiritually advanced than humanity. Flammarion had published a book called *La planète Mars et ses conditions d'habitabilité* (later translated as *The Planet Mars*) in 1892, where he claimed that "Mars seems to be the planet in the Solar System which most nearly resembles the Earth. We can repeat today what the great observer [William Herschel] wrote over a century ago, on 1 December 1783, about the inhabitants of Mars: Its inhabitants probably enjoy a situation in many respects similar to ours."[38] Flammarion had also published a novel entitled *Uranie* (later translated as *Urania: A Romance*) in 1889 where a narrator named Camille attends a séance and learns from its medium that his departed friends now live among the reddish vegetation and bizarre landscapes of the planet Mars. Smith's imagination echoed such motifs as she set Mars as a heavenly sphere. Her drawings and communications further presented its inhabitants as a community of equals established along the Martian canals (figure 2.1).

As with the previous romance, Flournoy concluded that the Martian performances were the result of Smith's imagination, suggestible to the desires and wishes of her surroundings, and regressing to childish fantasies. Remarking upon the glossolalia that accompanied the romance, he wrote that "all children are poets, and that in the original, the most extended,

Figure 2.1 Hélène Smith, drawing of the Martian landscape, n.d.
Papiers de la famille Flournoy, Bibliothèque de Genève, Ms. Fr.7843/3.

acceptation of the term. They create, they imagine, they construct—and language is not the least of their creation."[39]

Discoveries: From Mars to the Unconscious

In the preface to his work, Flournoy acknowledged the influence of contemporary authors who had pioneered understandings of trance, hypnosis, and the unconscious. Notably, he mentioned the work on "*mental disaggregation* of M. P. Janet . . . , the *hypnoid states* of MM. Breuer and Freud, and above all the *subliminal consciousness* of M. Myers."[40] The result of these influences, along with his own studies of the medium, was a conception of the unconscious as a creative force, capable of developing extraordinary abilities while formulating dream worlds and fantasies.

Contrary to many other psychologists and neurologists of the period, Flournoy rejected the definition of mediumship as pathology. Rather, he conceived the practice of mediumship as similar to acts of dreaming: somnambulism enacted the desires, fears, and influences of daily life and modified them through imaginative constructions. The main difference between the two states lay in the fact that mediums believed in the products of their trance imagination. Mediums' trance states, like dreams, provided access to the unconscious. Yet the subject's belief and interest in these states meant that they could be prolonged and observed over greater periods of time. Flournoy also noticed that trance proceeded through what Freud would simultaneously call the "dramatization" and "condensation" of ideas and memories in dreams. The performances of mediums transformed unconscious ideas into quite literal "dramas" or "plays," while their spirit personalities combined into one shape or voice various psychic conflicts and desires. Thus, Flournoy conceived the unconscious as multifarious.

First, Smith's performances illustrated for him the protective powers of the psyche. Through his analyses of Léopold, Flournoy indeed came to conceive her mediumship as a demonstration of the unconscious's defenses against difficulties. He therein found certain aspects of spiritualist practices to be highly beneficial. In his 1911 book, *Esprits et médiums*, Flournoy reiterated this claim by exploring the well-meaning spirits, hallucinations, and supernatural feelings that could be helpful to mediums. For instance, regarding the benefits of good spirits on a medium experiencing suicidal thoughts, he described the discourses of her guides:

> They do not lie. . . . They help, they encourage, they lend a hand, they protect; often they even save one's life . . . they represent psychological degrees (sometimes reaching up to the formation of a more or less complete secondary personality) superior to teleological automatism, which, in its lesser degrees, is only all that is happy inspiration and is confined to vulgar reflexes.[41]

In Smith, Cagliostro/Léopold played a similarly protective role, even long after the termination of Flournoy's investigations. In manuscripts later retrieved by art historian and director of the Musée d'Art et d'Histoire de Genève, Waldemar Deonna, Smith wrote: "Cagliostro, too, keeps watch, and he will always be there to divert what could be negative or bring harm around me."[42]

Second, Flournoy detected in Smith's trance a heightened memory and knowledge that remained archived in her unconscious. He thus defined the unconscious as a reservoir of "cryptoesthésies" (latent perceptions) and "cryptomnésies" (latent memories) that could re-emerge in altered states of consciousness.[43] Premonitions, he believed, originated from such latent knowledge, though spiritualists attributed them erroneously to independent forces and beings. From the first séances, Flournoy had concluded, as he wrote to William James, that the "great majority of the phenomena were evidently the automatic reproduction of forgotten memories—or memories registered unconsciously.... I have the definite impression that the extraordinary revelations obtained in the séances, for the most part, if not all (and certainly all those concerning me, as yet) are phenomena of 'Cryptomnesia.' "[44] Flournoy was here drawing from the work of Frederic Myers on hypermnesia in dreams, "where the memory of a subliminal perception" was said to appear "as a revelation in a dream of ordinary sleep, or under some other equivalent form of automatism."[45] Yet Flournoy also noted that the remembrances of trance were not necessarily exact. Rather, they appeared just as subject to embellishments and errors as ordinary memories. Not unlike Freud, who was then questioning the elements of fantasies and the states of suggestibility originating from hypnosis, Flournoy thus came to discover the inextricable connections between memory (or repression) and imagination (or desire).[46]

Third, and consequently, Flournoy noted that Smith's trance imagination not only revealed her own unconscious desires, but also those of her circle and culture at large. Suggestibility was an important concept in his study, for he realized that mediums were particularly sensitive to the ideas and desires produced around them. In *Nouvelles observations*, he therefore noted that, despite his various precautions, the investigator of mediumship "inevitably ends up shaping the subconscious, so suggestible, of his subject." He added that the investigation "threatens the medium, who knows herself—or believes herself—to be a constant object of study" and might thus subconsciously obey what she imagines to be his desire. Flournoy concluded that the investigator "must constantly ask himself, regarding all the mediums he studies, to what degree he might himself have become a preponderant cause of the phenomena obtained."[47]

In short, Flournoy came to see the unconscious as potentially possessing a higher degree of abilities than the normal self. The various personalities found in somnambulism could protect the person, help her realize dreams and wishes otherwise impossible, draw on a much more complete memory, and formulate creative solutions to life's challenges. Such an unconscious further took "pleasure in linguistic games" and delighted in "exotic and highly colored visual images."[48] Flournoy came to conclude that mediumship was an unconscious form of play that could ill correspond to the traditional conceptualizations of séances as sites of either genuine transcendence of conscious fraud. In *Nouvelles observations*, the psychologist stated: "The truth is probably between these two extremes and . . . the solution to this problem could be found, if not always, at least most of the time, in the psychological fact . . . of play. Indeed, play is . . . the essence and primary function of childhood and youth."[49] In mediumship, as in children's play, imaginary scenarios were shaped by daily preoccupations and wishes. Both mediums and children also generally believed in these scenarios, and their productions could become beneficial by offering solutions to unrecognized struggles.

Transference, or the Excesses of Desire

In Freudian terminology, *From India* also addressed the many traces of a latent sexuality informing the manifest contents of séances. The spirits' enactments of repressed fantasies indeed framed Flournoy's understanding of transference. Yet a certain blindness led him to dismiss the full implications of such discoveries.

In the section interpreting the Indian romance, for instance, Flournoy first appeared to recognize, from his reading of Freud and Breuer's *Studies in Hysteria*, the sexual nature of the transferential dynamic between the medium and himself. He wrote about the psychological origin of the Simandini/Sivrouka romance:

> From the point of view of psychopathology I should be tempted to cause this entire somnambulistic romance to be included in that which Freud calls *Abwehrpsychosen*, resulting from a sort of autonomy which frees the normal self from an affective idea incompatible with it; which idea revenges itself by occasioning very diverse perturbations. . . . Between these varied results may be found that in which the idea excluded from the consciousness becomes the germ of hypnoid developments, the point of departure of a secondary consciousness unknown to the ordinary personality, the center of a somnambulistic life in which the tendencies which the normal self has driven away from it may take refuge and give themselves free play.[50]

In other words, spiritualism would offer a beneficial solution to conflicting, unacknowledgeable desires, as these would be permitted expression through the séance's scripts and would thereby avoid conversion in physical symptoms. If Elise Müller could not express her attraction toward her married psychologist, Hélène Smith's "Hindoo" princess could, without guilt, tenderly embrace her reincarnated husband. What Freud and Breuer gave expression to in the psychoanalytic treatment was permitted and validated within spiritualist role-play. Flournoy added that, while nothing in Smith's conscious life would have caused the suspicion that she had entertained such "absurd sentiments which good sense would have condemned in advance," certain elements of her dreams and hints in her somnambulistic performances had demonstrated a latent conflict. With a revealing attempt at dissociation, he noted, addressing himself in the third person, that

> Mlle. Smith had several dreams concerning M.F. which she candidly related either to M. Lemaitre or to me, and which, under various symbolic images, betray a subliminal preoccupation. . . . It is certainly an enormous advantage for Mlle. Smith . . . that the *Abwehr* (defense) took the form of a somnambulistic romance, which avoided for her normal personality and her everyday life all the inconvenience of the *Conversion psychischer Erregung in's Körperliche*, to employ the terms of Freud.[51]

Indeed, in addition to the displays of love by the personality of Simandini, Flournoy had been aware of Smith's repressed desires toward him when her spirits frequently repeated the command that the psychologist "kiss her arm" to make it more pliable to automatic writing.[52]

Yet immediately after Flournoy suggested this hypothesis of sexual transference, he rejected it, adding a second, "on the whole, the most natural," possibility. He claimed that, though Freud and Breuer's *Studies* provided an interesting hypothesis, it was more likely that "the assimilation of Sivrouka to M. F. is only a coincidence due to the simple chance of Mlle. Smith having made the acquaintance of M. F. at the time when the Hindoo dream was about to begin."[53] Since the trance had not awakened "gross and more or less bestial tendencies" in the medium, he found much more likely this "hypothesis of a purely accidental identification."[54]

Why did Flournoy, after expanding upon the first hypothesis so convincingly, and after extrapolating on the manifestations of séances as highly complex products of the unconscious, now revert to simple coincidence? While *From India* gives no certain answer, it presents, from its very first pages, the signals of an unacknowledged desire in Flournoy himself. First noting that he "conformed [himself] strictly to the passive and purely contemplative attitude of the other sitters," Flournoy recounts how he was rapidly led to change his approach: "At the fourth sitting my discretion vanished. I could not resist a strong desire to ascertain the physiological condition of the charming seeress, and I made some vigorous elementary experiments upon her hands, which lay temptingly spread out opposite me on the table."[55] The psychologist's desire for scientific knowledge through "vigorous" experimentation thus finds its origins in what Flournoy defines as the charming, tempting passivity of the medium. From then on, the roles of medium and observer were redefined in Flournoy's desiring gaze: she became a passive, immobile object for experimentation, and he emerged as an active producer of scientific knowledge. The protagonists' desires for the other, one might add, was from then on interlaced with questions of agency, activity and passivity, and the production of knowledge.

After *From India* reached the market, Flournoy's correspondence with Smith indeed became marked by quarrels and misunderstandings about the proceedings of their collaboration—quarrels that seemed only to displace the frustrations of an unelaborated transference onto matters of intellectual property and the attribution of scientific discoveries.

It was only in July 1909, after nearly ten years of disputes, that Flournoy finally untied himself from the now unbearable relationship. In his last remaining letter to the medium, he wrote that he withdrew and canceled "all the letters that I wrote to you since March 1, 1901, letters that broadly betray a state of fatigue or nervous irritation that I cannot be excused for having given myself to."[56] This letter further gave her the entirety of the copyrights' proceedings (*droits d'auteurs*) generated from the fourth edition of his work. (Previously, Flournoy had decided to give her half the revenues generated from the publication of *From India* and to donate the other half to his scientific journal, *Archives de psychologie*.)

This gesture might have influenced Flournoy's later reception of a report from a psychiatrist named Dr. Émilie de Mé, who had been residing with him and his wife for a short period and who had determined to follow the latest developments in Smith's mediumship. On September 1, 1909, she sent him notes concerning her séances with Smith. In these, she identified a new turn in Léopold's spiritual manifestations: though speaking in his usual virile, accented voice, and beginning with his traditional recommendations for his sitter's health, the spirit now took an interest in revealing the erotic aspects of his rapport with Smith. Dr. de Mé noted in horror that Smith had taken "a lascivious attitude; the eyes are languid, the bust turned, the hands active, and finally . . . H.S. accuses an erotic spasm that leaves no doubt about the illusion of sexual encounter."[57]

The following notes indicate a reproduction of the legendary scene between Breuer and his patient. Here, after performing before de Mé certain acts "impossible to convey but which can be guessed at if one has studied individuals who have for long years practiced masturbation," Léopold explained that such amorous scenes between himself and medium had long taken place, though they had stopped when Flournoy had been present.[58] The notes went on:

> Where [Léopold] fails, and where he hates, at least momentarily, is during the love séances of Prof. F., who has long been Mlle S.'s lover. I exclaim: "It is not true, I say—the medium was never alone with Mr. F. and it is the most obvious material impossibility." Here the following narrative (from Léopold, of course): at the very beginning, many years ago, H.S. had entered the laboratory on a winter afternoon, under a pretext she could not remember—Mr. F. then confessing his "immoral" feelings toward her, she valiantly defended herself. But little by little, excited by his caresses (impossible to describe such rubbish!) . . . she surrendered completely. From this first encounter had resulted a pregnancy that, after three months, ended in a loss of blood.[59]

De Mé closed her remarks on this "impossible" pregnancy by diagnosing the transformed Hélène Smith as a "monomaniac suffering from delusions of grandeur." While such an account makes it impossible to ascertain whether Smith did experience what psychoanalysts would have termed a hysterical pregnancy, they certainly sharpen an evident connection between the medium's and Anna O.'s relationships to their savants. And like Breuer, Flournoy appears to have refused to acknowledge this unbearable excess of desire. As reported in Olivier Flournoy's account of his grandfather's life, Théodore's correspondence with the medium ceased entirely following the episode. For her part, although she had done what she could to examine Smith's unconscious, de Mé concluded that she had had to content herself with "the sad manifestations of an erotic cycle."[60]

Desire and Agency

The phantom pregnancies experienced by two pioneering figures of the unconscious send an important warning regarding the excesses of unacknowledged transference and countertransference within the analytic relationship. Freud interpreted the case of "B.'s baby" as such when he related it to various friends and disciples. Indeed, Freud had long considered the topic of desire in the Breuer/Pappenheim relationship. After her treatment had taken place, he wrote in a letter to his fiancé, Martha, about the effects of the provocative and clever Pappenheim on the medical community. The letter, dated October 31, 1883, stated:

> I know this from a colleague, the Assistant to the Chief Physician, who is well known there and who sometimes goes out there to substitute for Dr. Breslauer. He is completely enchanted by the girl, by her provocative appearance in spite of her grey hair, by her wit and her cleverness. . . . But, Martchen, discretion on all sides. And be discreet, too, about what I am about to tell you. Breuer too has a very high opinion of her, and gave up her care because it was threatening his happy marriage. His poor wife could not stand the fact that he was so exclusively devoting himself to a woman about whom he obviously spoke with great interest. . . . She fell ill, lost her spirits, until he noticed it and discovered the reason why. This naturally was enough for him to completely withdraw his medical attention from B.P.[61]

In 1932, almost fifty years later, Freud wrote to his friend Stefan Zweig that it took him years to reconceive the meaning of Breuer and Anna's desires.

> What really happened with Breuer's patient I was able to guess later on, long after the break in our relations, when I suddenly remembered something Breuer had once told me in another context before we had begun to collaborate and which he never repeated. On the evening of the day when all her symptoms had been disposed of, he was summoned to the patient again, found her confused and writhing in abdominal cramps. Asked what was wrong with her, she replied: "Now Dr. B.'s child is coming!" . . . Seized by conventional horror he took flight and abandoned the patient to a colleague. For months afterwards she struggled to regain her health in a sanatorium.[62]

From the individual difficulties of a threatened marriage to the denial of transference in Breuer's approach to analysis, the story of the relationship came to shape Freud's own narrative of the origins of psychoanalysis. Indeed, between the letter to Martha and the letter to Zweig, Freud published the paper "On the History of the Psychoanalytic Movement," in 1914. Here he returned once again to the story of Anna O. and remarked that although

Breuer had "said of his famous first patient that 'the element of sexuality' was astonishingly undeveloped in her and had contributed nothing to the very rich clinical picture of the case,'" he himself had later found "clear indications" that this was far from the truth. Freud added that, unaware of this erotic aspect, Breuer had made "use of a very intense suggestive rapport with the patient, which may serve us a complete prototype of what we call transference today." While Breuer could "have discovered from further indications the sexual motivation of this transference . . . the universal nature of this unexpected phenomenon" always escaped him. It was left to Freud to explore the sexual etiology of hysteria, the role of sexual fantasies in the unconscious, and the importance of transference in analysis, while Breuer retained only "distaste" for and "repudiation" of such claims.

While Freud's discoveries of the sexual nature of transference remain important in the formulation of psychoanalytic theories and approaches to this day, such an explanation may remain incomplete. In both Hélène Smith's and Anna O.'s stories, the symbolization of birthing (which both followed and finalized the separation from their doctor) may not only have expressed their latent desires, but also their labor toward, or their participation in, the conception of the ideas that had made their coauthors famous. Indeed, along with the traces of an impossible desire, a product of transference in analysis, what remains suspended in the relationships between the scientists and their women is their respective positions as subjects and objects of knowledge. What the eroticism of birthing metaphors may mask, in other words, is the equally difficult conflict of competing claims to agency and authorship. This conflict is particularly apparent through the Flournoy/Smith correspondence, where the themes of authoring, responsibility, and truth are continually debated.

The protagonists' dispute began following the publication of *From India*, after a rich American spiritualist provided Smith with a generous gift allowing her to retire from her work as a store clerk and to dedicate herself entirely to her mediumship. Following this event, Flournoy, who had earlier promised to give Smith all the revenues generated by his work, reconsidered the arrangement. The result of his decision could have been easily predicted considering the spiritualist and psychologist's hermeneutic practices: while Smith understood the word as Truth, both ahistorical and immutable, Flournoy saw truth as subject to interpretation, context, and change.

Thus, a letter from Flournoy, dated March 2, 1901, declared that his text had on the generous American "a psychological effect the likes of which would be hard to find, as far as I know, in all the history of Letters, both spiritual and secular," therefore making his previous arrangement null.[63] Smith responded: "What Mrs. Jackson has done for me concerns *no one but me*, and were I to possess a million, my happiness should not make you forget that you gave me your word and that about a year ago you told me: 'I consider the revenues of *From India to the Planet Mars* as not belonging to me but as being your due.'"[64]

Flournoy, whose practices of reading examined utterances based on their psychological and historical sources, could not understand Smith's objection. His response on the matter declared that she had chosen to follow the "known and convenient method that consists in isolating a text from its context to better falsify its meaning."[65] Of course, having accompanied her from France to India to Mars, Flournoy should have understood that Smith saw truth as transcending historical and material circumstances.

Accompanying this disagreement, however, was an even more fundamental—if incompletely acknowledged—dispute over the collaborators' respective roles in the creation of knowledge. Over the following years, financial disagreements would lead to a quarrel over the question of authorship, itself reproduced on a variety of platforms and occasions. So it was that in a letter from March 1901 Flournoy felt the need to reiterate his position as the sole "author" of *From India*, relegating Hélène to the role of its "main character." In response to Hélène's claim that the work's editors were equally engaged to their previous arrangement, Flournoy declared: "It would have been a commercial nonsense . . . for it is only with the *author* of a book that editors negotiate."[66] Though she had rewritten, directed, performed, and embellished the creations of Hugo, Dumas, Flammarion, and Marlès, Smith was thus relegated to the function of character in the story of her séances and excluded from commercial transactions.

But if both collaborators often forcefully claimed the importance of their own contribution to *From India*, at other times they vociferously denied *accusations* of authorship, as if the initial disagreement had to be reproduced and inverted on various stages. To mention but a few examples, after a review of Flournoy's work in the *Gazette de Lausanne* considered Hélène of a "stupid mentality," Flournoy wrote to the latter: "You are entirely wrong if you believe me the author or instigator of [this] article. . . . I have nothing to do with it."[67] Then, receiving a Christmas card portraying a miser and his bag of golden coins on which had been written "Des Indes a la Planète Mars," he reproached Hélène, noting that he had recognized her ink and calligraphy. She responded that she could see "no similarities, neither in the s, nor the m, v, f, and g." She added: "I have neither been its accomplice nor its author."[68] Both Flournoy and Smith therefore appeared highly ambivalent and anxious about their positionings as authors. Examination of their correspondence demonstrates that the topics of intellectual property and its revenues, along with the attribution or denial of authorship, occupied their exchanges entirely until Léopold's description of Smith's erotic encounters with Flournoy and her subsequent phantom pregnancy.

In a recent article, "From Electricity to Ectoplasm: Hysteria and American Spiritualism," Cathy Gutierrez addressed the correlation between hysteria and mediumship, paying particular attention to phenomena of hysterical pregnancies. She remarked that "incidents of hysterical pregnancies and birthing symbolism writ large are numerous" within nineteenth-century practices of mediumship. Even Margaret Fox, one of the founders of spiritualism, had found herself "appalled by the association of spirits and giving birth that she had witnessed" during a visit to London.[69] For Gutierrez, the prevalence of such symbolism indicates that "hysterical pregnancies were the vehicle for women's appropriation of an alternative discourse."[70] In the analytic framework, the bodily symptom indeed symbolizes the repressed and frustrated desires that could not be realized or verbalized consciously. As Juliet Mitchell explains, "A symptom is an alternative representation of a forbidden wish which has broken through from the unconscious, whence it was banished, into consciousness—but in an 'unrecognizable' form."[71] In this case, through symbols of pregnancy and childbirth, the body might symbolize, not only the repression of desires in the analytic relationship, as Freud had claimed, but also the role of women in the (pro)creation of a discourse of knowledge, a discourse in which they had been repositioned as objects.

As Sandra Gilbert and Susan Gubar famously argued in their now canonical work of feminist literary criticism, *The Madwoman in the Attic*, many nineteenth-century women suffered from an "anxiety of authorship" within patriarchal societies that largely restricted the means of literary and scientific production to male authors. Observing the denial of women's creativity in nineteenth-century literature, they asked: "If the pen is a metaphorical penis, with what organ can females generate texts?"[72] As many historians of the spiritualist movement in America and Europe have observed, mediumship provided an avenue for women to reconfigure their vocal organs, or deny ownership of their own hands, in order to carry the voices and writings of distinguished (and frequently male) authors. Mediums thus "took up the pen" only to deny their own enunciation of knowledge. Such a denial was fundamental to establish both the credibility and value of their elocution.[73] As Gutierrez notes: "The farther from the waking self and its perceived abilities, the more likely trance speech was to be regarded as authentic. One of the hallmarks of true mediumship was the ability to pass certain tests wherein the testers did not believe that the medium could discuss such topics due to a lack of education or intelligence. This was seen particularly in the case of women who were generally thought to be incapable of waxing eloquent about philosophy or politics."[74] Many of Smith's séances theatrically rendered her internalization of such anxiety of authorship. When she did not embody the "deep bass voice" of Léopold, she often carried the latter's knowledge through automatic writing. But the writing itself emerged only after significant struggles to control the medium's pen. In trance, Smith indeed often made gestures that indicated she was displeased with Léopold's manner of holding the pen. Comedic tussles between both personalities would frequently ensue and, more than once, Léopold exclaimed: "I do not make of her all that I wish . . . she is headstrong. . . . I do not know whether I shall succeed. . . . I do not believe I can master her today."[75]

Following the publication and success of *From India to the Planet Mars*, Smith's positioning as author became further complicated by the competing discourses of faith and medicine. On the one hand, though she achieved fame within the spiritualist community, such recognition could only be fleeting and momentary, for it was established on the denial of her authorship. On the other hand, while Flournoy's work reinterpreted her marvelous creations and spiritual wisdom as products of her own unconscious, she was perceived by the medical community as object for the scientific gaze of great men of genius, a case of "stupid mentality" that could nonetheless offer an enlightening perspective on the mind if subjected to the interpretation of medical authorities.

In this impasse, images of childbirth and labor could have served her as metaphors of female authorship and creativity. In contrast with Gilbert and Gubar's phallic analogy, the female womb has indeed long served as an imaginary space of creativity. In her preface to *Frankenstein*, Mary Shelley notably called her novel "my hideous progeny" and bid it to "go forth and prosper."[76] Jean Rhys later wrote, when she finished her masterpiece *Wide Sargasso Sea*: "I dreamt several times that I was going to have a baby—then I woke with relief. Finally I dreamt that I was looking at the baby in a cradle—such a puny weak thing. So the book must be finished, and that must be what I think about it really."[77] Such metaphors permitted women authors to reimagine the vocabulary of conception, (pro)creativity, (re)production, and mental and physical labor in terms reflecting female embodiment. Smith herself later used this metaphor to describe her attachment toward her creation. In 1912, after hearing that Flournoy, along with other members of the Catholic clergy of Geneva, might wish for her to expose her newest paintings, she wrote: "All these things disturb M.F. . . . with the fleet of our pastors who see in my work a danger. . . . [T]hey would like, I think, to make me expose my work so they can criticize it. . . . I desire that M.F. . . . never occupies himself with me again. I desire to give this *monsieur* no reason, for the present or future, to speak of all my children, the paintings."[78]

In other words, like Breuer's baby, Smith's "impossible" miscarriage problematizes the question of filiation in scientific discovery. Who bore the fruits of the collaborative labor between doctor and patient, between psychologist and medium? While Breuer refused the filiation, Smith and Flournoy debated for nearly ten years the question of authorship. In the end, he agreed to give Smith all the profits of his latest edition, thus perhaps finally recognizing her travail, before learning that their (phantom) child had long been lost.

Conclusion

Through the overdetermined meanings of their phantom pregnancies, both Anna O. and Hélène Smith placed their doctors in an impossible bind. Renewing the relationship, claiming "paternity" of the child, would amount to admitting the sexually motivated dynamic of transference and countertransference shaping their discoveries. By renouncing the child, on the other hand, Breuer and Flournoy also renounced their part in the creation of its symbolism: the discoveries conceived through this relationship. As John Forrester explains in "The True Story of Anna O.," "Dr. B's baby is quite obviously, on one level, psychoanalysis."[79] After Breuer rejected it, Freud could claim paternity and become the sole father of psychoanalysis. Flournoy followed a similar path, realizing that the only means of terminating the now unbearable relationship was to respond to Smith's demand by fulfilling his promise to give her the proceedings of *From India to the Planet Mars*'s *droits d'auteur* and, through this, recognize her claim to the book's authorship and discoveries.[80]

The women behind the figures of Hélène Smith and Anna O., frequently described as intelligent and hardworking, would certainly have felt suffocated by nineteenth-century conventions of middle-class domesticity. As Diane Hunter remarked, while Pappenheim's "intellectual and poetic gifts were remarkable, and she was a lively and charming person," she was assigned to household and nursing tasks while "her brother, one year younger than she and not nearly as bright, had recently entered the University of Vienna, an institution closed to women at that time."[81] For her part, Smith had had to leave school to begin an apprenticeship at the age of fifteen. Access to alternative futures may have initially appeared unreachable to these women. In developing hypnoid and trance states, they nonetheless found a path to intellectual life and scientific discussions. With Breuer, Pappenheim became involved in an exciting process of discovery, even formulating the expression "the talking cure," which would continue to define analysis to this day. The cure over, however, she remained anonymous, discredited, and even more closely confined than before. As Elizabeth Loentz explains, in what may have been "an attempt to escape the stigma of her mental illness, which was, according to her cousin, Paul Homburger, 'common knowledge' in Vienna," she moved from her family house to Frankfurt following her treatment.[82] Smith, for her part, gained much fame in spiritualist circles following the publication of *From India*. Yet this fame came at the cost of repeated attacks and denunciations in the public press.

Eventually, however, both women managed to redefine their experiences in their own terms. Neither of them ever married. Despite occasional relapses, Pappenheim accomplished much for herself and other women. In 1954, the Republic of West Germany honored her as a "Helper of Humanity" for her work as a feminist, a social worker, and a leader in organizations for Jewish women.[83] As for Smith, she remained active in spiritualist circles and redefined her position as an artist. She took lessons in painting and began to paint large tableaux of her spiritual visions. In her later life, she forbade reproduction of her work, reclaimed her paintings from Auguste Lemaitre, and considered publishing her own book about her experiences. In 1911, she wrote: "I must sign my paintings; I had not done so yet, not knowing whether I wanted to sign 'Hélène Smith' or my real name. Now, I think I am doing well by signing, in full, 'Élise Müller.'"[84]

Before this artistic phase, of her life, however, Smith would first transform the field of linguistics, entrancing, as the next chapter demonstrates, both its "father" and later explorers of language.

3

Languages

Extraplanetary Signs and the Haunted Origins of Modern Linguistics

Echo and Glossa

In Greek mythology, the story of Echo presents a beautiful nymph who becomes incapable of uttering her own enunciations and is condemned to repeat the words of others. On multiple occasions, when the goddess Hera could have found her husband consorting with the mountain nymphs, Echo held her in long, meaningless conversations, permitting her sisters to flee. In Ovid's Roman version, this constant blathering, along with her refusal to speak truth to the authority of the goddess, determine her punishment. Once the latter discovers her treachery, she exclaims: "I've been cheated enough by your prattling tongue. From now on, your words will be short and sweet!" Following this curse, Echo can "only repeat the words she heard at the end of a sentence and never reply for herself."[1] The nymph later encounters Narcissus and becomes the hunter's first mirror, repeating his every word. In this encounter, Echo and Narcissus come to embody various extremes of human personality, from self-love to selflessness. Yet Narcissus soon scorns and abandons her, and Echo recedes in shame to the caves and forests where we may still hear her, repeating the exclamations of delighted travelers.

In many respects, Echo's story could form an apt allegory for women's enunciation within the confines of patriarchy. The nymph personifies what linguist and psychoanalyst Luce Irigaray has described, in many of her works, as women's lack of discursive agency and consequent subjugation in social institutions. Drawing on Lacan's theory of subjectivity, Irigaray has highlighted the fact that the symbolic order, the realm of language and social institutions, creates a fundamental difficulty for women's appropriation of agency.[2] Created by men and passed on from fathers to sons, language, for Irigaray, has been conceived in masculine terms. Within such a frame, a woman's sense of self, established through discourse, will always

Hélène Smith. Claudie Massicotte, Oxford University Press. © Oxford University Press 2023.
DOI: 10.1093/oso/9780197680018.003.0004

be subjugated by the masculine. Thus, she writes: "We can assume that any theory of the subject has always been appropriated by the 'masculine.' When she submits to (such a) theory, woman fails to realize that she is renouncing the specificity of her own relationship to the imaginary."[3] In other words, since a woman is "alienated in this system of discourse as in her master and finding some hint of her own self, her own ego, only in another," she becomes, for Irigaray, condemned to repeat or reflect the male subject. In Judith Butler's later interpretation, "Luce Irigaray argues that women constitute a paradox, if not a contradiction, within the discourse of identity itself. . . . Within a language pervasively masculinist, a phallogocentric language, women represent the sex that cannot be thought, a linguistic absence and opacity."[4] Echoing the words of this masculine language, women are here considered unable to linguistically formulate a mastering relationship with the world. From self-love to selflessness, men and women are therefore well personified through the myth of Narcissus and Echo: while "he" finds himself reflected in her, "she" remains self-less, deprived of a language that could express her subjectivity.

In the nineteenth century, however, the figure of Echo reemerged in medical literature more specifically as a derangement of linguistic capacities. Afflicting both men and women, "echolalia" was an object of study among medical authorities, who defined it as "the vocal imitation of articulate and inarticulate sounds that come to our ears."[5] For one of Charcot's protégés, Gilles de la Tourette, echolalia represented an "almost irresistible need," more specifically a "need to repeat," that absorbed "all the intellectual faculties" of the afflicted.[6] It could appear when a patient would "hear one of the people around him speak; suddenly he repeats, with a jolt, the last word or words of the sentence he just heard. He is perfectly conscious, even quite decided."[7]

As we shall see in the following chapter, some psychologists of the late nineteenth and early twentieth centuries interpreted mediums' somnambulisms in similar terms. For them, mediumship only gave rise to mechanical reproductions of past events with very little contribution, agency, or originality from the medium's conscious or unconscious self. The entranced woman's words were echolalic, for they echoed, like other automatisms, previous thoughts or ideas received under hypnotic or suggestible states. By comparison to echolalia, however, another linguistic phenomenon puzzling medical authorities gained much popularity in nineteenth-century séances, a phenomenon that historian of spiritualism Christine Ferguson describes as "one of the most spectacular feats in the nineteenth-century Spiritualist repertoire."[8] Glossolalia, or speaking in tongues, formed the opposite of echolalia, for it appeared to present an excess of language, a need for expression defying the conventions of ordinary signification.

From the ancient Greek *glossa* (language or tongue) and *lalein* (to speak), glossolalia traditionally defines, as Roman Jakobson put it, "a special kind of verbal or quasi-verbal creative activity with the use of speech sounds totally deprived of a sense-discriminative role throughout an entire pronouncement, but nonetheless destined for a certain kind of communication and aimed at an actual audience or intended to be received and apprehended by a divine spirit."[9] Michel de Certeau confirms this conventional definition: "The experts repeat it over and over: glossolalia resembles a language but is not one. . . . Glossolalia is a trompe-l'oreille, just like a trompe-l'oeil, a semblance of language that can be fabricated when one knows its phonetic rules. 'It speaks for the sake of speaking' . . . and to return to the priority of a first telling." Glossolalia is generally defined, he adds, as "a fiction of discourse [that] orchestrates the act of saying but expresses nothing."[10] This excess of signs, these signifieds detached from clear signifiers, challenged the medical understanding of mediums' performances as simple echoes or automatic repetitions of ideas formed under suggestive states by reorganizing the very modalities of signification.

In Smith's séances, glossolalic expression was certainly legitimated and inspired by the occult and scientific desires of the sitters, who hoped to see, hear, and study the manifestations of another world. Indeed, Smith's very first foray into the utopian Martian landscapes in 1894 was described as the realization of a sitter's unconscious desire. Smith's descriptions of her marvelous visions were preceded by her exclamation, "Lemaitre, what you so desired!" Surprised by this remark, Lemaitre was then reminded by a fellow sitter that he had, more than one year earlier, suggested "it would be very interesting to know what is happening on other planets."[11] Yet, in Smith's séances, the glossolalic excess, the fictions of discourse produced by an indefatigable factory of languages, rendered possible the expression of a reality that both gave shape to and disrupted the audience's desires. If, as de Certeau continues, glossolalia is a "legitimate and necessary transgression of the order that makes one hold one's tongue or control one's voice when uttering sentences," its extraordinary, excessive production and multiplication in Smith's séances came to disrupt symbolic discourse, or to institute a new way of speech permitting the expression of diverse personalities.[12] Smith's languages were also more than mere facades or "trompe-l'oreille"; they constituted a variety of hieroglyphs, following their own rules, their own codifications of meaning and syntax.

Like Hera, who recognized that Echo's meaningless blathering formed a dangerous power threatening her authority, Flournoy saw a need to master and contain Smith's ever-increasing glossolalic utterances. After months of work to unlock the Martian ciphers, he remained puzzled by the words of Smith's Sanskrit romance and invited many scholars in Indian languages and history to offer their expertise. Among them, Ferdinand de Saussure was indubitably the most enthralled by the medium, and his persistent work on the language helped him establish foundational ideas that would later shape his theory of general linguistics. Yet Smith's voice remained unmanageable: the interest of acclaimed scholars in her linguistic inventions sparked new repertoires of unending creations, rendering her glossolalia impossible to contain. In retracing the variety of Smith's glossolalic expressions, from the Sanskrit to the Martian, and from the Ultra-Martian to the Uranian, this chapter argues that her trance communications became legitimate counterdiscourses to her savants' knowledge.

The First Languages: Martian and Sanskrit

Smith's first glossolalic expressions occurred at a séance on May 26, 1895. Taken by Auguste Lemaitre (A.L.), the séance notes explain:

> At 8:50, Mademoiselle experiences a heartbeat the likes of which she says she has never felt. . . . The table manifests the desire to speak and Mademoiselle, a little tired, asks me (A.L.) to spell. We get: *Koos* . . . Is it Hungarian? (Table:) Yes. New sign of the table; I (A.L.) spell: *oluu* . . . and after a short silence: *opoq* . . . Are these three words? (Table:) Yes. She continues: *Unly*. This sentence: "*Koos oluu opoq unly*" does it have any meaning? (Table:) Yes. Did Léopold dictate it? Yes. Is he alone? Yes. Is the sentence addressed to Mademoiselle? Yes.[13]

In following séances, Smith continued transmitting unknown words, through either table-rapping, automatic writing, or her own possessed voice. Thus, a few months later, in February 1896, she introduced the first sentences of her Martian language. While she orally described her auditory and visual sensations, Smith told her audience that she heard strange and incomprehensible words. Léopold, adopting his usual method of communication through rappings of the little finger, told the sitters that the language was in fact Martian and that Hélène would soon begin to speak it herself. As she opened her mouth, Lemaitre quickly took his pen and attempted to capture her words. Flournoy recounts: "Hélène begins to recite with increasing volubility an incomprehensible jargon, the beginning of which is as follows . . . 'Mitchma mitchmon mimini tchouainem mimatchineg masichinof mézavi patelki abrésinad navette naven mitchichénid naken chinoutoufiche'. . . . From this point the rapidity prevented the recognition of anything else."[14]

While these first words never found translation, future utterances became open to the understanding of her audience. As Léopold often described Smith's episodes, visions, and pantomimes, her guide Esenale (the Martian reincarnation of a sitter's departed son) helped translate her linguistic creations. Both spoken and written, the Martian language came to reveal itself in all its complexity. Flournoy's work introduces various examples of the extraplanetary language, which comprised some forty translated texts and three hundred words. These included the following sentence and its translation, in which Esenale reminded his previous mother of his love and attachment: "I modé mété modé modé iné palette is ché péliché ché chiré né ci ten ti vi," or "O mère, tendre mère, mère bien-aimée, calme tout ton souci, ton fils est près de toi" (O mother, tender mother, beloved mother, quiet all your worries, your son is near you).

In time, Flournoy systematically studied the writings and translations acquired from Smith and her guides. He developed a dictionary of Martian words as well as a system of correspondence between the Roman and Martian alphabets (See figure 3.1). Curiously, he noticed, the Martian language closely followed the grammar and syntax of the French sentence. A Martian sentence, in other words, generally contained the same number of words as its French translation and their order never differed. Further, its alphabet counted no sound additional to those of the French language, and many symbols were pronounced similarly to the corresponding French letters. For instance, he remarked that the Martian symbol corresponding to the letter c could, like the latter, become soft (as "s") before certain vowels or hard (like "k") before others, and even pronounced "ch," when paired with the symbol corresponding the letter h.

Thus, while the imagination of Martian inhabitants may have appeared plausible in Smith's late nineteenth-century circle, Flournoy noticed with

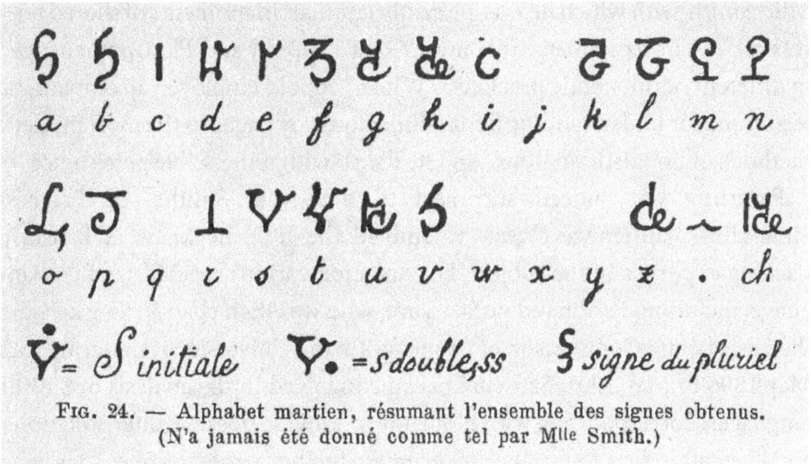
a b c d e f g h i j k l m n
o p q r s t u v w x y z . ch
= S initiale
=s double, ss
signe du pluriel
FIG. 24. — Alphabet martien, résumant l'ensemble des signes obtenus.
(N'a jamais été donné comme tel par Mlle Smith.)

Figure 3.1 Hélène Smith, Martian alphabet
Théodore Flournoy, *Des Indes à la planète Mars*, 201.

skepticism the lack of phonetic or grammatical distinction between Smith's Martian and French languages. He came to understand the Martian language as "a new indication of the infantile, primitive nature left behind in some way and long since passed by [Smith's] ordinary personality, of the subliminal strata which mediumistic autohypnotization with her puts in ebullition and causes to mount to the surface."[15] Having therefore unlocked the secret ciphers, he admitted, "I myself, I am ashamed to acknowledge, began, in 1898, to have enough of the Martian romance."[16]

Fortunately for Flournoy, simultaneous to the Martian romance, Smith's Indian imagination also came furnished with linguistic inventions and, by March 1895, she began expressing herself in what appeared to be Sanskrit. In episodes of somnambulism, Smith also wrote, sang, and performed in the embodiment of a fifteenth-century princess named Simandini.

Here, to the bemusement of Flournoy, Léopold's translations became freer and less closely aligned with the French grammar, thus making the language "less easy to explain than . . . the Martian because it has never been possible to obtain . . . a literal translation of it."[17] As Daniel Rosenberg explains in his recent article on Smith: "In the medium's own terms, there was a straightforward reason for this: Léopold could not speak Hindu. And so, when Princess Simandini would speak through Smith, Léopold himself could not understand the words. His interpretations were based on 'the innermost feelings of

Mlle. Smith' with which he was 'perfectly familiar' in moments of shared possession."[18] For Rosenberg, this meant that Léopold and Flournoy engaged in different hermeneutic practices: "While Léopold employed an empathetic technique for understanding Simandini, Flournoy engaged the most modern methods of linguistic analysis. And he did so with remarkable persistence."[19]

Flournoy was indeed surprised to note that Smith's—or Princess Simandini's—utterance closely resembled the little he knew of Sanskrit. Lacking expertise in the subject, he contacted various specialists of the language, including Ferdinand de Saussure, who was then chair in Sanskrit and the History and Comparison of Languages at the University of Geneva. From May 1896 to May 1901, Saussure became involved in the analysis of Smith's languages, corresponding with Flournoy to provide possible interpretations, and even attending four of her séances. He further wrote to colleagues, who then helped Flournoy decipher the historical and linguistic accuracies of Smith's romance. Saussure's involvement and interest in Smith's language was so significant, in fact, that Flournoy wrote in his preface that he owed a special gratitude to the linguist: "In particular," he wrote, "I must dearly thank M. de Saussure for the patience and the inextinguishable kindness he has brought to the examination of our 'Hindu' texts."[20] Examining Saussure's notes and letters to Flournoy, and the controversies that arose following his interpretations of the Indian romance, the following pages interrogate the hitherto obscure role Smith played in shaping Saussure's understanding of linguistic systems and the later associations between psychoanalysis and Saussurean semiology. Smith's séances here crystallized a privileged moment in the history of linguistics, as the emerging discipline began to evolve within the chiasm between comparative and historical studies of languages, that is, between the laws, systems, and rules of language and its contextual variabilities within specific languages and linguistic acts.

Atieyo Ganapatinâmâ: Saussure's Interpretations and the Structure of Language

Along with Saussure, Flournoy had contacted a variety of specialists to better situate his understanding of the romance. Unlike Saussure, however, many of them rejected Flournoy's theories of unconscious production. For instance, Auguste Barth (1834–1916), a founding member of the Ecole Française d'Extrême Orient, considered it more likely that Smith "was in all this more conscious than she appeared,"[21] and he asked Flournoy whether she might not have been "in relation with some student from whom she could have learned some snippets of Sanskrit and history?"[22] Saussure, on the other hand, accepted the possibility that Smith's romances were more than simple frauds, and he attempted to trace her glossolalia's origins. In what became the earliest linguistic study of glossolalia, Saussure came to interpret the medium's "Sanskrit" (which he termed "Sanskritoid" for its approximation of the language) through a methodology that prefigured his later definition of semiology in the 1911 *Course in General Linguistics*.[23]

Remarkably, Saussure's analysis began with a verification of the language's historical accuracy, demonstrating that he had at least considered the possibility of reincarnation. Noting that Sanskrit should have been reserved to officials, noblemen, and religious authorities, he argued that a fifteenth-century woman should have spoken the "vulgar" Prakrit dialect, rather than this "noble" tongue. He asked himself with irony, using the pejorative expression characterizing women of letters: "Was Simandini a bluestocking?"[24]

After rejecting the spiritualist viewpoint, Saussure observed that Smith's linguistic constructions could not be dismissed so easily. Having remarked upon the historical inaccuracies of Simandini's phrases, he nonetheless noted that many aspects of this language were strikingly just. Indeed, he noticed that the "Sanskritoid" contained some genuine words, and sometimes a series of syllables properly forming sentence fragments. The name Simandini itself, he revealed, could quite easily be associated with *sīmantinī*, sometimes a given name as well as the Sanskrit word for "woman." The words *mama priya*, which she lovingly pronounced to Flournoy/Sivrouka, could correctly be translated as "my dear" or "my beloved." Further, while Smith's communications also included a variety of incoherent syllables and "words" that corresponded to no known Sanskrit, he remarked, these still preserved a genuine Sanskrit aspect. When performing the Indian romance, for instance, Smith frequently used the sound of the letter *a* and never used the sound corresponding to the letter *f*, both of which are Sanskrit characteristics.

To illustrate to European readers how the Sanskritoid might appear to someone familiar with Sanskrit, Saussure even created his own glossolalia, inventing a "Latinoid" language that would correspond to Smith's approximation of Sanskrit, but using Latin as its basis.[25]

Once the historical and formalistic accuracy of the Sanskritoid had been analyzed, the question that most interested Flournoy remained open to interpretation: how could a woman—who was presumably untalented for languages, possessed little education, and had never traveled to India—create and maintain this convincing approximation of Sanskrit? To answer this question, Saussure offered the following analysis of her Sanskritoid sentence, "Atieyo Ganapatinâmâ," translated as "Je vous bénis au nom de Ganapati" (I bless you in the name of Ganapati):

> Her spirit works by the law that all familiar words are rendered by a substitute of an exotic aspect. It doesn't really matter what: above all, it must not have the look of French to her own eyes. . . . That given, I try to apply more closely this hypothetical procedure to the phrase below, for example: 1) "Je" [I] must be transformed. Can her memory provide an exotic alternative? Not one. So we randomly select *a* for "je." (Perhaps, in fact, this *a* is inspired from the English I, pronounced aï, but that is not necessarily so.) 2) "vous bénis"; or "bénis vous"; because if, for example, the word for "je" was suggested by English, it could follow that an English construction would be involuntarily followed in the words placed immediately after. One marks in consequence "bénis vous" [bless you] by: tiê yâ. The *yâ* could have been taken from the English *you*. . . . The *tiê*, "bénis," comes from nowhere, as in Martian. 3) *au nom de Ganapati* [in the name of Ganapati]; obviously the actual name Ganapati is not part of this process, and should be taken as it is. Which leaves "au nom de," which I will express by *nâmâ*, [and which] could be by recollection of the German *Name*, or could be by the revival of a Sanskrit *nâmâ*, also appearing sometimes. . . . In sum, gibberish that takes its elements from where it can, and invents them the rest of the time with the only rule not to allow the French basis from which it flees to be revealed.[26]

Therefore, Saussure demonstrated a certain systematicity in Smith's construction of Sanskritoid phrases. For him, the words employed were formed through a mixture of previously encountered Sanskrit words (such as the name of the deity Ganapati) and sounds that Smith created from the little she knew of other languages. Through apparently unconscious processes, Smith retrieved phonetic units and grammatical constructions, then combined them through various arbitrary associations to create a convincing imitation of language.

As Elliot Cooper remarks, in his article "Saussure and the Psychic," this process of interpretation "foreshadows Saussure's later characterisation of language as 'a structured system' or *Langue*."[27] His ability to reproduce

Smith's Sanskritoid through Latin further demonstrated this systematicity. Although Saussure did not yet deploy the famous terms of his *Course in General Linguistics*, he appeared to recognize that language is not "a naming-process only—a list of words, each corresponding to the thing that it names," but, rather, a system of signs arbitrarily connecting signifiers (or sound images) and signifieds (or concepts).[28] Johannes Fehr adds, in her study of Flournoy and Saussure:

> According to Robert Godei, "around 1894, the problem of the nature of language and the foundations of linguistics took on an obsessive character for [Saussure]." In reading Saussure's contributions to Flournoy's research . . . , we understand that Saussure was not simply willing to participate in Flournoy's research because it distracted him from his epistemological obsessions, but on the contrary because he could study the psychological functioning of a linguistic mechanism.[29]

In other words, Saussure was able to begin shaping his ideas about the rules of language underlying individual acts of speech through his study of Smith's glossolalic creations.

For Flournoy, Saussure's analysis further served to demonstrate the role of the unconscious in Smith's mediumship. Since she relied, according to Saussure, on knowledge of languages she had forgotten in her conscious life, her linguistic productions could indeed be understood as "cryptomnesia, pure and simple."[30]

After Saussure: Language, Symbolization, Desire

Following Saussure's analyses, various authors have attempted to discover the processes through which Smith could have invented such sophisticated systems of language. Victor Henry, then a professor of Sanskrit and Indo-European Languages at the Sorbonne, published a treatise entitled *Le language martien* (*The Martian Language*) in 1901. Closely examining Smith's forty Martian texts and three hundred words, he concluded that her séances revealed the necessity to rethink dominant conceptions about the genesis and evolution of language. For Henry, the Martian made possible such reflections through certain characteristics that the Sanskritoid lacked. While the latter language weaved incomprehensible jargon with known words, the former presented a systematic grammar and a rigid semantic. In other words, the Martian terms were used coherently and consistently through their repeated instances, and each was clearly defined through the exact translations of Léopold and Esenale. Analyzing Smith's alien glossolalia thus permitted Henry to pursue his previous investigations on the origins and development of human languages, the relations between language and thought, and the role of the unconscious in linguistic formations.[31]

For Henry, Smith's linguistic creations originated from the operations of a complex unconscious. Indeed, he wrote, her words appeared "unconsciously borrowed from the linguistic treasures, of which she is partly ignorant, and which lie within the depths of her subliminal memory."[32] Cryptomnesia could therefore play a role in this romance, as it had for the revelations of Princess Simandini. Henry's analysis reads similarly to Saussure's interpretation of the *Atieyo* (I bless you) in the sentence "Atieyo Ganapatinâmâ" earlier presented by Flournoy. While the Martian terms correspond to no known language, Henry explained, their formation might be due to some combinations or associations of words Smith knew—or once knew—from French, German, Hungarian, and Sanskrit. These associations could be formed through homophony, metonymy, synonymy, and contractions, among other processes.

Some words, Henry therefore declared, were associated through homophonic synonymous or near synonymous words, then contracted in the Martian form. Thus, he viewed the Martian *amêrê* (meaning to gather) as originating from the German *mehrere* (several), and he traced the Martian *nori* (never) back to the English *nor yet*. Meanwhile, *triné* (to speak) might be formed through the contraction of the French *doctrine* and *mervé* (superb) from the contraction of *merveille* or *merveilleux* (marvel, marvelous). Other words even appeared connected through infantile regression. Thus, *miza* (a rolling pavilion), was originated from the childish pronunciation of the French *maison* (house, home), while *mimâ* (parents) was said to reproduce the infantile vocalizations of *maman* (mother). Metonymy also played a role, as in the association of the Martian *chèke*, for paper, which Henry originated from the homonym *chèque* (check) forming a particular function of paper, and *chiré*, for son, originating from the French *chéri* (dear). Words could even originate from their semantic opposites, as he found to be the case in *luné* (day) from the French *lune* (moon) and *abadâ* (*little, not much*) from *abondant* (plenty).

As Saussure before him, Henry was also struck by the absence of the sound "f" in Smith's Sanskritoid. While Saussure had suggested a prior (though possibly unconscious) cognizance of this particular aspect of the Sanskrit language, Henry noted that a similar absence marked the Martian utterances, thus rendering this explication insufficient. Indeed, he remarked that the Martian sign corresponding to the letter *f* occurred only seven times in all three hundred words he analyzed. Henry therefore proposed a different interpretation, arguing that unconscious processes of symbolization were at the origin of this absence. He explained that the thought that most occupied all of Smith's somnambulism was to avoid speaking French. All her attention, thus being directed toward this effort, she may have avoided the letter "f," as a symbol par excellence of her mother tongue.[33]

In his correspondence with Flournoy, Saussure later qualified his colleague's theories as utter "foolishness," thus rejecting the possibility of precisely retracing the unconscious paths of ideas behind linguistic acts. In a letter from May 1901, he regretted being a possible inspiration for such unfortunate scholarship, having himself given to a "quasi-delirious conjecture" when he attempted to retrace the possible origins of Smith's "Atieyo Ganapatinâmâ."[34] The mechanisms behind new linguistic acts appeared for him much more uncertain, much more arbitrary, than Henry claimed.

For contemporary readers, Henry's absolute confidence in his series of associations indeed appears quite remarkable, if not exactly delirious. Toward the end of his analysis, he admitted that "some of my explanations must be held as forced or highly questionable," yet he claimed that "nearly all the Martian words have an assured etymology, drawn from real languages, more or less known, but certainly known, by Mlle Smith."[35] At the opposite of Saussure's, Henry's analyses thus appear to have belonged to what Olav Hammer has termed an "occult linguist," or a set of alternative linguistic theories that emerged in the nineteenth century and combined "monogenesis," attributing the origin of language to a primal divine act, "mimeticism," the idea that words must have originally reflected the reality they depict, "and, in some of their many versions, a third topos, namely the belief that clairvoyant investigation can uncover the truth about primeval speech."[36] Henry indeed summarized his findings by connecting Smith's linguistic creations to those of all humanity and to a primordial language, yet undiscovered, but still buried in mankind's unconscious:

> There remains still a large enough number of probable or assured [analyses] for the unexplainable residue to constitute an infinitesimal minority: it is therefore presumable that this residue itself would become reducible, were

we to possess more powerful or sagacious means of penetrating the secrets of the subconscious elaborations to which she has surrendered, and that it would then be apparent that she did not create a single word that did not already belong to her underlying memory.—Man, however he may want it, could not invent a language: He can only talk, he only talks, with his memories.[37]

While, with Saussure, Henry's readers might be keen to reject the value of his volume given his often seemingly far-fetched associations, others have found in it an important contribution to the study of linguistics. Tzvetan Todorov later returned to the Saussure/Henry controversy to retrieve the hitherto-forgotten discoveries of Henry's approach. He argued that Henry surpassed Saussure through his recognition of a logic of symbolization in the production of language. For him, we witness in Henry's study "the dawning of that other logic whose existence Saussure was unable to recognize."[38] Of course, for Todorov, Henry's work also failed to fully understand the work of symbolization and the unconscious processes that animate it. He wrote: "Henry's pages remain merely *haunted* by a Freudian spirit that never truly inhabits them. The new linguistics misses its first opportunity to embark upon the road of the symbolic (and thus its opportunity to open itself to psychoanalysis at its inception) . . . *Le Langage Martien* has no effect whatever on the evolution of science."[39] Yet, Henry was able to present the germs of ideas that would later connect, in Lacan, the Freudian unconscious with Saussure's linguistics.

Indeed, Henry's work offers a remarkable parallel to Freud's discoveries concerning the language of the unconscious. As in Freud's *The Interpretation of Dreams*, Henry detected a language of the unconscious where ideas expressed themselves through condensation (or contraction), displacement (or metonymy), and reversal into the opposite (or antiphrasis). Yet what distanced him from Freud's approach was the striking manner in which Henry established these associations of ideas, moving from what we might consider the manifest content of Smith's somnambulism (her Martian words) to their latent origins (or the "original" words from which they derived) without considering the history of his subject, or her own association of ideas. If Henry recognized Smith's position as a learner of French, German (for three years), and, perhaps, Magyar, Sanskrit, and English, it was only to regret that "she is obviously far too educated and too cultivated to have remained the intuitive [subject] which the construction of a primitive, spontaneous language would require; her subconscious is cluttered with too many conscious, linguistic, literary, and scholarly memories to show, under this confused and artificial veil, the far away memory of mysterious concordances of sound and meaning which created the language of our first ancestors."[40] In other words, for Henry, while Smith's mind contained a clutter of imaginative and cultivated memories, these only served to obscure the true object of linguistics: the discovery of the origins and evolution of human language.

Psychoanalysts would have to await the works of Lacan to discover, as Todorov suggests, a true engagement between Freudian analysis and Saussurean linguistics. In "The Instance of the Letter in the Unconscious," Lacan indeed claimed that the analyst was recipient of a letter, a series of words, which the analysand sent him, and which must then be read through examination of symbolization processes. Hence, Lacan wrote: "We can say that it is in the chain of the signifier that meaning *insists*, but that none of the chain's elements *consists* in the signification it can provide at that very moment."[41] In other words, while Henry could detach each Martian word to decipher its meaning individually, Lacan argued that meaning does not emerge from any specific word or element in the chain of signification. Rather, meaning emerges through the combination, through a certain structure or grammar, of symbolization.

A psychoanalyst and student of Lacan, Olivier Flournoy, Théodore's grandson, later came back to Smith's glossolalic inventions. Lacan, who had himself studied Smith's mediumship, referred to him as "Olivier Flournoy, famous name, third generation of great psychiatrists, the first being Théodore." He added, for the benefit of his students, "You know the famous case for which Théodore remains immortal in the analytic tradition, this delirious clairvoyant with a marvelous name about whom he composed a whole work, of which you could not profit enough were it to fall into your hand."[42] For Théodore's grandson, Smith languages revealed, neither cryptomnesia nor the origins and evolution of human language, but a regression to repressed stages of sexual development. Thus, Olivier Flournoy focused on the absence of the letter q in the Martian language, and the redoubling of the letter k in the Ultra-Martian. Through analysis of these linguistic acts (the French pronouncing the letter q as "cul" or "ass" and the letter k as "ca," as in *caca*), Flournoy came to conclude that the romance of the Red Planet illustrated a fixation in the anal stage. Its continuation on Uranus (with its reference to the anatomical part) only furthered demonstrated this fixation—as did the seventh planet's language, whose phrases resounded like those of a "child on the pot."[43]

As with Henry, I cannot avoid reading Olivier Flournoy's interpretations as analyses gone wild. (What to think, for instance, of his claim that, in the Uranian letter shapes, "one can see buttocks?" Or of his assertion that, in the two symbols following the letter z in figure 3.5, we may find "above the presumed orifice, the container. Envelop, matrix, uterus, ampulla recti for the first, feminine symbol . . . for the second, both destined to contain the poop-child?")[44] And yet I find myself drawn to the idea that Smith's languages formed regressions to a presymbolic stage—a stage that, with Irigaray, we might envision as the (female) imaginary, expressing a gendered self before the symbolic, or what Lacan calls "the Law of the Father."

Glossolalia and Smith's Linguistic Excess

How might one interpret the dynamic shaping the interpretation of Smith's séances? According to Mireille Cifali, Smith's speaking in tongues resulted from her suggestibility to the dreams of her savants. It was the latter, she claims, who shaped her imagination, while she ventriloquized their scientific dreams through her mechanical body: "We remain stuck with astonishment," Cifali writes, "when [Flournoy's suggestions] come close to a farce, when they manipulate Elise and make her a true puppet, a pure object of observation."[45] Certainly, Cifali is right to remark upon the collective nature of glossolalia: "We know that the phenomenon of glossolalia is always social and needs to be sustained by others, by ideology—religious or spiritual—which gives it a frame, authorizes it, valorizes it, and furnishes it with an external meaning. It requires an Institution that awaits the production by the subject in order to interpret it."[46] Yet, far from contained by this institution, far from a pure puppet echoing male subjectivity and desire, Smith offered continual inventions and reinventions of linguistic apparatuses and rules, thereby eluding audiences and thwarting her scholars' desires for knowledge and mastery.

While providing her linguists and psychologists the scene for new discoveries, Smith's imagination indeed operated a certain reversal of power relations at the séance table, for her spirit guides permitted her to offer a counterknowledge based on a distinct, and mysterious, system of legitimation. Constantly exceeding the scientific limits of Saussure's and Flournoy's methodologies, Léopold, Esenale, and Simandini intervened to authenticate opposing frames of interpretations. Despite her sex, her class, and her accompanying lack of education, Smith gained, through these personalities, access to an authoritative form of speech that would have been outside the realm of possibilities for a woman of modest upbringing. It is through such modes of legitimation that Léopold could oppose Flournoy's explanation of Smith's Sanskritoid; within the séance's hermeneutics, his access to knowledge relied on modalities of communication that the scientist could not access.

Similarly, Smith's personalities never accepted—and neither did she—the rationalist explanations of Flournoy and Saussure. As Flournoy noted, her subconscious even responded to their skepticism by adding new embellishments to her linguistic creations. Flournoy, who considered the Martian language a "puerile construction," notably wrote that he had shown Hélène his "full translation of the Martian texts" and "explained to her in detail the secrets of the language, its superficial originalities and fundamental resemblances to French," thus demonstrating his "utter skepticism as to the Martian."[47] While such a demonstration could have resulted in silencing her subconscious creativity, Smith's trance personalities did not abdicate so easily. Seventeen days after Flournoy made these statements, he was surprised to find that Smith's Martian language had been replaced by an "Ultra-Martian," which defined itself through its more pronounced originality and complete distinction from the French language.[48] Thus, while Flournoy had noted that the order of words within the Martian sentence was generally the same as in French, he now found that the Ultra-Martian had little comprehensible syntax. Further, while he had noted that Mars's alphabet was similar to French, possessing only twenty-one letters, but each corresponding to French sounds, he now found that the Ultra-Martian was "a language absolutely new, of a very peculiar rhythm, extremely rich in *a*, without any *ch* at all up to the present moment, and of which the construction is so different from the French that there is *no clear method of discovering it*."[49] Thus, to mention a few examples, the Martian *forimi ti zi romêti*, meaning *marque de l'attente* (symbol of waiting) became, in Ultra-Martian, *Abak*. The Martian *forimi ti mis mess mâti*, meaning *marque d'un grand chef* (symbol of a great chief), became the simpler *Touk* in Ultra-Martian.[50] After the publication of *From India to the Planet Mars*, Smith would continue to explore extraplanetary languages, and Flournoy was able to encounter some of her new inventions, which he reproduced in his *New Observations*. From the forty-eight

Ultra-Martian symbols he discovered, as it now appeared, the new language was impossible to decipher without Smith's personalities and resembled no European system of writing (see figures 3.2 and 3.3). His discoveries were thus subjected to Smith's interpretation and methodology.

By the summer of 1900, an Uranian romance also emerged in Smith's séances, as did a new alphabet and symbolization logic. On August 2, Smith wrote to Lemaitre that she had "heard the following words: afato matobi fomo zatomma idôto metta ato tadota moti tottizo zôtôta titô homato zito lopo lapedi lappoda alo to papéli" and was then struck by a "great desire to write." The result was the message in figure 3.4, which Flournoy reproduced and translated in *New Observations*. Once again, the psychologist found

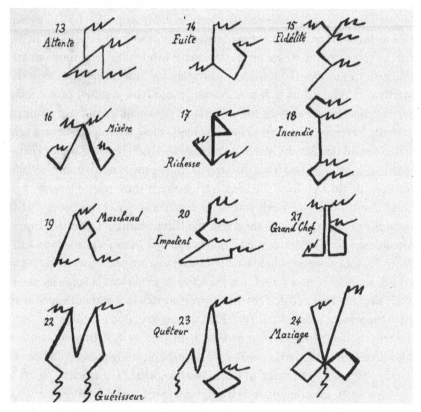

Figure 3.2 Ultra-Martian ideograms signifying Waiting, Flight, Loyalty, Misery, Wealth, Burning, Merchant, Impotent, Great Chief, Healer, Beggar, and Marriage

Flournoy, *Nouvelles observations sur un cas de somnambulisme*, 167.

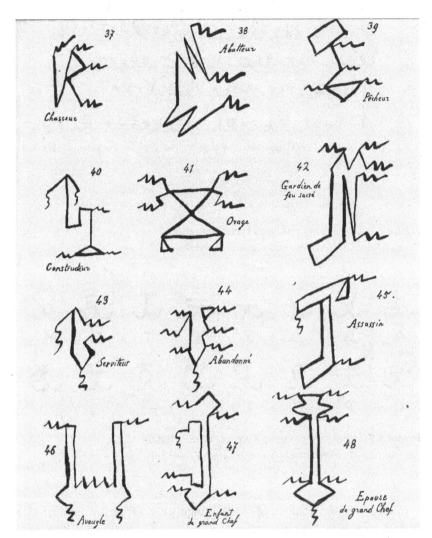

Figure 3.3 Last Ultra-Martian ideograms discovered by Flournoy, signifying Hunter, Slaughterer, Fisherman, Constructor, Thunderstorm, Warden of Sacred Fire, Servant, Merchant, Abandoned, Assassin, Blind, Great Chief's Child, and Great Chief's Wife

Flournoy, *Nouvelles observations sur un cas de somnambulisme*, 171.

himself unable to completely reproduce and understand its alphabet. Figure 3.5 demonstrates that four of the language's sixteen characters remained mysterious, as if they had been excesses unheard in the pronunciation of Smith's Ultra-Martian.

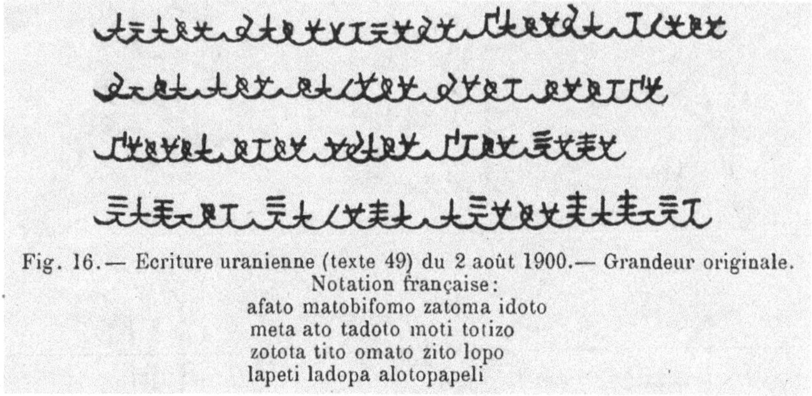

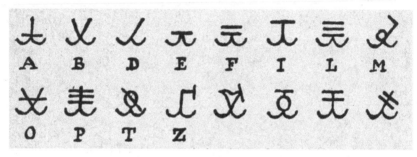

Fig. 16.— Ecriture uranienne (texte 49) du 2 août 1900.— Grandeur originale.
Notation française:
afato matobifomo zatoma idoto
meta ato tadoto moti totizo
zotota tito omato zito lopo
lapeti ladopa alotopapeli

Figure 3.4 Uranian symbols and French notation
Flournoy, *Nouvelles observations sur un cas de somnambulisme*, 185.

Figure 3.5 Uranian symbols and corresponding letters
Flournoy, *Nouvelles observations sur un cas de somnambulisme*, 185.

Considering the analysis of Smith's linguistic creations in light of Max Weber's notion of disenchantment illustrates the nuances and complexities of the relations between occultism, faith, and science at the turn of the nineteenth century. On the one hand, Saussure's analyses of her séances reframed glossolalia away from its religious interpretations. The most complex creations of spiritual languages were not, for him, a manifestation of transcendence, but an illustration of the psychology of language and of the arbitrariness of linguistic signs. On the other hand, Victor Henry perceived in the medium's linguistic exuberance a potential residue of humanity's first, and perhaps divine, language. Yet he also believed such mysteries could be conquered by science and rationality "were we to possess more powerful or sagacious means of penetrating the secrets of the subconscious elaborations."[51] As these analyses demonstrate, therefore, the thesis of disenchantment does not imply that the enchanted simply evaporated from nineteenth-century science and life. In the words of Wouter J. Hanegraaff, what rather emerged through modernity was, at the "foundation of modern natural science," a "conviction that, in principle and by definition, nothing in the natural world can be essentially 'mysterious' and 'incalculable,' that is to say, forever out of reach for intellectual understanding and human control."[52] And yet the key to the medium's ciphers remained out of reach for these savants. Despite Saussure's and Henry's contributions, Flournoy could only note that—at least for the time being—he remained without any "clear method of discovering" the deeper secrets of Smith's ever-increasing, perpetually evolving languages.[53]

Conclusion

I earlier alluded to Echo's mythology as a clear allegory for the intricacies of language, gender, and power, for the nymph points to our desire to be— and the impossibility of being—heard by the other. Through her encounter with Narcissus, she further personifies the problematization of sexual relations, as explored in the work of Luce Irigaray. I may now add that Echo also forms an interesting parallel with mediumship. Following Irigaray, we might indeed understand female mediumship as a paradoxical discursive performance that is reminiscent of the nymph's story: by renouncing their own embodied experiences, mediums were able to verbalize the identity of reputed men of science, religion, and the arts, just as Echo verbalized the personality of Narcissus before leaving her own body behind. Among believers, this repetition permitted mediums to enjoy the rewards of a masculine discursive positioning: mediums were frequently admired, their words taken as gospel, and their works praised and valued in spiritualist circles. As Flournoy reminded his readers, indeed, believers presented a "great respect shown to mediums, which is like that accorded to priests."[54] Irigaray's work on women's access to discourse and their oppression in symbolic language can thereby reveal how mediumship would constitute a compromise for nineteenth-century women, as the practice permitted them to speak and act with a new sense of agency, even though this linguistic positioning was obtained only through their renunciation of the embodied "I."

Furthermore, mediums' discursive acts could be interpreted according to the feminist strategy of mimicry defined by Irigaray. For the latter, "The exclusion of a female imaginary certainly puts woman in the position of experiencing herself only fragmentarily, . . . as waste, or excess, what is left of a mirror invested by the (masculine) 'subject' to reflect himself, to copy himself."[55] In this context, for Irigaray, mimicry forms a technique of apparently perfect echoing that nonetheless opens gaps within the systematicity of sameness.[56]

> One must assume the feminine role deliberately. Which means already to convert a form of subordination into an affirmation, and thus to begin to thwart it. . . . To play with mimesis is thus, for a woman, to try to recover the place of her exploitation by herself . . . so as to make "visible," by an effect of playful repetition, what was supposed to remain invisible: the cover-up of a possible operation of the feminine in language.[57]

Among believers, mediums' mimicry relied on tropes of feminine subordination to claim a greater capacity to become spiritually "possessed." This possession, in turn, opened the possibility of recognition in traditionally masculine realms of endeavors. Through their echoing of male (spiritual) voices, mediums were able to assume the authorial function of a masterful "I." Among skeptics, by contrast, mediums' performances could demonstrate that this masculine "I," with all its presumed mastery, is only a fictional position performed in discourse and legitimated by patriarchal institutions.

While mediums' spiritual discourses, by their very form, already challenge the symbolic order through playful mimicry, the practice of glossolalia furthers this challenge by establishing a different order of discourse, interpretation, and authority. Glossolalia has indeed generally been defined through its connection to the sacred, or as a way of communicating with the transcendent outside the rules of signification established within the linguistic community. Through its linguistic exuberance, glossolalia simulates language but disturbs it at the same time. In his article on glossolalia, de Certeau thus defines the term as a form of speech that defies the symbolic:

> Normally, in a society, institutions found, guarantee, and distribute the space of speech. They owe this role not to the capital of meaning that they preserve . . . but to their capacity to organize a checkerboard of positions that at once authorizes and limits verbal circulation, divides and controls it. Family, profession, and public function each define topics of illocutory acts,

that is to say, the network of spaces where speech is permitted (founded) but in a system of conventions that fixes its conditions and its pertinence: you can speak here but not there; you can say that here, but not under such and such circumstances, and nowhere else; and so on.[58]

Through the violent disarticulation of signifieds and their known signifiers, glossolalia can rearticulate the "checkerboard of positions" that permit or prevent certain pronouncements. In creating a multitude of ciphers, Smith reorganized the hierarchy of speaking positions at the séance table and became herself a subject of knowledge, a bluestocking, to reuse Saussure's expression. Smith also reframed the circumstances and conventions of "proper" discourse in order to express what we may consider a "female imaginary," a form of speech escaping the rules of symbolic discourse. For Irigaray, "If we [women] keep on speaking sameness, if we speak to each other as men have been doing for centuries, as we have been taught to speak, we'll miss each other, fail ourselves. . . . Words will pass through our bodies, above our heads . . . : we'll be spoken machines, speaking machines."[59] At the opposite of echolalia, Smith's glossolalia permits us to imagine a different economy of symbolization. Through this linguistic excess, the medium's personalities formed their own ciphers, structures, and conventions, which both resembled and diverged from existing languages. In the enchanted worlds she imagined, Smith thereby became indomitable, always escaping her scholars' attempts at mastery.

Like her linguistic creations, the medium's artistic oeuvre exceeded contemporaneous categorizations of art and thus required new frames of understanding. As the next chapter demonstrates, the surrealist poet André Breton attempted to decipher the mechanisms of her unbridled creativity and, in the process, uncovered the possibilities and powers of the unconscious. In these explorations, Breton gave new life to Flournoy's theories, which better addressed his own artistic experiments than increasingly dominant framings of the unconscious in twentieth-century France.

4

Creativity

The Muse of Surrealism, Automatism, and the Creative Unconscious

Léonie, Lucy, and the French Psychological Tradition

Akin to many psychopathologists of the late nineteenth century, Pierre
Janet (1859–1947) began his investigations of the mind with experiments
on a woman who presented many characteristics of spiritual mediumship.
In search of a subject for his doctoral dissertation, Janet had encountered
Léonie Leboulanger (1837–190?), a forty-five-year-old peasant woman who
had previously been a patient of a Le Havre doctor and who could apparently carry hypnotic commands without the means of direct communication. A professor of philosophy at the Lycée of Le Havre, Janet was enthralled
by the narrative of Léonie's abilities, and he began a series of experiments
that he soon published through several articles.[1] In consecutive trials, Janet
claimed to have hypnotized Léonie at a distance ranging from a few meters
to two kilometers and to have given her posthypnotic instructions while
she remained under the observation of invited witnesses.[2] Between 1885
and 1886, Janet reported having completed sixty-five experiments, of which
thirty-seven were successful. A success indicated that Léonie had properly
responded to the suggestion at about the same time as Janet had telepathi-
cally commanded it.[3] While Janet generally instructed Léonie to fall into a
hypnotic sleep, other suggestions were more improbable and ranged from
turning on a light at a certain moment of the day to opening an umbrella despite the beautiful weather.

During these trials, Janet discovered that this "poor peasant" (see figure
4.1), normally "a serious and somewhat melancholy woman, calm and slow,
very gentle and extremely timid," also possessed as second personality,
calling herself Léontine, who emerged when Léonie was entranced. While
Léonie was docile, Léontine appeared "gay, noisy, and restless to an insup-
portable degree; she [remained] good-natured" but had "a singular tendency

Hélène Smith. Claudie Massicotte, Oxford University Press. © Oxford University Press 2023.
DOI: 10.1093/oso/9780197680018.003.0005

Figure 4.1 The clairvoyant Léonie, n.d.
Collection of the Musée de Bsretagne, public domain.

to irony and bitter jests."[4] Janet seemed to marvel at Léonie's physical meta-morphosis, noting that "her face," when she became Léontine, was "no longer the same."[5] Further, like the mischievous personality of Anna O., Léonie "was far from being docile" in her second state, and she frequently disobeyed her investigator.[6]

Akin to Flournoy, Janet was thus deeply intrigued by mediums' and clairvoyants' alleged powers, and he made use of spiritualist methods to dis-cover hidden abilities of the mind. He notably communicated with Léonie's multiple personalities through automatic writing in addition to testing her clairvoyance and telepathic powers. However, by the late nineteenth and early twentieth centuries, prominent members of the new science of psychology began regarding the marvelous manifestations produced by mediums as unworthy of such clinical investigations. As increasing revelations of frauds and scandals tainted the fields of spiritualism and psychical research, the credibility of scientific experiments on séances largely suffered. Official psychiatric and psychological knowledge thus began to separate itself, not only from the study of alleged supranormal faculties among gifted spiritualists, but also, more generally, from any study conducted upon mediums.[7] In other words, many authors chose to abandon all inquiries into occult faculties of mind and to relegate them to the now autonomous discipline of psychical research. As historians have shown, Janet's trajectory both exemplified and shaped this separation, demonstrating how "French nascent psychology went through the study of 'marvelous phenomena' before recanting by claiming a higher scientific status than parapsychology/metapsychics."[8] In the late 1880s, Janet therefore left Léonie to psychical researchers (including Frederic Myers and Charles Richet), among whom she continued to build her reputation as a gifted somnambulist and clairvoyant.[9]

For his part, in 1889, Janet became director of the psychological laboratory at the Salpêtrière Hospital, where he worked closely with Jean-Martin Charcot. Early in their collaboration, Janet received the following advice from the Salpêtrière master: *Nihil admirari* (refuse wonder), advice that seems to have defined his later approach to the mind. As historian of psychology Régine Plas explains: "This warning, associated with the obstinate silence that Janet would keep his entire life on the sensational experiments of his youth [with Léonie], suggests that he had to disavow crediting his participants with extraordinary abilities."[10] At the Salpêtrière, Janet continued to explore automatisms through spiritualist practices but discovered only the symptomatic manifestations of disintegration. He stated in 1894: "There is no need to go back over the description of [automatic] writing discovered by spiritualists: if it no longer serves the religious purpose for which it was intended by the disciples of Allan Kardec, it may in many circumstances assume a medical role."[11]

Working with his Salpêtrière patients, Janet thus discovered only the pathological character of unconscious manifestations. In one of his experiments with automatic writing, he notably reported a conversation with his patient Lucy that highlighted the fragmentation of consciousness and the easiness with which unconscious personalities could form to divide the hysteric's psyche.[12] While the patient was distracted, he spoke with her and saw her hand respond through automatic writing.

> Do you hear me? I ask her—(she responds in writing) *No.*
> But to answer one must hear.—*Yes, absolutely.*
> So how do you do it?—*I do not know.*
> There must be someone who hears me?—*Yes.*
> Who?—*Other than Lucy.*
> Very well! Another person. Shall we name this person?—*No.*
> Yes, it will be more convenient.—*Well then, Adrienne.*[13]

Salpêtrière patients like Lucy/Adrienne therefore replaced Léonie/Léontine as a new locus for Janet's discovery of the unconscious. In this transition from the somnambulist to the hysteric, however, Janet's unconscious became devoid of wonder. Regarding his hysterics' automatic productions, he wrote that, even though "Lucy, Margaret, and many others present in a complete way the automatic writing and would make the fortune of a spiritualist cabinet,"[14] and that "the poor patients whom I studied had no genius; the phenomena which had become subconscious in them were very simple, and in others formed part of personal consciousness without exciting any admiration."[15] In the 1892 "Le spiritisme contemporain" ("Contemporary Spiritism"), Janet further reduced all phenomena of mediumship to hysteria, noting that phenomena emanating from spiritual séances "have laws and can be explained in the same manner by a serious trouble in the mental operation of perception, which we have described under the name of psychological disaggregation."[16]

Therefore, once Janet had abandoned his experiments with Léonie and reframed his understanding of the unconscious through the manifestations displayed by his hysterical patients, he came to see very little creativity, power, or marvel in the manifestations of the unconscious. This shift had important consequences for modern understandings of the subject: as Júlia Gyimesi remarks, a symptomatic view of the unconscious soon "gained the victory over other theories of the unconscious."[17] As Janet's theories and career gained prominence—the psychologist notably founded and presided over the French Societé de Psychologie in 1901—he reshaped the doxa of depth psychology in early twentieth-century France. The unconscious formulated within this doxa became far removed from the dangerously creative, highly powerful, and mysterious subliminal that experimental studies with mediums had claimed to uncover. While Janet acknowledged some intelligence in unconscious states, he reframed automatisms as repetitive—echolalic—and he therefore saw his entranced patients as "enfeebled minds . . . altogether devoid of creativity."[18]

Three decades later, the surrealist artist André Breton (1896–1966) would reject Janet's model of automatism as "sterile." In her study of Breton's and Janet's opposite understandings of automatism, Alexandra Bacopoulos-Viau explains that "by stripping his system of the 'marvellous' (le merveilleux), Janet also removed the potential for seeing in automatic manifestations of the mind a source of exalted creativity."[19] While Janet's work on automatism allowed "no creativity in elementary psychical states," which he saw as "vessels of repetition, disintegration," Breton's artistic project reframed automatism as a space of creativity.[20] As this chapter argues, Breton's attempt to recover the imaginative possibilities of unconscious creation was in part propelled by his fascination with modern occultism and, more specifically, with Hélène Smith.[21] Indeed, the year after Smith's death, Breton discovered many of her paintings and drawings,[22] and he later reproduced a number of her creations in his work "The Automatic Message."[23] Well aware of the scientific and psychological discourses on Smith, Breton read Flournoy's narrative and interpretation of her séances, and he came to draw on her performances as a model to unveil the limits and risks of subjectivity. Before his encounter with Smith, Breton had already conducted with his group a series of experiments in "psychic automatism" aimed at creating art without "any control exercised by reason [and] exempt from any aesthetic or moral concern" that drew upon spiritualist practices.[24] Notably, the surrealists' "period of sleeping fits," which revealed powerful mediumistic powers in Robert Desnos (1900–1945), had reproduced many of the motifs encountered in Smith's and other mediums' séances.

Although Breton encountered Smith's artistic creation after the publication of the first Manifesto, the medium's trance performances nonetheless offered him a parallel model of subjectivity that illuminated the excessive, dangerously powerful, creativity of automatic discourse. By contrast to Janet's hysterical "mediums," Smith's trance communications opened the way to interpretations of the unconscious, or subliminal self, as a reservoir of extraordinary creativity. Similarly, the surrealists' performances of automatism uncovered an unconscious that extended far beyond the productions of symptoms and functioned as a source of prodigious creativity and inexhaustible imagination. While such views of the psyche were becoming obliterated from the canon of depth psychology, Breton took seriously the performances of trance creativity displayed by mediums such as Smith. This chapter suggests that automatism thereby brought back to life important questions about both the limits and possibilities of authorial agency.

Smith's Spiritual Creations: From the Laboratory to the Museum

Akin to many nineteenth-century mediums, Smith developed in trance a capacity to enchant her audience through her artistic creations. While, following the spiritualist doctrine, she interpreted these creations as tangible demonstrations of a celestial world, other witnesses saw in her many productions a proof of the imaginative capabilities of the unconscious. In the Flournoy séances, Smith's fabulous art forms ranged from tragic performances to musical compositions, and from poetry to drawing. Well aware of Janet's work on disaggregation, Flournoy generally interpreted such events as demonstrations of unconscious creativity and opposed them to mechanical, repetitive, and symptomatic automatisms.

Relating Smith's dramatic representations of her past lives, Flournoy notably described the séance proceedings as multiple-course events. He noted that "the *menu* of the séances—if the expression is permissible—is always composed of one or two *plats de résistance*, carefully prepared in advance in the subliminal laboratories, and of various *hors d'oeuvres* left to the inspiration of the moment." These appetizers, Flournoy added, constituted, for instance, "the animated conversations, sometimes full of spirited repartee, between Léopold or Marie Antionette and the sitters." Flournoy admitted, with Janet, that in such spontaneous productions, some "repetition" and automatic phenomena "entirely mechanical and almost devoid of sense" presented themselves "on frequent occasions." Yet, by contrast to Janet's view of automatism, Flournoy added that many of Smith's royal performances "could not have been prepared in advance, and are all together opposed to the stereotyped repetition which is generally expected of automatic phenomena."[25]

Flournoy also marveled at Smith's literary creations. After noting that her writing in the royal romance followed the "archaic forms of orthography, *j'aurois* for *j'aurais*, etc.," he remarked: "It is undoubtably a matter for wonderment that Mlle. Smith, who has not gone very deep into literary studies, should, nevertheless, have retained these orthographic peculiarities of the eighteenth century; but we must not overlook the fineness of choice, the refined sensibility, the consummate, albeit instinctive, art which presides over the sorting and storing away of the subconscious memories."[26] Flournoy also noted that Léopold could quite easily compose beautiful poems, further emphasizing the creativity found in automatic writing. He remarked that, after receiving a letter from himself, Smith had been "seized with a vague desire to write, she took a pencil . . . and traced rapidly, in the characteristic handwriting of Léopold and with his signature, a beautiful epistle of eighteen Alexandrine lines addressed to me."[27] The psychologist concluded by connecting Smith's wonderful acts of literary creativity with a regression to the childhood state of play. As mentioned in Chapter 2, he noted: "All children are poets, and that in the original, the most extended, acceptation of the term. They create, they imagine, they construct—and language is not the least of their creations."[28]

Smith's romances were also accompanied by musical performances. In one of the séances attended by Ferdinand de Saussure, Flournoy remarked that the linguist, who was "very much better qualified than we to distinguish the Hindoo sounds," sat "quite near Hélène, who sang seated upon the ground."[29] Saussure took notes of the lyrics, which were later partially translated by Léopold. Flournoy added: "As to the melody of this plaintive ditty, M. Aug. de Morsier, who heard it at the séance of the 4th of September, 1898, has kindly noted it as exactly as possible" and he reproduced it in his own text.[30] Another musical séance is reported in the proceedings available at the Archives of Geneva. Dated March 4, 1900, the notes, taken by Auguste Lemaitre, explain that Smith "had a desire to play the piano, which gave me an unexpected little session of about 35 minutes. It seemed to her (6:25 am) that she was going to replay the romance she had already played to her mother last Sunday." Smith then "sang Hindu lyrics that she accompanied on the piano with a simple rhythm that did not lack charm. The very soft lyrics were unfortunately almost inaudible."[31] Lemaitre then transcribed the melody and the accompanying lyrics he had been able to identify.

Like many of Smith's other sitters, Flournoy was thus interested in recording her bursts of creativity. He proceeded similarly with her visual creations, as he collected and published ten images of drawings she made of her visions of the planet Mars, many of which can now be found in the Flournoy Collection at the Archives of Geneva (see figures 4.2, 4.3 and 4.4). Flournoy also reproduced some of Smith's later extraplanetary landscapes in the *Nouvelles observations*

Figure 4.2 Hélène Smith, drawing of Astané (Martian inhabitant), n.d.
Papiers de la famille Flournoy, Bibliothèque de Genève, Ms. Fr. 7843/3.

(*New Observations*, see figure 4.5). While not produced in complete trance, these drawings nonetheless reflected, for Flournoy, a certain amount of automatic creativity. He stated: "None of these pictures has been executed in complete somnambulism, and they have not, consequently, like the drawings of certain mediums, the interest of a graphic product, absolutely automatic, engendered outside of and unknown to the ordinary consciousness."[32] Yet, he added: "They represent a sort of intermediary activity, and correspond to a state of hemisomnambulism."[33] The psychologist provided an example in

Figure 4.3 Hélène Smith, drawing of the Martian landscape, n.d.
Papiers de la famille Flournoy, Bibliothèque de Genève, Ms. Fr.7843/3.

a letter Smith addressed to him regarding a strange flower from the Martian landscape she painted. "I greatly regret that you were not here to see me execute the drawing: the pencil glided so quickly that I did not have time to notice what contours it was making. I can assert without any exaggeration that it was not my hand alone that made the drawing, but that truly an invisible force guided the pencil in spite of me. . . . The whole was done so quickly that I marvelled at it."[34] Flournoy's interpretation was that the drawings were the product "of a quasi-automatic activity, which always gives great satisfaction to Mlle. Smith" and originated from "her subliminal self that holds the brush and executes, at its pleasure, its own tableaux, which also have the value of veritable originals."[35] Therefore, according to Sonu Shamdasani, Flournoy encountered in Smith's trances "a reversion to an earlier developmental stage of childhood that . . . is characterized by play. As play has a preparatory function, this reversion is compensatory, and enables access to a level of creativity that has been lost."[36] Throughout the rest of her life, Smith would reject this interpretation, despite her understanding of the wonderful power and creativity Flournoy

Figure 4.4 Hélène Smith, drawing of Martian vegetation, n.d.
Papiers de la famille Flournoy, Bibliothèque de Genève, Ms. Fr. 7843/3.

attributed to her unconscious. She wrote in her manuscripts in 1927, two years before her death:

Oh, this subconscious, this subliminal. . . . If it were to be felt capable of creating a work similar to mine, what should we think of it, of its power, of its strength? Shouldn't we devote a special cult to it, seek it out at every important, happy or unhappy, hour of our lives, make it act in our place for what we feel unable to do or to manage at times? And if we finally came to the point

Figure 4.5 Ultra-Martian landscape, signed by Hélène Smith
Flournoy, *Nouvelles observations sur un cas de somnambulisme*, 161.

where we could do nothing but admit its existence, should we not see in it a personality, more spiritualized than the first one, a help that God would have created to enlighten us at times, a second consciousness emanating from Him, helping Him in His mission concerning His children?[37]

After the termination of Smith's séances with Flournoy, the medium's approach to spiritualism evolved. Less is known about the following period of her life, but she appears to have dedicated herself more completely to her visual creations. After a rich American provided her with the means to live independently, Smith took lessons in painting and began a series of visual creations reflecting her spiritual encounters. Most records of Smith's existence during this period appear in the work of Waldemar Deonna, then archaeology professor at the University of Geneva and director of the Musée d'Art et d'Histoire de Genève. Responsible for the paintings, letters, and manuscripts of Hélène Smith following her death, Deonna offered an exhibition of her work in Geneva in 1929, before it moved to Paris in 1932.[38] Deonna also published an account of her creations, beliefs, and artistic methods in *De la planète Mars en Terre Sainte* (*From Mars to the Holy Land*) in 1932.

Here Smith again explained how her spiritual creations responded to a certain dissatisfaction with expectations of domesticity placed upon women. She noted that, after the death of her mother, a sense of loneliness and a profound sadness had nearly convinced her to marry. Yet, it was on the very day she "was about to make up [her] mind at the idea of marrying," that she "started [her] first painting"[39] Following this loss of her mother in 1905, Smith completed in trance various paintings representing her visions of Christian religious figures. Each of these portraits was first announced by a spirit or angel before Smith completed it in moments of somnambulism. The medium now appeared to realize Flournoy's wish for a "graphic product, absolutely automatic,"[40] for she completely lost consciousness during their creation. Almost immediately after the beginning of this new production, she further drew the interest and curiosity of Geneva society. As Auguste Lemaitre explained, in an article for *Archives de psychologie* in 1907: "Thousands of people have marched in her quaint little apartment over the past three months to contemplate her somnambulistic masterpieces. The most enthusiastic appraisals were expressed. There were a few discordant notes: but these were quickly stifled in the general concert of praise and admiring outbursts: so much so that, for a while, the illustrious medium's salon would have seemed well on its way to becoming a new place of pilgrimage and devotion."[41]

Deonna established the chronology of these works as follows, indicating a creative process lasting between weeks and years for the completion of each piece. Her longest work emerged during First World War as a peace offering to a troubled world but was never completed.

Painting	Announcement	Beginning
Head of the Christ	1905	Three weeks later
Head of the Virgin	March or April 1905	November 1905
Jesus in Gethsemane	November 1905	October 1906
Crucified	October 1906	March 1908
Jesus in Emmaus	August 1908	Christmas 1909
Transfiguration	April 1909	February 1911
The Saint Family	August 1911	November 1911
Hélène and the Angel	August 1911	June 1912
Judas	1912	July 1913
Angel of Peace	August 1914	March 1918*

*Deonna, De la planète Mars, 308.

Figure 4.6 Hélène Smith, *Cagliostro*, 1913. Oil painting.
Deonna, *De la planète Mars en Terre Sainte.*

Beyond these important figures of Christianity, Smith's paintings during this period also included *Cagliostro*, completed 1909 (figure 4.6), and *The Daughter of Jairus* completed in 1913 (figure 4.7).

Between 1905 and 1915, Smith devoted herself nearly entirely to her creations, even moving to a new apartment when she felt her work could benefit from the change. She wrote in 1909: "I needed a special room in which to paint, and where I could sleep, without having to reduce myself to an alcove behind paintings that had to be moved every night and where I lacked air. There, I will have air and greenery, peace and quiet to finish my work, which I feel is crying out for it."[42]

As per her creative process, we possess, thanks to Deonna's publication and an earlier article by Auguste Lemaitre, numerous descriptions of her method. The creations generally began with Smith's hearing of voices announcing that a new painting would soon emerge. She would then have visions of the painting, in its actual size, so that she could take measurements and order

Figure 4.7 Hélène Smith, *The Daughter of Jairus*, 1913. Oil painting.
Musée LaM. Public domain.

the appropriate frames and panels. Once the material arrived, the paintings themselves would mostly take place under complete trance. On occasion, Smith would find herself encircled by a dense fog and feel a loss of control over her hands. At other times, her room would transform itself to represent the scene of the image to be painted. As a part of this environment, the image would then juxtapose itself upon the panel. In either case, Smith would then lose consciousness and, upon awakening, discover that part of the painting had been completed. She explained: "I completely lose consciousness. I wake up from this state to find that the piece of painting I had glimpsed is actually painted this time . . . the color that still adheres to my fingers is proof of this."[43] Her portraits would often begin with the eyes of her subjects, before she completed the rest of their bodies and their surroundings (see figures 4.8, 4.9). Once the works were finished, she would, in her awakened state, decorate their frames through her own conscious creations. According to Deonna, these adornments made plain the contrast between her conscious

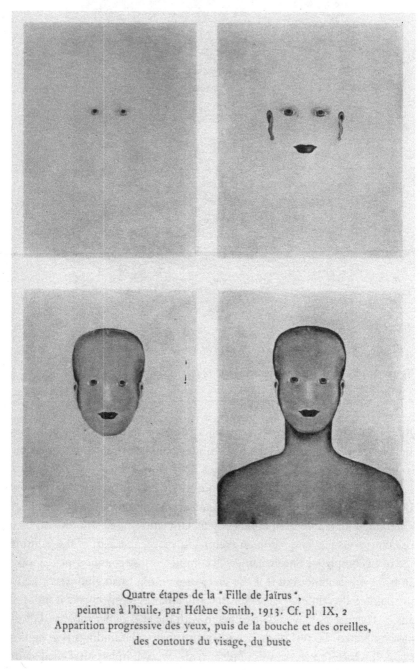

Quatre étapes de la " Fille de Jaïrus ",
peinture à l'huile, par Hélène Smith, 1913. Cf. pl. IX, 2
Apparition progressive des yeux, puis de la bouche et des oreilles,
des contours du visage, du buste

Figure 4.8 Four steps of the daughter of Jairus, 1913

Deonna, *De la planète Mars en Terre Sainte.*

Quatre étapes de la " Fille de Jaïrus ",
peinture à l'huile, par Hélène Smith, 1913. Cf. pl. IX, 2, et pl. XV

Figure 4.9 Four more steps of the daughter of Jairus, 1913

Deonna, *De la planète Mars en Terre Sainte*.

and unconscious artistic abilities, for they were, "we won't hesitate to say it, of the worst possible taste."[44]

During this period, Smith also fell in love with a man whom she called her "great Italian friend." Beginning in 1907, the two exchanged letters, and Smith in time came to see him as her true soulmate. After his death in 1915, her unconscious creativity greatly diminished. A painting that had been announced the previous year would begin in 1918, but no other painting would be completed. According to Deonna, it was the mourning of her friend, and his manifestation as a new spiritual guide, that reshaped her unconscious activity. The Italian friend's messages indeed became more numerous than those of her guiding angels, and they occupied her mind in other ways. The Italian friend's postmortem messages were, he wrote, "the cause of the halt in her pictorial production. . . . She now lives only in the memory of her friend, waiting for his visions and automatic dictations, which from then on fill her manuscripts."[45] While her creations had begun against expectations of marriage and domesticity, it appears they ended with the reunion with her true love, now idealized in spiritual form. After this death, Smith thus rebuilt her world through different preoccupations; she lived largely without society, but remained surrounded by Léopold, her Italian friend, Jesus, and the many angels who offered her protections against various perceived plights. Even after she had stopped painting, the characters in her tableaux remained active beings, speaking and moving bodies embellishing her life. She wrote in 1927, about a new vision surrounding her painting of the angel Gabriel (figure 4.10),

> At that moment, the painting seemed to slip, and it was on top of the painting of the angel Gabriel surrounding me with his arm that the ever more radiant and beautiful star came to rest. The angel detached himself from the painting and, surrounding me with his arm, showed me the sky radiating a thousand lights. Then, as he tilted his face toward mine, his soft and sweet voice whispered to me: Friend, always walk in the footsteps of the Master. I am your guardian angel, the companion of your Immortality who will protect you here below from the wickedness of men.[46]

In the words of a follower and contemporary of Smith, "The Christ whom Hélène saw lived, walked, approached her, put his hand on her shoulder, even spoke words of peace and comfort to her, and left her troubled and moved to

Figure 4.10 Hélène Smith, *Helen and the Angel*. Oil painting. This painting was also reproduced in Breton's 1933 "Le Message Automatique."
Art Brut / Collection ABCD.

tears. It is easy for those who have not seen or felt anything similar to talk of hallucinations."[47]

After her death in June 1929, Smith bequeathed her paintings to the Musée d'Art et d'Histoire de Genève. Although she by then tried to protect her works against renewed scientific investigations, her last wish was not granted. Indeed, Deonna explained that, despite Smith's hope that "her works would not fall into the hands of her enemies, spiritists, magnetizers, and envious people of any caliber, or scholars of the race of a Flournoy, nor would they serve as study documents in a psychology laboratory," the Geneva museum had "put them on deposit for some time precisely at the Psychology Laboratory of our University!"[48] As Allison Morehead reveals in a study of Smith's will and the ensuing Geneva exhibition, the medium's gift was not entirely appreciated by members of the museum direction. Louis Gielly (1876–1951), then responsible for the fine arts collection, stated that he had examined "the paintings from Miss Müller's estate" and found that "they are of no interest to our collections and are unexposable." He concluded: "I therefore propose that this bequest be declined."[49] To rescue the paintings, Deonna pleaded to the president of the administrative counsel of Geneva that, while he agreed that "these works, executed by Miss Müller herself, do not have sufficient artistic interest to be exhibited in our painting collections," they nonetheless presented a "very important scientific psychological interest."[50] He added, noting a loophole in Smith's legacy, "The will does not contain any restrictive clause obliging the city of Geneva to exhibit her paintings, [and] it will be easy, once they are in our possession, to deposit them in the most appropriate place, namely the Psychology Laboratory of the University of Geneva."[51] Deonna then worked with Edouard Claparède (1873–1940), cofounder of the *Archives de psychologie* with Théodore Flournoy and newest director of the laboratory, who accepted the paintings on behalf of the laboratory "with the greatest interest."[52]

Deonna also managed to exhibit Smith's collection in the museum for a brief time, not as works of art, but as psychological documents of scientific importance for the community of Geneva. The exhibition was announced in a press release: "The City of Geneva has just received a collection of paintings of very special interest, bequeathed by their author, Mademoiselle Elise-Catherine MULLER, better known in the scientific world under the pseudonym of Hélène Smith." These paintings, it added, would be exposed "in the exhibition hall of the Decorative Arts section, not for their aesthetic value but only for their psychological interest."[53] In 1929, the paintings therefore found at least a temporary home in the Musée d'Art et d'Histoire de Genève, where they were exhibited for some weeks and garnered a "large influx of visitors."[54] The paintings further had profound effects on some of these visitors, as a review of the exhibition for *La Suisse* attested. The author remarked that the museum had presented a dozen paintings of various dimensions, some enormous, such as the *Transfiguration* and the *Crucifixion*, others smaller. A total absence of craft is revealed, at first glance, and even to a layman. Some features are vaguely reminiscent of the Primitives or the Byzantine icons; others show a childish naiveté and make one think of children's scribbles. The colors are hard, brutal, or bland, without nuances, and offer the spectacle of a striking disharmony. But the feeling that emanates from these strange canvases, haunting like a night-mare, is in no way similar to the feeling one gets from the candid freshness of a Fra Angelico. I know nothing more painful than the smile of the two prophets of the *Transfiguration*. . . . Beneath this smile, which is meant to be supernatural, one guesses a grimace. Beneath the simplicity of the whole, one discerns something extravagant, something reticent, abnormal, and in fact demonic, which makes one shudder. . . . If I were forced to live, even if only for twenty-four hours, in the atmosphere of such sinister images, I know that I would be good for the attic.[55]

In the following year, the will was contested by a lawyer representing dis-tant members of Smith's family, and their consequent trajectory remains little documented. Another exhibition took place in Paris in 1932, the same year Deonna published his near four-hundred-page account and discussion of Smith's religious oeuvre. Most of the paintings then disappeared in the late 1930s, but not before Breton encountered them and reproduced many in his writings. It was through these museum displays and Deonna's work that the artist learned of Smith and began to integrate her influence into the surrealist corpus.

The Siren of Knowledge: Smith and Surrealist Explorations of the Occult

Along with other modern artists who drew on the "discourses of the oc-cult dominant during [this] period," Breton was intrigued by the artistic possibilities of enchantment.[56] For him, as for other artists of the late nine-teenth and early twentieth centuries, occult practices, including those of spiritual mediums, provided a useful tool to explore the complexities of sub-jectivity and authorship. As Tessel Bauduin remarks, "The innovative char-acter of mediumistic art lies . . . predominantly in their claims to authorless creation or authorial displacement. This clearly resonated with one of modernism's main motifs: a thorough destabilising of authorship and the locus of creative genius."[57] Breton thus drew on such practices to explore the yet mysterious artistic abilities of subliminal states.

For various authors, Breton's investigations through spiritualist practices emerged as a slightly embarrassing illustration of his scientific naiveté and a demonstration of his misunderstanding of contemporaneous theories of the unconscious. Jean Clair noted that "the unconscious that André Breton evokes and that permits him to give, so he believes, a theoretical, if not scientific, foundation to automatic writing . . . is an unconscious that, however, by the year 1920, had become archaic, obsolete."[58] This view echoed the reflections of Jean-Louis Houdebine, whose 1971 *Tel Quel* article examined the "misunderstanding of psychoanalysis in surrealist discourse."[59] Houdebine saw in Freudian psychoanalysis a radical break from earlier conceptions of the unconscious that derived from psychical and occult research. For him, Breton's "mystico-poetic eclecticism" failed to recognize such advances in resorting to unfounded, obsolete views of subjectivity through his use of occult experiments.[60]

A different view of the psychological tradition, however, might suggest that Breton's automatist discourses entailed serious research into the modalities of unconscious creativity. As the doxa of depth psychology in interwar France—largely fashioned by Janet's theories—developed a restrictive view of the unconscious through its symptomatic manifestations, Breton devised with his group a series of experiments with spiritualist practices that tried to retrieve the mysterious creative faculties of the psyche. These experiments, aimed at "systematically exploring the unconscious," formed an important moment in the history of the unconscious, now recuperated as both a destructive *and* creative force.[61] Breton thus joined the symptomatic (Freud's and Janet's) and mythopoetic (Myers's and Flournoy's) traditions of the unconscious.

As many of the psychical researchers, psychiatrists, and psychopathologists who studied trance communications before him, Breton rejected the possibility of possession. Indeed, he claimed repeatedly that he did not believe in spiritual communications and found the mediums' attachment to the spiritualist hypothesis "unfortunate." Already in the 1922 text, "The Mediums Enter," he declared: "It goes without saying that at no time, starting with the day we agreed to try these experiments, have we ever adopted the spiritualist view point. As far as I am concerned, I absolutely refuse to admit that any communication whatsoever can exist between the living and the dead."[62] However, as an important part of the psychological tradition that preceded him, he also saw experiences of trance and automatic writing as valuable strategies to access unconscious creativity. Breton thus largely rejected the newly formed division between occult practices and the study of the unconscious, as he conceived the practices of spiritualism and the experiments of psychical research as powerful illustrations of yet ill-understood forms of creativity. For Tessel Bauduin, therefore, "Breton created an all-encompassing surrealist universe, something simultaneously marvellous, enchanted, secular and scientifically oriented, in a unity of paradoxes that only Surrealism would be able to pull off."[63] Breton participated in this investigative tradition by adopting for himself the positions of both medium and psychological interpreter. This partial identification with the figure of the medium participated in his opposition to the institutional violence of modern psychiatry.[64]

Breton's first systematic experiments with hidden faculties of mind occurred in the spring of 1919. That year, he created with Philippe Soupault what he would later conceive as the "first purely surrealist work."[65] *The Magnetic Fields*, written through automatic writing in six consecutive days, became a turning point for the French surrealist movement, whose members increasingly resorted to writing techniques aimed at liberating inhibited forces of creativity. Years later, Breton remembered these experiences in sharp contrast to Janet's perception of hysterical automatism in "Lucy, Margaret, and many others."[66] Breton wrote:

> All of a sudden, I found, quite by accident, beautiful phrases, phrases such as I had never written. . . . And there were still more coming. . . . It was as though some vein had burst within me, one word followed another, found its proper place . . . my pencil could not keep up with them, and yet I went as fast as I could, my hand in constant motion, I did not lose a minute. The sentences continued to well up within me. I was pregnant with my own subject.[67]

Breton's use of the procreation metaphor will recall an important motif in Smith's unconscious explored in Chapter 2. Akin to Breton, the medium saw her body as a vessel for the voice of the other and appeared enthralled by her creative process. In her later life, Smith also deployed the vocabulary of bearing in relation to her oeuvre. She notably used the metaphor to describe a then nearly completed painting of "[her] little Jesus": "What a delicious and adorable child! With what joy have I seen him move forward!

With what joy have I seen all its little limbs forming! It seems to me now that he is flesh and blood, my property, a child of my own. I would like to press him into my arms." But while Breton deployed this imagery to indicate the "birth" or realization and discovery of a voice and power within himself, Smith elaborated it to illuminate the life, power, or autonomous reality of her creations. Thus, remarking on the comparative laboriousness of her own creative process, she added: "Every mother finds her baby charming, and since my paintings are my children, it is natural that I have a penchant for admiring them and finding nothing wrong with them. This painting, however, took its time to come into the world. Delayed and eagerly awaited births usually bring nothing but disappointment. For my Jesus on the cross, the fourth great child, this is not so."[68] While deploying a materialist understanding and vocabulary of automatic production, Breton nonetheless shared with Smith and other mediums an understanding of the mechanical body as a feminine or femininized canvas for the voice of the other, a fertile vessel ready to be taken over by mysterious and creative forces.

In the following years, Breton continued to experiment with this emerging subject—creating through highly different rhythms than the conscious self—as he explored the creative possibilities of trance states. Some of these experiments were reported in the 1922 "The Mediums Enter," which proposed the first definition of surrealism as "a certain psychic automatism that corresponds rather well to the dream state, a state that is currently very hard to delimit."[69] "The Mediums Enter" presented the surrealists' inquiries into this dream state as it recounted episodes of the group's "period of sleeping-fits." In settings meant to reproduce the spiritualist séance, members of the group began to experience phenomena of trance, somnambulism, and dual personality. The text presented the trance communications of members of the group during the séances, whose regular sitters included Breton, Max Morise (1900–1973), Paul Éluard (1895–1952), Max Ernst (1891–1976), René Crevel (1900–1935), Benjamin Péret (1899–1959), and Robert Desnos. Of these, the latter three had been able to fall into somnambulistic states or, as Breton put it, "to fall asleep."[70]

Crevel had been the first to introduce the group to séances, after himself being initiated by a medium named Madame Dante. On the evening of September 25, 1922, he held a séance with Breton, Desnos, and Morise, during which he rapidly fell into a hypnotic slumber and uttered "a kind of defense or indictment that was not copied down at the time."[71] On the following evening, Desnos, Morise, and Breton conducted a second séance, and, this time, an entranced Desnos began compulsively scratching the tabletop. When Crevel suggested that such an attitude might reveal a desire to write, a pencil and paper were placed in Desnos's vicinity and a second phase of automatism emerged, in which members of the group began to produce original stories, writings, and drawings under trance. Soon, Crevel began to recount stories of a woman accused of murdering her husband through a "declamatory diction, interspersed with sighs, sometimes transforming into a kind of song," and Péret began to predict the future and make swimming motions on the séance table.[72] However, none could surpass the wonderful creativity of Desnos, whose spontaneous artistic productions enthralled the group. Breton recounted that, following such productions, "the most self-assured among us [stood] confused, trembling with gratitude and fear," losing their composure before the marvel.[73]

In successive séances, Desnos established contact with Marcel Duchamp's own alter ego, Rrose Sélavy, and rapidly created poetic phrases and images that, while reminding the surrealists of the artist's inventive style, fascinated the group for its own originality. Interestingly, Katherine Conley suggests that Desnos's production of a female alter ego may have determined by the cultural and scientific interpretation of mediumship and automatism as traditionally female or feminine.[74] Years later, in the largely autobiographical novel *Nadja* (1928), Breton recalled:

> Once again, now, I see Robert Desnos at the period those of us who knew it called the Nap Period [sleeping fits]. He "dozes," but he writes, he talks. It is evening, in my studio over the Cabaret du Ciel . . . and Desnos continues seeing what I do not see. . . . He borrows the personality of the most singular man . . . Marcel Duchamp. . . . What in Duchamp seemed most inimitable through some mysterious "plays on words" (Rrose Sélavy) can be found in Desnos in all its purity and suddenly assumes an extraordinary resonance. Those who have not seen his pencil set on paper—without the slightest hesitation and with an astonishing speed— . . . cannot conceive of everything involved in their creation at the time, of the absolutely oracular value they assumed.[75]

Just as Smith had found herself incapable of learning languages while awake, but produced in trance wonderfully inventive linguistic systems, alphabets, and translations, Desnos was, Breton remarked, "as incapable as the rest of us" of producing such fabulous creations outside the séances.[76]

The performance of trance, however, provided him access to a powerful form of creativity. Accordingly, before the break with Desnos, Breton could claim that the latter had come closest to realizing the surrealist ideal of creativity.[77]

However, as the surrealists soon discovered, the state of trance also freed the destructive, symptomatic forces of the unconscious, constantly threatening the subject with its own dissolution. Remembering the compulsive dangers of the sleeping fits, Aragon wrote about the "sleepers" in 1924:

> [They] live only for these moments of oblivion, when they talk with the lights out, without consciousness, like drowning men in the open air. These moments multiply by the day. They want to spend more and more time in oblivion. When told what they have uttered they are intoxicated by their own words. They fall into trances everywhere. . . . Those who submit themselves to these incessant experiments endure a constant state of appalling agitation, become increasingly manic.[78]

The surrealist somnambulists began to lose weight, entered sleeping states ever more often, and became increasingly difficult to awaken. Breton remarked that Desnos would "just go off, even in the middle of a meal. What was more, it was harder and harder to wake him by the usual methods. One evening, I absolutely couldn't . . . and I had to go out and get a doctor."[79] In early 1923, Breton put an end to the sleeping fits after an episode of trance nearly led to the mediums' deaths. As Ruth Brandon reveals, through a succession of strange events, the surrealists discovered the menacing powers of trance:

> On one astonishing occasion . . . a large party of guests was invited to a grand house belonging to Marie de la Hire, a friend of Picabia's. The rooms were cavernous and dimly lit, and before long ten or more of the guests were entranced, sleepwalking, gesticulating, uttering strange prophecies. At about two in the morning, Breton suddenly realized that a number of them had disappeared [and] finally discovered them in some dark anteroom, where they were trying to hang themselves from the coat hooks. They had plenty of rope. . . . Crevel was one of them, it was apparently he who had put the idea into their heads.[80]

Although Breton remained cautious in his following investigations of the unconscious, he never abandoned his fascination with spiritualist practices.

Published five years after his 1925 "Letter to Seers," the 1930 *Second Manifesto*, for instance, linked specifically surrealist art with spiritual mediumship and proclaimed the artistic value of the latter.[81] Breton demanded, "once again, that we submit ourselves to the mediums who do exist, albeit no doubt in very small numbers, and that we subordinate our interest—which ought not to be overestimated—of what we are doing to the interest which the first of their messages offers."[82] In this work, Breton also defended the possibility of telepathy—a phenomenon encountered among mediums that had fascinated researchers from Myers to Flournoy to Freud.[83] Akin to Flournoy, Breton thus claimed to discover hidden functions of the mind through experiments with play, trance, and creativity. It was another surrealist experiment—the collective game of Cadavre Exquis—which, he claimed, provided evidence of "a strange possibility of thought, that of its *pooling*."[84]

As per Smith, Breton's first public mention of the medium's name appeared in the 1928 *Nadja*. The latter text indeed included a note reflecting his fascination with the medium and connected her to the eponymous character. Breton remarked that Nadja had had the impression of having participated in his earlier work, "Soluble Fish," in "a scene whose precise meaning . . . I have never been able to determine and whose characters are as alien, their agitation as enigmatic as possible . . . and even . . . played the—if anything obscure—part of Hélène." Breton began with this "obscure" name and connected it to Nadja and other mediums' precognitive forms of knowledge. He concluded: "I have never known personally any woman of this name . . . . Yet Madame Sacco, clairvoyante, 3 Rue des Usines, who has never been mistaken about me, assured me early this year that my mind was greatly preoccupied with a 'Hélène.' Is this why, some time after this period, I was so greatly interested in everything concerning Hélène Smith? . . . 'Hélène, c'est moi,' Nadja used to say."[85]

In the following years, Breton indeed became fascinated by Smith. The exhibitions held in Paris and Geneva, as well as Flournoy's work on the medium, introduced Breton to many of her creations.[86] In "The Automatic Message," published in *Minotaure* in 1933, Breton described her as "the prolific Élise Müller, who became famous under the pseudonym Hélène Smith."[87] He here found himself so enthralled by her creations that he even identified her as the muse of surrealism and considered her "by far the richest of all" cases of mediumship.[88] He reproduced many of her creations in the article, alongside those of other mediums and "naïve" (or folk) art. Breton remained enthralled by the medium in the following years: he identified her as a "celebrated medium, painter and inventor of languages" in the 1938 *Abbreviated Dictionary of Surrealism*, written with Éluard, and he celebrated her in the 1940 *Jeu de Marseilles* (a surrealist deck of cards). Created before Breton's and other surrealists' exile from fascist-controlled France, the game included new court cards replacing the king, queen, and jack with the characters of Genius, Siren, and Magus. The suits reflected the four major preoccupations of Love (Flame), Dream (Star), Revolution (Wheel), and Knowledge (Lock). Smith appeared in the latter suit and was thus symbolized as Siren of Knowledge, or Locks, next to Hegel, Genius of Locks, and Paracelsus, Magus of Locks.[89] Breton further reiterated Smith's long-lasting influence in his 1952 *Entretiens*, where he remarked that his understanding of the unconscious was shaped by such work as "Théodore Flournoy's fascinating communications on the medium Hélène Smith," in conjunction with his "other ways of seeing thanks to the enthusiastic admiration I have for Freud."[90] Last, in the 1965 re-edition of "Surrealism and Painting," Breton returned once again to the medium, adding to his text the four images of *The Daughter of Jairus* in order to better illustrate her creative process.[91]

Although Breton's encounter with Smith emerged after he had begun to develop the surrealist project, this extraordinary medium and the fascination she invoked permitted the poet to better understand his own investigations into the possibilities of automatic discourse. The surrealists' spontaneous productions of language had indeed enlightened a dangerous, yet highly creative subjectivity in excess that would find powerful confirmation through Flournoy's analytic vocabulary. In her recent study of Smith's interplanetary languages, Marina Yagello explains: "What distinguishes the glossolalist from someone speaking an ordinary language is that he or she isn't the person speaking. The relationship to the person is missing. There is no I standing at the source of the utterance. . . . In glossolalia there is certainly an ego at the center, but it is a non-linguistic ego . . . unlike the I of the linguistic system."[92] More powerfully than any other medium, for Breton, Smith provided a dissolution of the self-transparent locutor as the center of discourse, a dissolution that the surrealists had themselves experienced through the performances of the automatic body. Smith's romances and linguistic systems had thus introduced, like Freudian discoveries of the unconscious, a profound threat to the transparent cogito. But Smith's séances, akin to the surrealists' experiments, additionally emphasized the fertile, playful modalities of a prodigiously creative unconscious. Smith could thus reveal, for Breton, an important, yet mysterious, form of knowledge regarding the secrets of creativity.

Conclusion: Breton, Smith, and the Automatic Artist

In recent years, various scholars have disputed the intellectual influences behind the surrealists' automatism. In a seminal article, Jean Starobinski suggested that, despite Breton's repeated acknowledgment of Freud, the surrealists' concept of psychic automatism derived primarily from Janet's automatism and Myers's subliminal realm.[93] Starobinski notably found support in the 1933 "The Automatic Message," where—along with Smith's—Breton acknowledged Myers's influence upon the surrealist undertaking. Placing Myers's discoveries besides those of James and Flournoy, Breton wrote: "We are much more widely tributaries than what we believe to what William James, quite justly, has termed the gothic psychology of F.W.H. Myers, which, in an entirely new, fascinating world, has later brought us the admirable explorations of Th. Flournoy."[94] Starobinski's conclusions, however, were later rejected by Marguerite Bonnet, who demonstrated, through in-depth study of Breton's notebooks and manuscripts, that the author had followed an erroneous chronology. Noting that Breton never acknowledged the influence of Janet and that he only discovered the works of Myers in 1925, she argued that it is Freud's theories that provided the surrealists with the decisive impulse toward the discovery of automatism as key to the unconscious.[95]

While Bonnet is certainly right to recognize the importance of Freud at the origins of surrealism, she fails to recognize the complexity of an author's intellectual context. Indeed, as Bertrand Méheust argues, Bonnet's article acts "as if the influences of a writer . . . could be limited to those he or she recognized in writing; as if Freud's thought was itself exempt of the magnetico-hypnotic-spiritist traditions; as if one could attribute to chance the fact that the sleeping fits coincided exactly with the apogee of French psychical research."[96] Thus, although Breton only discovered Myers in 1925 and Smith in the late 1920s, the surrealists' experiments in automatism cannot be fully understood outside the context of spiritualism and the infatuation of scientists and psychologists for its revelation of a dangerously creative unconscious.[97]

Similarly, although Smith was not, chronologically, at the origins of Breton's creations, her trance practices can shed an important light on the artistic productions of automatism. Particularly, Flournoy's theorization of a fabulously imaginative unconscious, derived directly from her automatic imagination, can frame a deeper understanding of the surrealist movement than single attention to now dominant models of depth psychology. Indeed, while many depth psychologists, including Janet and Freud, uncovered the pathological nature of an unconscious and its production of unwanted symptoms, Smith's marvelous productions led Flournoy to trace an unconscious marked by artistic possibilities. As Mireille Cifali wrote in a 1983 French reedition of *Des Indes à la planète Mars*, Flournoy was interested "in the entanglements that link the unconscious to artistic and fictional creation, to the creative imagination of works and scientific discoveries, to the immense yet silent treasures that suddenly spring up and overwhelm."[98]

To this day, in the words of historian of psychology Henri Ellenberger, "We seldom hear of the mythopoetic unconscious. What psychoanalysts call fantasies represent a minute part of mythopoetic manifestations. We have lost sight of the importance of this terrible power—a power that fathered epidemics of demonism, collective psychoses among witches, revelations of Spiritualists. . . . Unfortunately, neither Freud nor Jung became aware of the role of the mythopoetic unconscious."[99] Similarly, in France, Janet's move from Léonie to Lucy and other Salpêtrière hysterics illustrated a transformed understanding of automatic or unconscious productions. From mysterious, marvelous, and creative, automatism came to represent a pathological tendency toward dissociation expressed in repetitive acts. In the words of Bacopoulos-Viau: "In order to create a new science, the official psychologist of inter-war France erected barriers and distanced himself from both Spiritism and psychical research."[100] Through his retrieval of spiritualist practices, Breton could therefore hope to reclaim those creative faculties of the unconscious that were being relegated to the margins of psychology. Thus, the 1924 *Manifesto* proclaimed: "Under the pretense of civilization and progress, we have managed to banish from the mind everything that may rightly or wrongly be termed superstition or fancy: forbidden is any kind of search for truth which is not in conformance with accepted practices."[101] Although he may not have encountered Smith's trance performances before the writing of *Nadja*, this "richest" of all mediums presented through her paintings, romances, and languages the marvelous unconscious faculties that Breton wished to elaborate.

Conclusion

The Enchanted Unconscious

In October 1894, before he encountered his famous medium, the psychologist Théodore Flournoy wrote to his friend William James about the difficulty he experienced in pursuing his writing and scholarship. He described his "torment" through a marked psychopathological vocabulary, noting: "If graphophobia is not yet officially a form of neurasthenia, it is nevertheless real and causes me torment, whether it is a question of revising a lesson or of writing very freely to a friend." Flournoy further indicated the symptoms of his graphophobia, adding: "The mere fact of taking up a pen and sitting down before a blank piece of paper paralyzes me completely. It is only after several useless attempts, separated by days and even weeks in which it is impossible even to make a new attempt, that I give birth, with great effort, to a few lines."[1] Admitting that his incapacity to write was truly "becoming an illness," Flournoy remarked that he had even considered "the idea of resorting to the Brown Sequard injections," a questionable treatment named after physicist Charles-Édouard Brown-Séquard, who had introduced it in a paper at the Société de Biologie in Paris in 1889. To "give birth" to new writings, Flournoy considered injecting himself with the serum, a preparation made from the testicles of dogs and guinea pigs that had apparently made its inventor feel rejuvenated, better able to concentrate, and physically stronger.[2] A disillusioned James, however, warned Flournoy against it: he had himself, in a moment of great "fatigue" and "in desperation," tried "the famous injections." Unfortunately, he added, "The result after eight of them was an abscess" that had kept him in bed for five weeks.[3]

One might easily imagine, then, how Flournoy would have found himself entranced with the formidable creative capabilities of Hélène Smith, whom he encountered a few months afterward. Perhaps this writing paralysis even explains why Flournoy—despite trying to conform himself "strictly to the passive and purely contemplative attitude of the other sitters"—had not been able to resist reaching for her marvelous hands. As earlier noted,

Hélène Smith. Claudie Massicotte, Oxford University Press. © Oxford University Press 2023.
DOI: 10.1093/oso/9780197680018.003.0006

he explained: "At the fourth sitting my discretion vanished. I could not resist a strong desire to ascertain the physiological condition of the charming seeress, and I made some vigorous elementary experiments upon her hands, which lay temptingly spread out opposite me on the table."[4] Grasping at the marvel, touching his seeress, Flournoy perhaps sought to capture some of her magic, as in desperation James had earlier reached for the Brown Sequard elixir with devastating consequences. Unlike his, Smith's writing was indeed uninhibited, glossolalic, spontaneous, and limitless. The medium embodied the possibilities of a creativity unbound by norms of appropriate discourse and the anxieties of authorship. Following her various productions through the final years of the nineteenth century, Flournoy could thus formulate a complex and creative unconscious, reconciling the emerging trajectories of psychoanalysis and psychical research.

Shortly after Flournoy complained of his "graphophobia" to his friend, Sigmund Freud also became afflicted by his own writing paralysis. (I suspect many authors have indeed diagnosed themselves with such a condition.) Like Flournoy, the psychoanalyst shared his distress in his correspondence with a friend, deploying a similarly psychopathological vocabulary. On August 14, 1897, Freud declared to Wilhelm Fliess that "the chief patient" he was now occupied with was himself. Referring to his "little hysteria," Freud added that his illness had been intensified by his work and now affected his writing. He noted that his self-analysis was "the thing that paralyses the power of writing down and communicating what so far I have learned."[5] A few days later, Freud further seemed to indicate that the illness had affected the very movements of his hand, telling Fliess: "My handwriting is more human again, so my tiredness is wearing off. Your writing, I see with pleasure, never varies."[6] Freud's hand thus seemed affected by a force independent of his conscious agency. The psychoanalyst was only able to regain control over his motor reactions—to make his writing "more human again"—by overcoming the resistances of censorship.

Over the following month, Freud appeared to dispel his writing paralysis as he refashioned his conception of the unconscious. Writing that he "no longer believe[d]" in his theory of the neuroses as responses to sexual seduction in childhood, Freud explained that what he had earlier perceived to be revelations of abuse in his patients' infancy had in fact been expressions of unbearable incestuous desires.[7] Remarking upon the impossibility of retrieving pure memories of infancy, he wrote: "When one thus sees that the unconscious never overcomes the resistance of the conscious, one must abandon the expectation that in treatment the reverse process will take place to the extent that the conscious will fully dominate the unconscious."[8] Many years later, the psychoanalyst would explain his rejection of the seduction theory by observing that, under the influence of hypnosis, many of his patients had reproduced from their childhood scenes of sexual abuse by adult persons. After believing these narratives, however, he "was at last obliged to recognize that these scenes of seduction had never taken place, and that they were only phantasies which my patients had made up or which I myself had perhaps forced on them. . . . When I had pulled myself together, I was able to draw the right conclusions from my discovery; namely, that the neurotic symptoms were not related directly to actual events but to wishful phantasies."[9]

While Flournoy's graphophobia had led to his fascination with the unbridled creativity of his entranced seeress, Freud's writing paralysis had announced the discovery of incestuous desires and their repression, later giving rise to his landmark theory of the Oedipus complex. Such a discovery further came to demarcate psychoanalysis from competing understandings of the psyche. Indeed, as Carl Jung would recount many years later, Freud conceived his theory of sexuality as foundational to the establishment of psychoanalysis as a scientific enterprise, opposed to the superstitions and pseudosciences of occultism. Jung thus remembered Freud telling him: "You see we must make a dogma of it, an unshakable bulwark." When "in some astonishment" Jung asked him, "A bulwark—against what?" Freud allegedly responded, " 'Against the black tide of mud'—and here he hesitated for a moment, then added, 'of occultism.' "[10] Freud's theory of sexuality indeed emphasized the biological nature of the unconscious against the more transcendental view of the subconscious expressed in psychical research. Certainly, Frederic Myers and William James, among other SPR members, had formulated theories of the mind that lent credence to spiritualist beliefs and opened the way toward transcendence. In this context, Freud's theory of sexuality served a demarcating function that was, to him, essential for the scientific establishment of the unconscious.[11]

In recent years, many scholars have reviewed the disenchantment thesis in light of the now well-recognized popularity of occult practices from the nineteenth century on. In a 2000 article, Richard Jenkins interpreted the thesis as a dialectic of disenchantment and re-enchantment, suggesting that "modern societies are an array of opposing tendencies, themes, and forces."[12] Despite such opposing forces, Jenkins nonetheless recognized the value of Weber's notion, writing: "That we have grounds for scepticism about the impact of scope of disenchantment does not mean that we should abandon the notion, or the wider concept of rationalization. There is too much evidence for both, in our own experience and in the social science literature, to encourage such recklessness."[13] More recently, Jason Josephson-Storm has similarly rejected the interpretation of disenchantment as a linear progression of "magic's exit from the henceforth law-governed world."[14] By contrast, however, he viewed the notion, not as a dialectic process, but as a tale or myth.[15] As he wrote in *The Myth of Disenchantment*, while the idea of a linear and progressive rejection of the marvelous continues to dominate many historical approaches to modernity, "This narrative is wrong . . . we have never been disenchanted."[16] Perhaps the most nuanced approach to Weber's thesis emerges in the work of Egil Asprem, who, like Jenkins, recognized the concept's validity but reframed it, not as a "process" that rendered modernity increasingly secularized, but as a "problem" that required new categorizations and negotiations between science, religion, and the occult.[17] Asprem remarked: "Reconceptualising disenchantment as a historically situated first and foremost creates a new conceptual tool, 'the problem of disenchantment,' that can do some interesting analytical work in the interdisciplinary field strung out between the history of religion, the history of science, and the history of esotericism."[18] As a particular episode in modern intellectual history, Smith's story similarly problematizes simplistic understandings of disenchantment as a transparent and uncontradicted progression toward secularization. Whether they believed in some or none of her enchanted experiences, her savants shared a belief that scientific experimentations could lead to greater understandings (and negations) of the marvelous. They examined spiritualist practices to discover yet unexplored continents, whether internal or other worldly. In approaching her manifestations from diverse disciplinary and occult (or skeptical) perspectives, they sometimes drew, sometimes erased, and sometimes reshaped boundaries between the enchanted and the scientific.

Also common among the scientists, authors, spiritualists, and artists introduced in this work is a shared conception of the (traditionally female and feminine) entranced body as a passive recipient for the voice of another. From the Salpêtrière hysterics who channeled the voices of medical authorities on their very skin, to the spiritual mediums said to bear the voices of celestial beings, and to the "feminized" bodies of surrealist artists "giving birth" to inner, mysterious voices within the self, the otherness of the female body provided a bridge between the marvelous and the scientific. In the secularized experiments of Charcot and Janet, the enchanted could be displaced within the mysteries of femininity. For many psychical researchers and spiritualists, by contrast, this mysterious embodiment formed a gateway to the scientific exploration of the enchanted. Flournoy's discoveries of the unconscious came from what he perceived to be a neutral and open position toward the occult. Thus, for him, Smith's trance and subliminal states came to illustrate greater power, creativity, and knowledge than the psychopathological approaches of Freud allowed.

Centering psychoanalysis on Freud's theory of sexuality, historians of the discipline have also traditionally promoted the idea of a clear demarcation between psychoanalysis and the occult, defining Freud's new science as an extension of the Enlightenment project rationally examining the nature of the human psyche through its attention to sexual instincts. As this work argued, such narratives of a disenchanted psychoanalysis have erased much of the complex history of practices, experiences, and encounters shaping discoveries of the unconscious. And indeed, beyond their initial bouts of graphophobia, Freud's and Flournoy's writings more often intertwined than such narratives would suggest. Many years following his encounter with Smith, Flournoy indeed went on to teach psychoanalysis in Switzerland, thus shaping the history of the institution in the country. His grandson, Olivier Flournoy, who retraced the story of the fabulous medium many years later, himself became president of the Switzerland Psychoanalytic Association and a student of Jacques Lacan. Elsewhere, Flournoy stated that, if he could live his life again, he would have liked to study psychoanalysis and Freud's sexual theory more closely. Freud, for his part, produced research on telepathy, even noting, in the 1930s, that he felt the scientific position of psychoanalysis was strong enough to integrate a theory of telepathy. In a letter to Weiss from 1932, he remarked that "to take flight, in a cowardly fashion and behind the shelter of disdain, from the allegedly 'supra-natural' shows very little confidence in the trustworthiness of our scientific Weltanschauung."[19] He published many papers on the subject and even resolved to claim, in "Dreams and the Occult," that 'taking all the evidence together there remains a heavy weight of probability in favour of the reality of thought transference.'[20] He included the essay in the 1933 *New Introductory Lectures on Psychoanalysis*, thus demonstrating a commitment to frame the topic among the theoretical apparatus of psychoanalysis. And while Flournoy had regretted not devoting more of his life to psychoanalysis, Freud wrote, in answer to an invitation to write on the occult: "If I were at the beginning rather than at the end of a scientific career, as I am today, I might possibly choose just this field of research, in spite of all the difficulties."[21] Thus, as I hoped to demonstrate in this work, it is perhaps not so much their fascination with the occult, as their consequent framing of the unconscious that came to differentiate Freud's and Flournoy's work. While Freud came to focus on the sexual etiology of its manifestations, Flournoy remained fascinated by the marvelously creative possibilities of subliminal states he had discovered through Hélène Smith.

Notes

Introduction

1. My translation from "Le phénomène des tables parlantes n'amoindrit pas le XIXè siècle, il l'agrandit." Cited in Boivin, "Preface," 18. Throughout this work, all citations will be presented in English. In cases where translations are mine (when no existing translations were found), I have added the original in notes.
2. Strachey, "Editor's Introduction," xx.
3. Together, these three editions included twenty-five hundred printed copies, according to Flournoy's grandson (Flournoy, *Théodore et Léopold*, 166).
4. "un beau livre qui devrait faire un jour l'objet d'un film" and "trouverait en Élise une réplique d'Adèle Hugo" (Roudinesco, "Des Martiens," 26).
5. "Qu'est-ce qui sépare *Des Indes à la planète Mars* de *L'Interprétation des rêves* publié par Sigmund Freud exactement à la même date? Tout et rien. . . . Freud raconte les mêmes histoires que Flournoy, mais dans une autre langue, une langue venue du crépuscule, une langue nouvelle." And Flournoy "semble assis le cul entre deux siècles, une fesse dans la tradition épistémologique et romanesque du XIXe siècle, une autre dans ce sol mouvant du XXe siècle vers lequel il regarde désespérément. . . . À l'opposé de Freud, Flournoy n'est donc ni thérapeute, puisqu'il refuse de soigner, ni théoricien . . . voilà pourquoi il n'est pas un novateur, mais un magnétiseur à l'ancienne" (Roudinesco, "Des Martiens," 26).
6. While Flournoy uses the term "subliminal" in this text, he considers it as synonymous with unconscious. Thus, he notes, "The words *subliminal* (*sub limen*; *unter der Schwelle*; under the threshold) and *subconscious* or *unconscious* are practically synonymous and designate phenomena and processes that one has some reason to believe are conscious even though they are unknown to the subject, since they take place so to speak below the level of its ordinary consciousness" (Flournoy, *From India*, 8).
7. My translation from "Freud déterre un inconscient marqué davantage par les effets de la censure, du déguisement, et de son lien avec le symptôme; Flournoy est par contre plus sensibles aux enchevêtrements qui lient l'inconscient à la création artistique" (Cifali, "Introduction," 374).
8. Notable exceptions include Ellenberger, *Discovery of the Unconscious*; Devereux, *Psychoanalysis and the Occult*; Plas, *Naissance*; and Moreau, *Freud et l'occultisme*. More recent works on depth psychology and the occult include Brottman, *Phantoms of the Clinic*; Pierri, *Occultism*; Plas, "Naissance" and "Psychology and Psychical Research"; Raia, *The New Prometheans*; and Totton, *Psychoanalysis and the Paranormal*.
9. Ellenberger, *Discovery of the Unconscious*, 98.

10. A note on the works cited in this book: for ease of reading, I have opted to introduce all titles in their English translations. In cases where no English translation has been published, I have used the original title and presented my own translations in the following parenthesis.

11. See Hustvedt, *Medical Muses*, 33–142; Didi-Huberman, "L'incarnation figurale" and *The Invention of Hysteria*; and Enquist, *Story of Blanche*.

12. See Hunter, "Hysteria, Psychoanalysis, and Feminism"; Rosenbaum and Muroff, *Anna O.*; Guttmann, *Enigma of Anna O.*; Jackowitz, "Anna O / Bertha Pappenheim"; and Ticktin, "Anna O's Other Story."

13. See Bernheimer and Kahane, *In Dora's Case*; Muslin and Gill, "Transference"; Glenn, "Freud, Dora"; Marcus, "Freud and Dora"; Moi, "Representation of Patriarchy."

14. Flournoy, *From India*, 19.

15. Flournoy, *From India*, 26.

16. Flournoy, *From India*, 9.

17. See Shamdasani, "Encountering Hélène"; Henry, *Le language martien*; Flournoy, "Nouvelles observations."

18. Todorov, *Theories of the Symbol*, 256–257.

19. Le Clair, *Letters of James and Flournoy*, 17.

20. Le Clair, *Letters of James and Flournoy*, 29.

21. Le Clair, *Letters of James and Flournoy*, 29.

22. Flournoy, *From India*, 266.

23. Flournoy, *From India*, 12. The language here used by Flournoy to express his perception of the medium as both passive and seductive illustrates well the eroticism shaping relations between female spiritualists and their observers. In Chapter 2, I come back to such seductive relations to interrogate more fully the erotic representations of female mediums in cultural and scientific discourses.

24. My translation from "Je serais pourtant curieux de savoir en quoi l'explication par le subliminal est plus normale que l'explication par l'esprit, en quoi notre explication est plus occulte que la sienne. Car enfin, un subliminal . . . qui a de la promptitude, de la finesse, un flair étonnamment exquis et délicat . . . une imagination remarquablement calme, pondérée, attachée au réel et au vraisemblable; une subconscience merveilleusement douée et prodigieusement féconde . . . , un subliminal qui fait écrire au médium des écritures qui ne sont pas les siennes; qui change une douce voix de femme en une voix d'homme profonde, grave, lente et basse, . . . un tel subliminal me paraît d'une explication, pour le moins, aussi occulte, aussi invraisemblable que celle défendue et admise par les spirites" (Société, *Autour "Des Indes à la planète Mars"*, 101–102).

25. "une grande affluence de visiteurs" (Deonna, *De la planète Mars*, 1).

26. Audinet et al., *Entrée des médiums*, 78.

27. Morehead, "Symbolism, Mediumship," 77.

28. Shamdasani, "Encountering Hélène," xxxiv.

29. "presque tous mes correspondants pour recueillir leurs observations et éclaircissements" and "cahiers de notes, procès-verbaux, essais d'écriture et de dessin automatique, etc." (Flournoy, *Esprits et mediums*, 6).

30. "en somme rien qui sortît de l'ordinaire en ce genre, rien, par exemple, qui approchât la belle imagination subliminale, créatrice de langues et de mythes, qu'à la même époque je voyais se déployer dans les somnambulismes de Mlle Smith" (Flournoy, *Esprits et mediums*, 2).

31. Flournoy, *Spiritism and Psychology*, vii.

32. See Flournoy, *La philosophie de William James*.

33. In this work, I have adopted the term "spiritualism" instead of "spiritism," a term preferred by many historians to describe the history of the movement in France (see, for instance, Lachapelle, *Investigating the Supernatural*; Sharp, *Secular Spirituality*). *Spiritisme* was commonly used in French-speaking Europe to distinguish the movement and its practices (speaking with the dead, holding séances, etc.) from *spiritualisme*, conceived as a philosophical approach opposed to materialism, a belief in the existence of a human soul or spirit that did not necessarily lead to communion with the dead. The term "spiritualism," however, is not only more familiar to English-speaking audiences, but also applicable to the movement outside of Francophone contexts. This book will position Smith's séances in the larger landscape of her imagination, readings, and inspiration as well as in the vast intellectual network of Flournoy, whose work attempted to bridge the discoveries of Myers and James with those of Janet and Freud. Thus, "spiritualism" serves to better describe the European development of the movement.

34. On the Fox sisters, see notably Leonard, *People from the Other Side*; Ruben, *The Reluctant Spiritualist*; and Weisberg, *Talking to the Dead*.

35. My translation from "L'Europe entière, et que-dis-je, l'Europe? en ce moment le monde a la tête tournée d'une expérience qui consiste à faire tourner une table. On n'entend parler de toutes parts que de la table qui tourne: lui-même Galilée, il a fait moins de bruit le jour où il prouva qu'en effet c'était la terre qui tournait autour du soleil" (*Le courrier des États-Unis*, May 28, 1853; quoted in Sylvain, "Quand les tables dansaient," 222).

36. Jung, "On Spiritualistic Phenomena," 93.

37. Asprem, "Aren't We Living," 16. In *The Place of Enchantment*, Alex Owen similarly ponders "why, in this quintessentially 'modern' moment, late-Victorian and Edwardian women and men became absorbed by metaphysical quests, heterodox spiritual encounters, and occult experimentation, each of which seems to signal the desire for unorthodox numinous experience in a post-Darwinian world" (7). Her work demonstrates the central place of occultism in shaping modern understandings of rationality and consciousness.

38. Hanegraaff, *Esotericism and the Academy*, 252.

39. The entanglements of science and the séance were so profound, indeed, that a recent collection of essays on the topic was introduced as "united by a willingness to . . . insist that the relevance of spiritualism to the history of science is no longer unknown nor in question" (Ferguson and Sera-Shriar, "Spiritualism and Science Studies," 2). On the relations of science and spiritualism, see also Brain, "Materialising the Medium"; Brower, *Unruly Spirits*; Ferguson, "Recent Scholarship" and "Other Worlds"; Lachapelle, "Attempting Science"; Monroe, *Laboratories of Faith*; Noakes, *Physics*

and Psychics; Oppenheim, *The Other World*; Parot, "Psychology Experiments"; Raia, "From Either Theory"; Robertson, *Science of the Séance*; Sharp, *Secular Spirituality*; Treitel, *Science for the Soul*; and Walkowitz, "Science and the Séance."

40. "Objects of the Society," 3.

41. On this topic, see Sconce, *Haunted Media*, 21–58.

42. Enns, "Psychic Radio," 139.

43. Or, in the words of Jenny Hazelgrove, "Mediumship became analogous with the telephone and wireless. Just as people 'tuned in' to wireless broadcasts, so 'sensitives' 'tuned in' to the 'other world'" (Hazelgrove, *Spiritualism and British Society*, 21). On mediumship, science, and telecommunications, see also Braude, *Radical Spirits*; Galvan, *The Sympathetic Medium*; and Sconce, *Haunted Media*.

44. Hanegraaff, *Esotericism and the Academy*, 254. Hanegraaff does not refer here to the spiritualist movement specifically but, more largely, to Western esoteric traditions in the wake of the Enlightenment. This definition, of course, aptly applies to spiritualist practices.

45. Hanegraaff, *Esotericism and the Academy*, 254. See also "Modernization" in Hanegraaff, *Western Esoterism*, 119–142.

46. Bogdan, *Western Esotericism and Rituals*, 7.

47. Bogdan, *Western Esotericism and Rituals*, 7.

48. Ellenberger, *Discovery of the Unconscious*, 85. On spiritualism and the history of psychology, see also Brower, *Unruly Spirits*; Coon, "Testing the Limits"; Gyimesi, "The Problem of Demarcation"; Laborde-Nottale, *La voyance et l'inconscient*; Lachapelle, *Investigating the Supernatural*; Meheust, *Somnambulisme et médiumnité*; Parot, "Le bannissement des esprits"; Plas, *Naissance*; Shamdasani, "Automatic Writing"; and Sharp, *Secular Spirituality*.

49. Jasen, "Mind, Medicine," 7.

50. On the importance of animal magnetism in the history of depth psychology, see Ellenberger, *Discovery of the Unconscious*; and Crabtree, *From Mesmer to Freud*. On the influences of mesmerism on the spiritualist movement, see McCorristine, *Spiritualism, Mesmerism*; and Monroe, *Laboratories of Faith*.

51. Charcot, "Spiritisme et hystérie."

52. See Levack, *The Devil Within*, 128, 293 n.76.

53. Janet, "Notes sur quelques phénomènes."

54. For further information on Janet's experiments with Léonie, see Leloup, "Pierre Janet"; and Luckhurst, *The Invention of Telepathy*. I also briefly address these experiments in Chapter 4.

55. For Flournoy's influence on Jung (which later became part of the rift between Freud and Jung), see Charet, *Spiritualism and the Foundations* and Shamdasani, "Encountering Hélène."

56. Cited and translated by Shamdasani in "Encountering Hélène," ix.

57. See Jung, "Psychology and Pathology."

58. See Ferenczi, "Spiritism."

59. On Ferenczi's approach to the occult, see also Fodor, "Sándor Ferenczi's Psychic Adventures"; Gyimesi, "Sándor Ferenczi"; Lorin, "Sandor et les fantômes";

Thurschwell, "Ferenczi's Dangerous Proximities"; and Rabeyron and Evrard, "Perspectives historiques et contemporaines."

60. Brabant et al., *Correspondence*, 274.

61. Rudinesco, "Des Martiens," 26.

62. Freud, "Occult Significance of Dreams," 88.

63. Freud, "Occult Significance of Dreams," 89.

64. Jones, *Life and Work*, 393. On Freud and the occult, see also Granoff and Rey, *L'occulte*; Massicotte, "Psychical Transmissions"; Moreau, *Freud et l'occultisme*; Totton, *Psychoanalysis and the Paranormal*; and Turnheim, "Freud le medium."

65. Gyimesi, "The Problem of Demarcation," 465.

66. Shamdasani, "Misunderstanding Jung," 462.

67. James, "Frederic Myers's Service," 384.

68. My translation from "De connexes, ces questions devinrent inacceptables" (Le Maléfan, "L'Hallucination télépathique," 21).

69. Le Clair, *Letters of James and Flournoy*, 104. On the history of the institute, see also Lachapelle, "Attempting Science."

70. See Le Maléfan, "L'hallucination télépathique," 20.

71. Quoted in Cerullo, *Secularization of the Soul*, 160 and Gyimesi, "The Problem of Demarcation," 467. For an analysis of the "Note" with regards to psychoanalysis's distinction from psychical research, see also Keeley, "Subliminal Promptings."

72. Freud, "Note on the Unconscious," 260.

73. Gyimesi, "The Problem of Demarcation," 468.

74. Marvin, *The Philosophy of Spiritualism*, 35.

75. Marvin, *The Philosophy of Spiritualism*, 35.

76. Hammond, *Spiritualism and Allied Causes*, 256.

77. See Burlet, *Du spiritisme*.

78. Le Clair, *Letters of James and Flournoy*, 47.

79. Levack, *The Devil Within*, 129.

80. Beizer, *Ventriloquized Bodies*, 3.

81. Levack's exploration of the history of demonic possession indeed suggests that, "consciously or not, demoniacs followed scripts that were encoded in their religious cultures" and that such scripts were "strikingly different for Catholics and Protestants" (*The Devil Within*, 20). The historian Asti Hustvedt has noted, regarding Charcot's hysterics, how such scripts may be "learned" and enacted. She writes: "Charcot described the characteristics of hysteria in great detail, and repeatedly produced visual representations of its various poses in photographs, drawings, wax casts, as well as reenactments. Blanche and the other hysterics were surrounded by the images and therefore, even if no one was verbally coaching them, they certainly knew what was expected of them" (Hustvedt, *Medical Muses*, 49).

82. Bronfen, *The Knotted Subject*, xiii.

83. Breton, *Manifestoes*, 26.

84. On the closet episode, see Thompson, "The Automatic Hand," 10.

85. Ellenberger, *Discovery of the Unconscious*, 56.

Chapter 1

1. "L'hypothèse de Flournoy / Me trouble et me rend perplexe: / L'homme aurait un second moi / De nature fort complexe. / Au moi naturel ce moi sous-jacent / Damerait le pion . . . et, c'est renversant! / Se travestirait, changerait de sexe . . . / Certes, pour un moi, ça n'est pas banal. / Cet original / A reçu le nom de Subliminal" (quoted in Grasset, *L'occultisme*, 199).

2. For the details of Blanche's life at the Salpêtrière, see Hustvedt, *Medical Muses*, 33–142.

3. Showalter, *The Female Malady*, 2–3.

4. According to Amanda du Preez, "The rate of diagnoses at Salpêtrière between 1841 and 1842" indicates that "648 women patients were admitted, of which only one percent were diagnosed with hysteria. Between 1882 and 1883, at the height of Charcot's 'reign,' 500 women were admitted and between eighteen to twenty percent were diagnosed as hysterical." The male asylum of Bicêtre, however, saw only two men diagnosed as hysterical in 1883 (du Preez, *Gendered Bodies*, 12 n. 46).

5. Hustvedt, *Medical Muses*, 50–52.

6. Foucault, *The History of Sexuality*, 56 n. 1.

7. "Un phénomène singulier dû à une excitabilité spéciale de la peau qui consiste dans l'apparition de saillies œdémateuses, entourées de rougeurs, semblables aux plaques ortiées, pouvant former des figures variées à volonté, sous l'influence des excitations du tégument" (Féré and Lamy, "La dermographie," 283).

8. "Mathilde était totalement anesthésique et il suffisait de tracer sur sa peau blanche, d'une douceur pareille à une peau d'enfant, les caractères qu'on voulait pour qu'aussitôt, à la place touchée par l'ongle ou le crayon du docteur, une saillie rouge apparût, d'une proéminence telle qu'en tâtant ces caractères, on pût reconnaître la lettre que venait d'écrire là [le docteur]" (Claretie, *Les amours d'un interne*, 312).

9. "on peut lui traverser de part en part la peau des membres, du ventre, des seins, de la face, sans qu'elle ressente la moindre douleur. . . La sensibilité au froid, à la chaleur, au chatouillement ne se rencontre pas davantage" and "exécuter . . . les dessins les plus divers, écrire des noms de dix à quinze lettres" (Dujardin-Beaumetz, "Notes sur des troubles," 198–199).

10. See Hustvedt, *Medical Muses*, 56.

11. On the medical use of *femme-cliché* and *femme-autographe*, see Dujardin-Beaumetz, "Notes sur des troubles," 199–200.

12. "maître de la pensée et des sensations de cette masse de chair, devenue plus facile a pétrir entre ses doigts que le bloc de terre sous le pouce du sculpteur" (Claretie, *Les amours d'un interne*, 178).

13. De la Tourette, *L'hypnotisme*, 126.

14. "En thèse générale, celui qui, lors d'une première hypnotisation, voudra violer une femme, devra bien plutôt profiter de la léthargie, où elle est inerte" (de la Tourette, *L'hypnotisme*, 126).

15. "dans ce domaine, notre puissance ne rencontrera guère de limites; car, en réalité, nous pouvons faire varier notre action, presqu'à l'infini" (Charcot, "Sur deux cas," 340).

16. De la Tourette and Richer, "Hypnotisme," 94.

17. Beizer, *Ventriloquized Bodies*, 1.

18. Beizer, *Ventriloquized Bodies*, 9.

19. Hayward, *Resisting History*, 35.

20. Hayward, *Resisting History*, 37.

21. "Disons encore que la partie éclairée des populations a su, à part quelques rares exceptions, ne voir dans le spiritisme qu'une grossière duperie pratiquée sur une large échelle. Et effectivement, des femmes, des jeunes filles surtout, avec bon nombre d'ouvriers plus ou moins ignorants ou paresseux, forment l'immense majorité des fidèles" (Burlet, *Du spiritisme*, 7).

22. Braude, *Radical Spirits*, 23. For other studies focusing on mediumship and femininity in the nineteenth and early twentieth centuries, see, in America, Carroll, *Spiritualism in Antebellum America*; Goldsmith, *Other Powers*; McGarry, *Ghosts of Futures Past*; Lowry, *Invisible Hosts*; in Canada, Massicotte, *Trance Speakers*; Robertson, *Science of the Séance*; in England, Barrow, *Independent Spirits*; Owen, *The Darkened Room*; Tromp, *Altered States*; and in France, Edelman, *Voyantes, guérisseuses et visionnaires*.

23. Sconce, *Haunted Media*, 12.

24. Sconce, *Haunted Media*, 22, 36.

25. Warner, *Phantasmagoria*, 241.

26. Sharp, *Secular Spirituality*, 54.

27. "douées d'une certaine dose d'électricité naturelle, véritables torpilles humaines, produisant par le simple contact tous les effets d'attraction et de répulsion" (Kardec, *Le livre des mediums*, 162).

28. "La question est de savoir si les personnes électriques auraient une aptitude plus grande à devenir médiums à effets physiques; nous le pensons" (Kardec, *Le livre des mediums*, 163).

29. I recuperate this expression from André Breton in *Les vases communicants* (later translated as *Communicated Vessels*).

30. "Le somnambule agit sous l'influence de son propre Esprit; c'est son âme qui, dans les moments d'émancipation, voit, entend et perçoit en dehors de la limite des sens . . . ; en un mot, il vit par anticipation de la vie des Esprits" (Kardec, *Le livre des mediums*, 168).

31. "Le médium, au contraire, est l'instrument d'une intelligence étrangère; il est passif, et ce qu'il dit ne vient point de lui. En résumé, le somnambule exprime sa propre pensée, et le médium exprime celle d'un autre. Mais l'Esprit qui se communique à un médium ordinaire peut tout aussi bien le faire à un somnambule" (Kardec, *Le livre des mediums*, 168).

32. My translation from "pas la moindre conscience de ce qu'il écrit" and "inconscience absolue . . . est précieuse en ce qu'elle ne peut laisser aucun doute sur l'indépendance de la pensée de celui qui écrit" (Kardec, *Le livre des mediums*, 173).

33. Hustvedt, *Medical Muses*, 57.

34. "Ils endormirent, convulsionnèrent toute une génération, et exploitèrent, surtout à leur profit, les malades hystériques et la crédulité publique" (Brouardel, "Preface," iii).

35. "nous sommes loin de cette date. Grâce à [Charcot], grâce aux travaux de ses élèves, nous sommes en possession d'un terrain véritablement scientifique" (Brouardel, "Preface," v).

36. "L'amour du merveilleux et la crainte du surnaturel sont innés en nous. Ces sentiments sont plus ou moins manifestes et peuvent, suivant les cas, caractériser un peuple, une époque ou un âge, mais, qu'il s'agisse de peuples ou d'hommes, ils existent chez tous, plus profonds chez ceux qui sont au début de leur développement intellectuel. L'imagination de l'enfant y puise ses jouissances et ses terreurs les plus vives" (Brouardel, "Preface," i).

37. "tout ce qui frappe vivement l'esprit, tout ce qui impressionne fortement l'imagination, favorise singulièrement, chez les sujets prédisposés, l'apparition de l'hystérie. Parmi tous ces traumatismes des fonctions cérébrales, il n'en est peut-être point de plus efficace, et dont l'action ait été plus souvent signalée, que cette croyance au merveilleux, au surnaturel, qu'entretiennent et qu'exagèrent, soit les pratiques religieuses excessives, soit, dans un ordre d'idées connexe, le spiritisme et sa mise en œuvre" (Charcot, "Spiritisme et hystérie," 229).

38. Sharp, *Secular Spirituality*, 129.

39. Sharp, *Secular Spirituality*, 98.

40. "La raison se révolte à l'idée des tortures morales et corporelles auxquelles la science a quelquefois soumis des êtres faibles et délicats en vue de s'assurer s'il n'y avait pas supercherie de leur part; ces expérimentations, le plus souvent faites avec malveillance, sont toujours nuisibles aux organisations sensitives; il pourrait en résulter de graves désordres" (Kardec, *Le livre des mediums*, 197).

41. "Nous avons, assurément, des faits et des manifestations qui sont de l'ordre scientifique . . . des Myers, des Hodgson, des Wollace, des Aksakof, de tant d'autres qui, après de longues hésitations et de patientes recherches, en viennent à conclure comme nous" (Société, *Autour "Des Indes à la planète Mars"*, 22).

42. "On sait quel rôle considérable joue la suggestion dans les expériences psychiques, jusqu'où va la suggestibilité des médiums. Ce fait, dûment constaté, quel est le devoir de l'observateur? S'efforcer de rester neutre, faire le possible et l'impossible pour laisser au phénomène toute sa sincérité et toute sa spontanéité. Au lieu de cela, que voyons-nous? Des interventions actives qui tendent à le modifier à tout bout de champ, soit que l'on tente des expériences physiologiques sur le sujet, soit que l'on interrompe la communication par des questions et des observations qui en entravent la libre allure, ou la dévient vers d'autres directions. Celte façon de procéder peut avoir ses avantages; elle a sûrement de très graves inconvénients. Une étude aussi délicate exige une grande délicatesse" (Société, *Autour "Des Indes à la planète Mars"*, 41).

43. "Notre monde s'en allait à la dérive, sans gouvernail pour guider sa course, sans phare pourlui indiquer le port. . . . La matière triomphait avec le matérialisme. Les espérances, quant au futur, s'évanouissaient les unes après les autres. La mort devait être la fin de tout. Nous savons maintenant—nous savons de science certaine—qu'elle n'est que le passage d'une vie à une autre. Ce que nous affirmions naguère sous la risée et le mépris publics, les savants, chaque jour, les savants les plus positifs, les plus rebelles aux vains rêves et aux mirages décevants, le confirment de plus en plus" (Société, *Autour "Des Indes à la planète Mars"*, 181).

44. See Carroll, *Spiritualism in Antebellum America*; Castellan, *Le spiritisme*; Monroe, *Laboratories of Faith*; Oppenheim, *The Other World*; Owen, *The Darkened Room*; Massicotte, *Trance Speakers*.

45. Owen, *The Darkened Room*, 1.

46. Sharp, *Secular Spirituality*, 112.

47. Davis, *The Temple*, 224.

48. Braude, *Radical Spirits*, 57.

49. Sharp, *Secular Spirituality*, xix.

50. "et les premières médiums spirites en particulier, s'appuient sur cette nouvelle religion pour prendre la parole, une parole bien souvent critique. . . . Enfin, l'état modifié de conscience dans lequel elles sont réellement (ou disent être) leur confère un masque protecteur propice à la prise de parole ou à l'écriture, par ailleurs difficiles d'accès aux femmes du XIXᵉ siècle, on le sait. Le spiritisme serait donc pour ces femmes un moyen, original et détourné certes, pour des prises de positions politiques et sociales" (Edelman, "Spiritisme et Politique," 3).

51. "Lors donc qu'un enfant naît, il ne vient pas seulement sur la terre, il y revient. Notre habitacle nous connaît et nous le connaissons. Nous y avons déjà vécu, nous y vivrons probablement encore. Les uns y ont séjourné plus souvent, les autres moins" (Société, *Autour "Des Indes à la planète Mars"*, 210).

52. Edelman, "Spiritisme et Politique," 3.

53. This inscription is why if I have opted to retain the pseudonym Hélène Smith rather than to refer to her birth name, Elise Müller.

54. "Je n'ai pas voulu être leur chose, leur machine" and "J'ai toujours estimé que mon travail, ainsi que les admirables et inoubliables visions qui l'accompagnent, n'avait nullement besoin du contrôle des hommes; que je n'avais à rendre compte à personne de mes actions. Que même il y aurait comme une profanation, un sacrilège, à vouloir y mettre une direction humaine. Aussi suis-je restée ferme, énergique, prudente, surtout en présence de la mission qui m'était confiée de l'Au-Delà, ne sentant en tout temps le besoin que du contrôle de Dieu seul" (Deonna, *De la planète Mars*, 37, 5).

Chapter 2

1. Anna O.'s story has now become a site of contestation regarding the origins of psycho-analysis, the importance of the sexual etiology in hysteria, and the role of transference in analysis. See, in addition to others cited below, Jones, *Life and Work*, 1:223–26; Ellenberger, "Story of 'Anna O.'"; Forrester, "True Story of Anna O."; Skues, *Sigmund Freud*; and Breger, *Dream of Undying Fame*.

2. Freud and Breuer, *Studies in Hysteria*, 24.

3. Freud and Breuer, *Studies in Hysteria*, 24.

4. Freud and Breuer, *Studies in Hysteria*, 25.

5. Freud and Breuer, *Studies in Hysteria*, 26.

6. Freud and Breuer, *Studies in Hysteria*, 26.

7. Golomb Hoffman, "Archival Bodies," 6.

8. Freud and Breuer, *Studies in Hysteria*, 35.

9. Freud and Breuer, *Studies in Hysteria*, 129.

10. Freud and Breuer, *Studies in Hysteria*, 129.

11. Freud and Breuer, *Studies in Hysteria*, 21.

12. See Freud and Breuer, *Studies in Hysteria*, n1, p. 40–41.

13. Hunter, "Hysteria, Psychoanalysis, Feminism," 472.

14. Flournoy, *From India*, 295.

15. Flournoy, *From India*, 259.

16. Flournoy, *From India*, 111.

17. Flournoy, *From India*, 181.

18. See Hugo, *Le livre des tables*.

19. Flournoy, *From India*, 30.

20. In 1907, Smith appears to have remained subconsciously influenced by Dumas's literary imagination. After wearing a necklace recently received from a female acquaintance, she felt the hand of a man detaching it from her neck, while whispering in her ear, "It's me, Philippe." Smith understood the vision as a foreboding, warning her not to wear the necklace, but she could not retrace its origins. She wrote in her journals: "But who is he? No one among my relations bears the name of Philippe, and from those who have left this world, I do not remember that there was one of this name" ("Mais qui est-il? Je n'ai dans mes relations aucune portant le prénom de Philippe, et dans celles qui seraient déjà parties d'ici-bas, je ne me souviens nullement qu'il en fut une de ce nom") (Deonna, *De la planète Mars*, 18). In Dumas's novel, *Le collier de la Reine*, the character of Philippe emerges in association with a necklace offered to Marie Antoinette in the narration of the famous "affair of the diamond necklace."

21. The most famous of these poems, "Demain dès l'aube" ("Tomorrow at Dawn"), was published in the volume *Les contemplations* (*The Contemplations*) in 1856. On the selected alias of Cagliostro, Smith herself later offered a different hypothesis. After learning that the historical figure had been imprisoned and died in a village named San Leo, she wrote, in 1908: "I understand now why Cagliostro wished that we named him Léopold, or simply Léo, as he would say to us. It is the name of the cemetery where he was sleeping his last rest" ("Je comprends maintenant pourquoi Cagliostro a désiré qu'on le nommât Léopold, ou Léo tout court, nous disait-il. C'était le nom du cimetière où il dormait de son dernier sommeil") (Deonna, *De la planète Mars*, 45).

22. Flournoy, *From India*, 66.

23. "Une formation hypnoïde de nature et d'origine essentiellement psycho-sexuelle" (Flournoy, *Nouvelles observations*, 119).

24. Flournoy declared that no less than four suiters had asked for her hand during the year following the publication of *Des Indes*. Flournoy, *Nouvelles observations*, 120.

25. Flournoy, *From India*, 52.

26. Flournoy, *From India*, 211.

27. Flournoy, *From India*, 210.

28. Flournoy, *From India*, 221.
29. Flournoy, *From India*, 217.
30. Flournoy, *From India*, 174.
31. Flournoy, *From India*, 174.
32. Flournoy, *From India*, 178.
33. Flournoy, *From India*, 183.
34. Flournoy, *From India*, 183.
35. Flournoy, *From India*, 186.
36. Flournoy, *From India*, 95.
37. Crossley, *Imagining Mars*, 129.
38. Flammarion, *The Planet Mars*, 511.
39. Flournoy, *From India*, 164. It may worth noting that, in all her romances, Smith appears to emphasize the immutable nature of sex—her soul, in all her incarnations, remains female—while nonetheless demonstrating the artificiality of class. The fantasies that psychologists called mediums' "delusions of grandeur" demonstrated, for middle- and working-class audiences, that social inequalities were not the result of a natural order. This aspect, as Lynn Sharp remarks, made the spiritualist movement generally democratic and progressive. In France, she notes, "Spiritists varied from the elite to the worker. The bulk of the movement was made up of middle and working class people. In Paris, rentiers, accountants, and butchers met together to talk to kin who had passed on" (Sharp, *Secular Spirituality*, xv). In suggesting that a store clerk could hide the reincarnation of a queen, Smith's séances might indeed have supported ideals of social progress and equality. However, her romances also appeared to emphasize the immutable nature of sex; while various spiritualist authors following reincarnation doctrines saw the soul as androgynous, sexed only through physical embodiment on earth, Smith's soul, in all her incarnations, remained female and all her loving relationships heterosexual.
40. Flournoy, *From India*, 7.
41. "Ils ne mentent pas. . . . Ils aident, ils encouragent, ils tirent d'embarras, ils protègent; souvent même ils sauvent la vie. . . . ils représentent les degrés psychologiquement supérieurs (atteignant jusqu'à la formation d'une seconde personnalité plus ou moins complète) de l'automatisme téléologique, lequel à ses degrés moindres, embrasse tout ce qui n'est qu'heureuses inspirations, et confine par en bas aux vulgaires réflexes" (Flournoy, *Esprits et medium*, 295).
42. "Cagliostro, aussi, veille, et saura toujours détourner ce qui pourrait m'être nuisible ou apporter quelque méfait autour de moi" (Deonna, *De la planète Mars*, 36).
43. Flournoy, *From India*, 314.
44. Le Clair, *Letters of James and Flournoy*, 47.
45. Flournoy, *From India*, 245.
46. On Freud's simultaneous studies of memory constructions, see Freud, "Screen Memories."
47. "finit inévitablement par façonner la subconscience si suggestible de son sujet," "menace le medium qui se sait—ou se croit—un objet constant d'étude de la part de son observateur," and "Aussi l'investigateur doit-il sans cesse se demander, a l'égard

de chacun des mediums qu'il étudie, jusqu'à quel point il n'est pas à la longue devenu lui-même tout à la fois une cause prépondérante des phénomènes qu'il obtient" (Flournoy, *Nouvelles observations*, 116).

48. Flournoy, *From India*, 155.

49. "la vérité est probablement entre ces deux extrêmes et . . . la solution du problème se trouverait dans le fait psychologique . . . qui constitue le jeu" and "En effet . . . le jeu est . . . l'essence et la raison d'être de l'enfance et la jeunesse" (Flournoy, *Nouvelles observations*, 248).

50. Flournoy, *From India*, 207.

51. Flournoy, *From India*, 322.

52. Flournoy, *From India*, 259.

53. Flournoy, *From India*, 208.

54. Flournoy, *From India*, 209. In 1910, Flournoy would be invited by Cécile Vé, director of an Evangelical institute and a mystic, to cure her of her inner "raw beast," which continuously precipitated in her a "furnace of sexual emotions" (Flournoy, *Une mystique moderne*, 20) The case was published in Flournoy's *Une mystique moderne* (*A Modern Mystic*) in 1915. Placing her under hypnosis, Flournoy attempted to free her from her guilt and to convince her to treat such natural instincts with greater indifference in order to reduce their power over her psychic life. In this relationship, Flournoy was once again blind to the eroticism shaping the dynamic of transference and countertransference; he noted that his and Cécile's relationship was agreeable, "free of hidden motives," and devoid of "manifest or latent passions" (*Une mystique moderne*, 36). Thus, when a divine friend from the heavens appeared to her and, over several nights, provided her with religious experiences through sexual ecstasies, Flournoy remained unaware of his own similitude with the ghostly friend. On this episode and Flournoy's inattention to the transferential dynamic, see also Hamon, "Une mystique moderne."

55. Flournoy, *From India*, 12.

56. "toutes les lettres que j'ai pu vous écrire depuis le 1 mars 1901, lettre dont la plupart trahissaient un état de fatigue ou d'irritation nerveuse auquel je suis inexcusable d'avoir cédé" (Flournoy, *Théodore et Léopold*, 170).

57. "une attitude lascive; les yeux sont languissants, le buste renversé, les mains *actives* et enfin . . . H.S. accuse un spasme érotique qui ne laisse pas de doute sur l'illusion d'un rapprochement sexuel" (Flournoy, *Théodore et Léopold*, 172).

58. "impossibles à rapporter, mais qui se devinent si on a étudié les individus qui pratiquent la masturbation depuis de longues années" (Flournoy, *Théodore et Léopold*, 173).

59. "Là où il échoue, et où il *hait* au moins momentanément, c'est au cours des . . . séances amoureuses du Pr. F. qui a été longtemps l'amant de Mlle S. Je me récrie: 'Ce n'est pas vrai, dis-je—le medium ne s'est jamais trouvé seule avec Mr. F et c'est l'impossibilité matérielle la plus probante.' Ici le récit suivant (de Léopold bien entendu): tout au commencement, il y a de longues années, H.S. est entrée au laboratoire un après-midi d'hiver sous un prétexte dont elle ne se souvient plus—Mr F. lui ayant avoué des sentiments « d'ordre immoral » elle s'est défendue vaillamment. Mais peu à peu

excitée par des caresses (impossible de décrire ces immondices!) . . . Elle s'est livrée entièrement. De cette première entrevue est résulté un commencement de grossesse qui au bout de trois mois et demi s'est terminée en une perte de sang" (Flournoy, *Théodore et Léopold*, 173).

60. "des tristes manifestations du cycle érotique" (Flournoy, *Théodore et Léopold*, 174).

61. Cited in Forrester, "True Story of Anna O.," 331. While Freud's interpretation of the end of the treatment is contentious (Bertha herself had set the date for the termination of her analysis), this does not preclude the possibility that Breuer may have been affected by an unconscious desire toward his patient, a desire that would have shaped the transference and countertransference in the analysis and, perhaps, led to his readiness to accept her termination of the cure.

62. Cited in Forrester, "True Story of Anna O.," 328.

63. "un effet psychologique dont il existe peu d'exemples, que je sache, dans l'histoire des Lettres, tant spirites que profanes" (Flournoy, *Théodore et Léopold*, 118).

64. "Ce que Madame Jackson a fait pour moi ne *regarde personne* et possèderais-je in million que mon bonheur ne devrait point vous faire oublier la parole donnée et vous faire souvenir qu'il y a une année environ vous m'avez dit: 'je considère le revenu des Indes a la planète Mars comme ne m'appartenant pas et comme devant vous revenir'" (Flournoy, *Théodore et Léopold*, 121).

65. "le procédé connu et commode qui consiste à isoler un texte de son contexte afin d'en mieux fausser le sens" (Flournoy, *Théodore et Léopold*, 123).

66. "C'eut été un non-sens commercial . . . car ce n'est qu'avec *l'auteur* d'un livre que traitent les éditeurs" (Flournoy, *Théodore et Léopold*, 123).

67. "mentalité débile" and "Vous vous trompez totalement me croyant l'auteur ou l'inspirateur de l'article de la *Gazette de Lausanne*; je n'y suis pour rien" (Flournoy, *Théodore et Léopold*, 143).

68. "aucun rapprochement ni dans les s, m, v, f, et g" and "Je n'ai pas été plus complice qu'auteur" (Flournoy *Théodore et Léopold*, 145).

69. Gutierrez, "From Electricity to Ectoplasm," 70.

70. Gutierrez, "From Electricity to Ectoplasm," 71.

71. Mitchell, *Psychoanalysis and Feminism*, 9–10.

72. Gilbert and Gubar, *Madwoman in the Attic*, 7.

73. See, for instance, Sword, *Ghostwriting Modernism*; London, *Writing Double*; and Massicotte, *Trance Speakers*.

74. Gutierrez, "From Electricity to Ectoplasm," 68.

75. Flournoy, *From India*, 65.

76. Shelley, *Frankenstein*, 10.

77. Rhys, *Jean Rhys Letters*, 301. On women's creativity and the symbolism of pregnancy, see also Friedman, "Creativity."

78. "Toutes ces choses troublent M. F. . . . avec la flotte de nos pasteurs qui voient un danger dans mon œuvre . . . [I]ls voudraient, je pense, me faire exposer mon œuvre afin de la critiquer. . . . Je désire que M. F. . . . ne s'occupe plus jamais de moi. Je désire ne donner à ce monsieur aucun sujet, soit pour le présent, soit pour l'avenir, d'avoir à parler de tous mes enfants les tableaux" (Deonna, *De la planète Mars*, 52–53).

79. Rhys, *Jean Rhys Letters*, 301.

80. Brady Brower's excellent article "The Medium Is the Message" also examines the Flournoy/Smith correspondence and claims that "in this case, the unitary subject of liberal philosophy and of law (the author and proprietor) was opposed on the one hand by the transcendent subject of spiritualism and, on the other, by the internally riven subjectivity of the new psychology" (32). Brower concludes that we should take seriously "the disposition of property" presented in this correspondence, because "the ideal of authorship and ownership invoked by both was illusory . . . neither Hélène nor Flournoy were really the authors of their own histories" (54).

81. Hunter, "Hysteria, Psychoanalysis, and Feminism," 469.

82. Loentz, *Let Me Continue*, 199.

83. See Gay, *Freud*, 66.

84. "Il faut que je signe mes tableaux; je ne l'avais pas encore fait à ce jour, ne sachant si je voulais signer 'Hélène Smith' ou de mon vrai nom. Maintenant je pense bien faire en signant en toutes lettres 'Élise Müller'" (Deonna, *De la planète Mars*, 40). Yet it should be noted that Léopold prevented her from adding *any name* to the paintings. Smith adds: "As I was about to sign . . . I felt a hand resting on my arm, and the well-known voice of Cagliostro whispered in my ear: 'Stop, you do not need to be in such a hurry; wait a little still.' Thus . . . I put the brush down, and said, 'I will wait'" ("Au moment où j'allais me mettre en devoir de signer . . . j'ai senti une main se poser sur mon bras, puis la voix bien connue de Cagliostro a murmuré à mon oreille: 'Arrête, tu n'as pas besoin de tant te presser; attends encore un peu . . .' Alors . . . j'ai posé le pinceau, et ai dit, 'J'attendrai'") (Deonna, *De la planète Mars*, 40).

Chapter 3

1. Ovid, *Metamorphoses*, 110.

2. While drawing from Lacan's notions of the real, imaginary, and symbolic realms, Irigaray thus also rejects Lacan universalization of the symbolic. She writes: "There is lacking in Lacan a theory of enunciation which would be sufficiently complex, and which would allow him to account for the effect of sexual difference in the production of language" (cited in Hass, "Style of the Speaking Subject," 67).

3. Irigaray, *Speculum*, 133.

4. Butler, *Gender Trouble*, 9.

5. "l'imitation par la voix de sons articulés ou non qui viennent frapper notre oreille" (de la Tourette, "Clinique nerveuse," 177). Today, the term appears in the literature on autism spectrum disorders, particularly in works regarding the clinic with children. See, for instance, Sterponi and Shankey, "Rethinking Echolalia," and Neely et al. "Treatment of Echolalia."

6. "besoin presque irrésistible," "besoin de répétition," and "toutes les facultés de l'intelligence" (de la Tourette, "Clinique Nerveuse," 175–176).

7. "entend parler une des personnes qui l'entourent; aussitôt il répète, avec une secousse, le ou les derniers mots de la phrase qu'il vient d'entendre. Il est parfaitement conscient, tout à fait décidé même" (de la Tourette, "Clinique Nerveuse," 175).

8. Ferguson, *Determined Spirits*, 77. Ferguson is here referring to xenoglossia, a particular expression of speaking in tongues whereby the medium uttered sentences in foreign languages or approximations of foreign languages. Smith's glossolalia often took the form of xenoglossia, though the foreign languages she created either did not exist (as was the case of her Martian and Uranian) or presented only similarities with existing language (as was the case for her Sanskritoid), as I explain below.

9. Jakobson, *Selected Writings*, 214.

10. de Certeau. "Vocal Utopias," 29.

11. "Lemaître, ce que tu désirais tant" and "Il serait bien intéressant de savoir ce qui se passe dans d'autres planètes!" This episode is explored in Cifali, "La fabrication," 40.

12. De Certeau, "Vocal Utopias," 31.

13. In Cifali, "A propos de la glossolalie," 321–322.

14. Flournoy, *From India*, 95.

15. Flournoy, *From India*, 164.

16. Flournoy, *From India*, 165.

17. Flournoy, *From India*, 193.

18. Rosenberg, "Speaking Martian," n.p.

19. Rosenberg, "Speaking Martian," n.p.

20. Flournoy, *From India*, 5.

21. "Smith a été en tout ceci plus consciente qu'elle ne le paraît" (Flournoy, *Théodore et Léopold*, 209).

22. "a-t-elle été en relation avec quelque étudiant, de qui elle aurait pu prendre quelques bribes de sanscrit et d'histoire?" (Flournoy, *Théodore et Léopold*, 182).

23. On Saussure's being the first modern study of glossolalia, Cooper, "Saussure and the Psychic," 259.

24. "Simandini aurait-elle été un bas bleu?" (Flournoy, *Théodore et Léopold*, 186).

25. See Flournoy, *Théodore et Léopold*, 199–203.

26. Flournoy, *From India*, 316.

27. Cooper, "Saussure and the Psychic," 258.

28. Saussure, *Course in General Linguistics*, 65.

29. "Au dire de Robert Godei, 'autour de 1894, le problème de la nature de la langue et des fondements de la linguistique a pris pour lui un caractère obsédant.' Or, à lire les contributions de Saussure aux recherches de Flournoy..., on comprend que Saussure n'était pas simplement disposé à participer à la recherche de Flournoy parce que cela le détournait de ses obsessions épistémologiques, mais tout au contraire parce qu'il y pouvait étudier le fonctionnement psychologique d'un mécanisme linguistique" (Fehr, "Le mécanisme de la langue," 99).

30. Flournoy, *From India*, 243.

31. On Henry's larger body of works, see Puech, *Linguistique et partages*.

32. "empruntés inconsciemment au trésor linguistique, d'elle en partie inconnu, qui git dans les profondeurs de sa mémoire subliminale" (Henry, *Le langage martien*, 4).

33. Henry, *Le language martien*, 22–23.
34. "folichonneries" and "conjecture quasi-divagante" (Flournoy, *De Théodore à Léopold*, 211).
35. "quelques-unes de mes explications doivent être tenues pour forcées" and "presque tous les mots du martien ont une étymologie assurée" (Henry, *Le langage martien*, 140).
36. Hammer, "Stages in the Development," 143–144.
37. "Il en reste encore un assez grand nombre de probables ou de sûres, pour que le résidu inexplicable ne constitue qu'une infime minorité: il est donc à présumer que ce résidu lui-même deviendrait réductible, si nous disposions de moyens plus puissants ou plus sagaces pour pénétrer les secrets de l'élaboration subconsciente à laquelle elle s'est livrée, et qu'il apparaitrait dès lors qu'elle n'a point créé un seul mot qui n'appartint d'ores et déjà à sa mémoire sous-jacente.—L'homme, quand il le voudrait, n'inventerait pas une langue: il ne peut parler, il ne parle qu'avec ses souvenirs" (Henry, *Le langage martien*, 140).
38. Todorov, *Theories of the Symbol*, 262.
39. Todorov, *Theories of the Symbol*, 264.
40. Henry, *Le langage martien*, 139.
41. Lacan, "Instance of the Letter," 419, §502.
42. "Olivier Flournoy, nom célèbre, troisième génération de grands psychiatres, le premier étant Théodore ... et vous savez le cas célèbre par quoi Théodore reste immortel dans la tradition analytique, cette clairvoyante délirante au nom merveilleux dont il a fait tout un ouvrage et dont vous ne sauriez trop profiter si l'ouvrage vous tombe sous la main" (Lacan, *Séminaire XV*, 32).
43. Flournoy, *Théodore et Léopold*, 100.
44. "On y retrouve les fesses" and "au-dessus de l'orifice présumé, le contenant. Enveloppe, matrice, utérus, ampoule rectale, pour le premier, symbole féminin pour le second, destinés l'un et l'autre à contenir 'l'enfant caca'" (Flournoy, *Théodore et Léopold*, 101).
45. Cifali, "Appendix One," 285.
46. Cifali, "Appendix One," 285.
47. Flournoy, *From India*, 166.
48. Flournoy, *From India*, 168.
49. Flournoy, *From India*, 170. Emphasis mine.
50. Flournoy, *Nouvelles observations*, 154.
51. Henry, *Le langage martien*, 140.
52. Hanegraaff, *Esotericism and the Academy*, 253–254.
53. Flournoy, *From India*, 170.
54. Flournoy, *From India*, 52.
55. Irigaray, *This Sex*, 30.
56. Exploring Smith's Martian travels within the larger history of "telepresence," Christopher Keep elegantly explains the apparent merging of the medium's identity with her interlocutors' and her consequent destabilization of discursive categories. He writes: "Such interactions are distinctly reciprocal: as she enters into the everyday lives of her Martian companions, so they, in turn, enter deeply into her own terrestrial

concerns and customs, speaking through her even as she speaks to them. In the course of this complex and often perplexing exchange, in which the self becomes other even to itself, the normative distinctions . . . of an active sender and passive receiver . . . give way to a dynamic relation of mutual entanglement in which both sender and receiver are ineluctably caught up in and become part of the other" ("Hélène Smith," 540).

57. Irigaray, *This Sex*, 76.
58. De Certeau, "Vocal Utopias," 39.
59. Irigaray, *This Sex*, 205.

Chapter 4

1. See Janet, "Note sur quelques phénomènes," 1885, "Deuxième note sur le sommeil," 1886, "Les actes inconscients," 1886, "Les phases intermédiaires de l'hypnotisme," 1886, "L'anesthésie systématisée," 1887.
2. For further information on Janet's experiments with Léonie, see Eisenbud, *Paranormal Foreknowledge*, 140–146; Luckhurst, *The Invention of Telepathy*, 143; and Plas, *Naissance*, 93–98.
3. See Evrard, Pratte, and Cardeña, "Pierre Janet," 103.
4. Cited in Stead, *Real Ghost Stories*, 45.
5. Cited in Stead, *Real Ghost Stories*, 45.
6. Janet, "Note sur quelques phénomènes," 1885, 32.
7. On this separation, see Coon, "Testing the Limits"; Keeley, "Subliminal Promptings"; and Parot, "Le bannissement des esprits."
8. Evrard, Pratte, and Cardeña, "Pierre Janet," 101.
9. Gauld, "Notes on the Career," 141.
10. Plas, *Naissance*, 144.
11. "Inutile de revenir sur la description de cette écriture que les spirites ont découverte: si elle n'a plus aujourd'hui le rôle religieux auquel la destinaient les disciples d'Allan Kardec, peut-être peut-elle avoir dans maintes circonstances un certain rôle médical" (Janet, *L'état mental*, 59).
12. On Lucy and Léonie, see Brown, "Pierre Janet," 282.
13. "M'entendez-vous, lui dis-je?—(Elle répond par écrit) Non.—Mais pour répondre il faut entendre.—Oui, absolument.—Alors, comment faites-vous?—Je ne sais.—Il faut bien qu'il y ait quelqu'un qui m'entende?—Oui.—Qui cela?—Autre que Lucie.—Ah bien! une autre personne. Voulez-vous que nous lui donnions un nom?—Non.—Si, ce sera plus commode.—Eh bien Adrienne" (Janet, *L'automatisme psychologique*, 317–318).
14. "Lucie, Marguerite et bien d'autres présentent, d'une façon complète, l'écriture automatique et ferait la fortune d'un cabinet spirite" (Janet, *L'état mental*, 204).
15. Cited in Baccopoulos-Viau, "Automatism, Surrealism," 267.
16. "ont des lois et s'expliquent de la même manière par un trouble grave dans l'opération mentale de la perception, que nous avons décrit sous le nom de désagrégation psychologique" (Janet, "Le spiritisme contemporain," 419).

17. Gyimesi, "The Problem of Demarcation," 468. In France, experimental explorations of so-called psi phenomena were relegated to the Institut Métapsychique International, established in 1919, under the direction of Gustave Geley.

18. Baccopoulos-Viau, "Automatism, Surrealism," 262.

19. Baccopoulos-Viau, "Automatism, Surrealism," 260.

20. Baccopoulos-Viau, "Automatism, Surrealism," 266.

21. Many studies have addressed Bretonian surrealism and the occult. See, for instance, Bauduin, *Surrealism and the Occult*; Choucha, *Surrealism and the Occult*; Ferentinou, "Surrealism, Occulture and Gender"; Ferentinou, Bauduin, and Zamani, *Surrealism, Occultism and Politics*; Rabinovitch, *Surrealism and the Sacred*. My focus here is on Smith's influence and Breton's use of (secularized) spiritualist practices to reframe the creative unconscious.

22. Morehead, "Symbolism, Mediumship," 77.

23. Breton, "The Automatic Message," 20.

24. Breton, *Manifestoes of Surrealism*, 26.

25. Flournoy, *From India*, 49.

26. Flournoy, *From India*, 69.

27. Flournoy, *From India*, 100.

28. Flournoy, *From India*, 164.

29. Flournoy, *From India*, 200.

30. Flournoy, *From India*, 200–201.

31. "Hélène eut une envie d'aller au piano, ce qui me procura une petite séance imprévue, d'environ 35 minutes. Il lui sembla (6h.25) qu'elle allait rejouer la romance que dimanche dernier elle avait déjà joue à sa mère. 'Hélène' chanta des paroles hindoues qu'elle accompagnait au piano sur un rythme simple qui ne manquait pas de charme. Les paroles très douces étaient malheureusement presque insaisissables" (Lemaitre, "Compte-rendu," 27).

32. Flournoy, *From India*, 110.

33. Flournoy, *From India*, 109.

34. Flournoy, *From India*, 110.

35. Flournoy, *From India*, 110.

36. Shamdasani, "Encountering Hélène," xxv.

37. "Oh! Ce subconscient, ce subliminal. . . . S'il fallait le sentir capable de créer une œuvre semblable à la mienne, que faudrait-il penser de lui, de sa puissance, de sa force. Ne faudrait-il pas lui vouer un culte spécial, le rechercher à chaque heure importante, heureuse ou malheureuse de notre vie, le faire agir à notre place pour ce que nous nous sentons incapable par moment de faire ou de débrouiller? Et si nous arrivions enfin à ne pouvoir faire autrement que de l'admettre, ne faudrait-il pas voir en lui une personnalité, plus spiritualisée que la première, une aide que Dieu se serait créée pour nous éclairer parfois, une seconde conscience émanant de Lui, l'aidant dans sa mission autour de ses enfants?" (Deonna, *De la planète Mars*, 50).

38. For an excellent study of the complex legacy of Hélène Smith's religious paintings, see Morehead, "Le legs et l'exposition." The author retraces in fascinating detail the

contestation of Smith's will and the complex movements of her paintings between psychology laboratory, museum, and distant heirs, before their near complete disappearance.

39. "J'étais sur le point de me décider à l'état du mariage, quand . . . a commencé mon premier tableau" (Deonna, *De la planète Mars*, 102).

40. Flournoy, *From India*, 110.

41. "Des milliers de personnes ont défilé, depuis trois mois, dans son coquet petit appartement pour contempler ses chefs-d'œuvre somnambuliques. Les appréciations les plus enthousiastes se sont fait jour. Il y a bien eu quelques notes discordantes: mais elles ont été vite étouffées dans le concert général d'éloges et d'explosions admiratives: si bien que, pour un peu, le salon de l'illustre médium serait en passe de devenir un nouveau lieu de pèlerinage et de dévotion" (Lemaître, "Un nouveau cycle," 63).

42. "Il me fallait une chambre spéciale pour peindre, où je puisse coucher, et non pas me réduire comme ici dans une alcôve derrière des tableaux qu'il fallait remuer tous les soirs et ou je manquais d'air. Là-bas, j'aurai de l'air et de la verdure, du calme pour terminer mon œuvre, qui, je sens, le demande à grand cris" (Deonna, *De la planète Mars*, 39).

43. "Je perds tout à fait conscience de ma personnalité. Je m'éveille de cet état pour constater que la parcelle de peinture entrevue est bien véritablement peinte cette fois-ci . . . la couleur qui adhère encore à mes doigts en est le témoignage" (Deonna, *De la planète Mars*, 316).

44. "nous n'hésiterons pas à le dire, du plus mauvais gout" (Deonna, *De la planète Mars*, 304).

45. "la cause de l'arrêt dans la production picturale. . . . Elle ne vit plus que dans le souvenir de son ami, elle attend ses visions et ses dictées automatiques, qui dès lors remplissent ses manuscrits" (Deonna, *De la planète Mars*, 259).

46. "A ce moment, le tableau sembla glisser, et ce fut sur celui de l'Ange Gabriel m'entourant de son bras que l'étoile toujours plus rayonnante et plus belle se posa. L'Angle se détacha du tableau et m'entourant de son bras, me montra le ciel rayonnant de mille clartés. Puis, inclinant son visage sur le mien, sa voix douce et suave me murmura: Amie, marche toujours sur les traces du Maitre, je suis ton ange gardien, le compagnon de ton Immortalité qui te garantira ici-bas de la méchanceté des hommes" (Deonna, *De la planète Mars*, 99).

47. "Le Christ que voyait Helene vivait, marchait, s'approchait d'elle, lui mettait la main sur l'épaule, lui adressait même des paroles de paix et de réconfort, et la laissait troublée et émue jusqu'aux larmes. Il est facile à qui n'a rien vu, n'a rien senti, de parler d'hallucinations" (Cuendet, *Les tableaux*, 25).

48. "ses œuvres ne tomberont pas dans les mains de ses ennemis, spirites, magnétiseurs, et envouteurs de tout calibre, ou savant de la race d'un Flournoy, et [qu']ils ne serviront pas de documents d'études dans un laboratoire de psychologie!" and "les a mis en dépôt quelque temps précisément au Laboratoire de psychologie de notre Université!" (Deonna, *De la planète Mars*, 371).

49. "les tableaux provenant de la succession de Mlle Muller" and "Ils n'offrent aucune espèce d'intérêt pour nos collections et sont inexposables. Je propose donc que ce legs soit refusé" (cited in Morehead, "Le legs et l'exposition," 108).

50. "ces toiles, exécutées par Mlle Muller elle-même, n'ont pas un intérêt artistique suffisant pour pouvoir être exposées dans nos collections de peinture" and "un très grand intérêt scientifique et psychologique" (cited in Morehead, "Le legs et l'exposition," 108).

51. "le testament ne contient aucune clause restrictive obligeant la Ville de Genève à exposer ses tableaux [et] il sera facile, une fois ceux-ci entrés en notre possession, de les déposer dans l'endroit qui serait le plus approprié, soit le Laboratoire de Psychologie de l'Université de Genève" (cited in Morehead, "Le legs et l'exposition," 108).

52. "avec le plus grand intérêt" (cited in Morehead, "Le legs et l'exposition," 112).

53. "La Ville de Genève vient de recevoir une collection de peintures d'un intérêt tout spécial, léguées par leur auteur, Mademoiselle Elise-Catherine MULLER, plus connue du monde scientifique sous le pseudonyme d'Helene Smith" and "la salle d'exposition de la section des Arts décoratifs, non pour leur valeur esthétique mais uniquement pour leur intérêt psychologique" (cited in Morehead, "Le legs et l'exposition," 116).

54. "une grande affluence de visiteurs" (Deonna, *De la planète Mars*, 1).

55. "de dimensions diverse, les unes énormes, comme la 'Transfiguration' ou la 'Crucifixion,' les autres plus réduites. Une absence totale de métier s'y révèle, du premier coup d'œil et même à un profane. Certains traits rappellent vaguement les Primitifs ou les icônes byzantines, d'autres attestent d'une naïveté puérile et font songer à des gribouillages d'enfants. Les couleurs sont dures, brutales ou fades, sans nuances et offrent le spectacle d'une criante inharmonie. Mais le sentiment qui se dégage de ces toiles bizarres, obsédantes comme un cauchemar, n'est semblable en rien à celui que l'on éprouve devant la fraîcheur candide d'un Fra Angelico. Je ne sais rien de plus pénible que le sourire des deux prophètes dans la 'Transfiguration.' . . . Sous ce sourire qui veut être surnaturel, on devine une grimace. Sous la simplicité de l'ensemble, on discerne quelque chose d'extravagant, un je ne sais quoi de réticent, d'anormal, et pour tout dire de démoniaque, qui fait frémir. . . . Si l'on me contraignait de vivre, ne fût-ce que vingt-quatre heures dans l'ambiance d'images si funestes, je sais bien que je serais bon à mettre au cabanon" (cited in Morehead, "Le legs et l'exposition," 117–118).

56. Wilson, *Modernism and Magic*, 1. Also cited in Bauduin, "Surely Modern Art," 29. The latter adds: "Without a doubt there are strong strains of esotericism and occultism in modern Western art. . . . Occulture permeated general culture, including the field of modern(ist) art" (29–30). For additional studies of occultism and modern arts and literature, see notably Bauduin and Johnsson, *Occult in Modernist Art*; Bramble, *Modernism and the Occult*; Cardinal and Lusardy, *Art Spirite, Médiumnique, Visionnaire*; Clinton, *Mechanical Occult*; Materer, *Modernist Alchemy*.

57. Bauduin, "Surely Modern Art," 36.

58. Clair, "Le surréalisme," 79. Clair's work on surrealism was the object of polemical debates in French media following his publication of "Le surréalisme et la démoralisation de l'Occident" in *Le Monde* in 2001. In it, Clair rejected what he considered a critical impunity accorded to the surrealists and condemned, following

the attacks of September 11, the anti-Western and anti-American stance he retrieved from surrealist works (Clair, "Le surréalisme et la démoralisation," 1). In 2002, *Jean Clair ou la misère intellectuelle française* gathered a collection of "pro-surrealist" responses to Clair's article from artists, writers, and scholars (Abbou et al., *Jean Clair*). Clair's article followed this polemic, along with his 2003 monograph (*Du surréalisme*).

59. This translates the original title, "Méconnaissance de la psychanalyse dans le discours surréaliste." See Houdebine, "Méconnaissance de la psychanalyse," 67–82.

60. Houdebine, "Méconnaissance de la psychanalyse," 72. See also the article's criticism in Lomas, *The Haunted Self*, 66–69.

61. Breton, "For Dada." 54.

62. Breton, "The Mediums Enter," 92.

63. Bauduin, *Surrealism and the Occult*, 106.

64. As Roudinesco demonstrates, this identification notably occurs through Nadja, who, as will later be made clear, is herself identified with Smith ("in the manner of Hélène Smith" Nadja believed that "she had lived in the past under the reign of Marie Antoinette," Roudinesco reminds us). After noting the institutionalization of Nadja in the Vaucluse asylum, Breton declares his "contempt . . . for psychiatry, its rituals and works" and concludes that "Beauty will be CONVULSIVE or it will not be." Through this identification, Roudinesco argues, "the Madwoman" thus allowed Breton to "attain his desire to write and to achieve that convulsive beauty of which he dreamed" (Roudinesco, *Jacques Lacan & Co.*, 27).

65. Breton, *Manifestoes*, 35.

66. Janet, *L'état mental*, 204.

67. Breton, *Manifestoes*, 22–23.

68. "Quel délicieux et adorable enfant! Avec quelle joie je l'ai vu avancer! Avec quel bonheur j'ai vu se former tous ses petits membres! Il me semble maintenant qu'il est de chair et d'os, mon bien, un enfant bien à moi. Je voudrais le presser dans mes bras." And: "chaque mère trouve son bebe charmant, et comme mes tableaux sont mes enfants, il est naturel que j'aie un penchant à les admirer et à n'y rien trouver de défectueux. Ce tableau a pourtant pris son temps pour venir au monde. Les naissances retardées, et attendues avec beaucoup d'impatience, n'apportent ordinairement que des déceptions. Pour mon Jésus crucifié, le quatrième grand enfant, il n'en est pas ainsi" (Deonna, *De la planète Mars*, 101).

69. Breton, "The Mediums Enter," 91.

70. Breton, "The Mediums Enter," 95.

71. Breton, "The Mediums Enter," 92. Through the terms "hypnotic slumber" and "sleeping fits," the surrealists both reaffirmed the distinction between their and spiritualist practices of automatic writing (the former refusing the spiritual hypothesis) and alluded to traditions of somnambulism in France. Notably, through the writings of Allan Kardec, practices of mediumship had indeed been largely understood, in France, in continuity with phenomena of mesmerism, hypnotism, and somnambulism. See Lachapelle, *Investigating the Supernatural*; Brower, *Unruly Spirits*; and Méheust, *Somnambulisme et Mediumnité*.

72. Breton, "The Mediums Enter," 92, 95.

73. Breton, "The Mediums Enter," 92.

74. Conley, *Robert Desnos*, 30–31.

75. Breton, *Nadja*, 31–32.

76. Cited in Brandon, *Surreal Lives*, 205.

77. Breton, *Manifestoes of Surrealism*, 29.

78. Aragon, "A Wave of Dream," 6.

79. Breton, Parinaud, *Entretiens*, 91.

80. Brandon, *Surreal Lives*, 206.

81. Breton, "Letter to Seers," in *Manifestoes of Surrealism*, 195–204.

82. Breton, *Manifestoes of Surrealism*, 179.

83. I have written on Freud's fascination with telepathy in Massicotte, "Psychical Transmissions," as well as in Evrard, Massicotte, and Rabeyron, "Freud as a Psychical Researcher." Flournoy also addressed the possibilities of various psi phenomena, including telepathy, in Smith's séances. However, he explained that "although personally in favor of telepathy, I have failed in finding striking proofs of it in Mlle. Smith, and the few experiments I have attempted with her on this subject offered nothing encouraging. I tried several times to make an impression upon Helene from a distance and to appear before her during the evening, when I thought she had returned to her home, which is a kilometre distant from mine. I obtained no satisfactory result" (Flournoy, *From India*, 236).

84. Breton, *Manifestoes of Surrealism*, 179.

85. Breton, *Nadja*, 79–80.

86. See Morehead, "Symbolism, Mediumship," 77.

87. Breton, "The Automatic Message," 20.

88. Breton, "The Automatic Message," 20. On the female medium as muse of surrealism, see also Conley, *Automatic Woman*.

89. On the *Jeu de Marseille*, see Mesch, "Serious Play," 65–68; and Brockington, "Creative Occupation," 40–42.

90. "passionnantes communications de Théodore Flournoy à propos du médium Hélène Smith" and "autres façons de voir à la faveur de l'admiration enthousiaste que je porte a Freud" (Breton, Parinaud, *Entretiens*, 76).

91. See Breton, *Le surrealisme et la peinture*.

92. Yaguello, *Lunatic Lovers of Language*, 96.

93. See Starobinski, "Freud, Breton, Myers."

94. Breton, "Le message automatique," 168–169.

95. See: Bonnet, *André Breton*.

96. "Comme si les influences subies par un écrivain . . . se limitaient à celles qu'il a bien voulu reconnaître par écrit. Comme si la pensée freudienne elle-meme n'était pas tributaire de la fermentation magnéto-hypnotico-spirite. Comme si l'on pouvait attribuer au hasard le fait que l'époque décisive des sommeils coïncide exactement avec l'apogée de la métapsychique française" (Méheust, "Annexes," 159).

97. Méheust's description of such a context could well illustrate what Christopher Partridge has termed "occulture." The term describes a constant yet evolving "resource on which people draw, a reservoir of ideas, beliefs, practices, and symbols."

Partridge adds, "Occulture is the spiritual bricoleur's Internet from which to download whatever appeals or inspires; it is the sacralizing air that many of our contemporaries breathe; it is the well from which the serious occultist draws; it is the varied landscape the New Age nomad explores; it is the cluttered warehouse frequently plundered by producers of popular culture searching for ideas, images and symbols" (Partridge, *Re-enchantment of the West*, 84–85. See also Partridge, "Occulture and Everyday Enchantment").

98. "aux enchevêtrements qui lient l'inconscient à la création artistique, fictionnelle, à l'imagination créatrice d'œuvres et de découvertes scientifiques, à l'immense richesse silencieuse qui tout à coup jaillit et supéfie" (Cifali, "Postface," 374).

99. Ellenberger, "Freud in Perspective," 56.

100. Bacopoulos-Viau, "Automatism, Surrealism," 269.

101. Breton, *Manifestoes*, 10.

Conclusion

1. Le Clair, *The Letters*, 37.
2. Le Clair, *The Letters*, 37. On the injections, see Aminoff, "Life and Legacy."
3. Le Clair, *The Letters*, 35.
4. Flournoy, *From India*, 12.
5. Freud, *Complete Letters*, 214.
6. Freud, *Complete Letters*, 214.
7. Freud, *Complete Letters*, 215.
8. Freud, *Complete Letters*, 215.
9. Freud, "An Autobiographical Study," 34.
10. Jung, *Memories, Dreams, Reflections*, 173.
11. On this topic, see Gyimesi, "The Problem of Demarcation."
12. Jenkins, "Disenchantment, Enchantment and Re-enchantment," 13.
13. Jenkins, "Disenchantment, Enchantment and Re-enchantment," 20.
14. Josephson-Storm, *The Myth of Disenchantment*, 3.
15. The term "myth" is used by Josephson-Storm in a dual sense. On the one hand, disenchantment is a myth in that it never happened. On the other hand, it is a myth, a foundational story or grand narrative, around which scholars and intellectuals have constructed their sense of self.
16. Josephson-Storm, *The Myth of Disenchantment*, 3.
17. Asprem, *The Problem of Disenchantment*, 17–48. See also Asprem, "Aren't We Living," 18.
18. Asprem, *The Problem of Disenchantment*, 6.
19. Weiss, *Sigmund Freud*, 70.
20. Freud, "Dreams and the Occult," 100.
21. Freud, *Letters of Sigmund Freud*, 334. In recent years, Freudian writings on telepathy have further gained increasing interest in the field of relational psychoanalysis, a field that has challenged the narrative of psychoanalysis as a transparent step in a

progressive process of disenchantment. The field's intersubjective framework and interest in the transferential dynamic might explain its authors' greater openness to the topic and to research on paranormal or extraordinary experiences more generally. While this field has not, to the best of my knowledge, reignited Flournoy's and other psychical researchers' vision of a creative and quasi-transcendent unconscious, it has certainly opened the discipline to new and original collaborations with the domain of parapsychology and psychical research. On this topic, see Boyle, "Esoteric Traces"; Brottman, *Phantoms of the Clinic*; De Peyer, "Telepathic Entanglements," "Uncanny Communication," and "Traversing the Ineffable"; Eshel, "Where Are You," "Beam of Chimeric Darkness," "Patient-Analyst 'Withness,'" "Would Clinical Psychoanalysis," and *Emergence of Analytic Oneness*; Farber, "Becoming a Telepathic"; Hewitt, "Legacies of the Occult"; Rabeyron, Renaud, and Massicotte, "Es gibt Gedankenübertragung" and "Psychoanalysis and the Sour Apple"; Reichbart, *The Paranormal Surrounds Us*; Ahmed, *Parapsychologie et psychanalyse*; Widlöcher, "The Third in Mind"; and Wooffitt, "Relational Psychoanalysis."

Bibliography

Abbou, Malek, et al. *Jean Clair, ou la misère intellectuelle française*. Paris: Association des amis de Benjamin Péret, 2002.

Ahmed, Djohar Si. *Parapsychologie et psychanalyse*. Paris: Dunod, 1990.

Alvarado, Carlos S., and Stanley Krippner. "Nineteenth-Century Pioneers in the Study of Dissociation: William James and Psychical Research." *Journal of Consciousness Studies* 17, no. 12 (2010): 19–43.

Ambrose, Kevin. "Witches Plan to Curse Trump: We Will Counter With Prayer." *Christian Nationalism*, February 23, 2017. https://www.christiannationalism.com/2017/02/23/witches-plan-curse-president-trump/.

Aminoff, Michael J. "The Life and Legacy of Brown-Séquard." *Brain* 40, no. 5 (2017): 1525–1532.

Aragon, Louis. "A Wave of Dreams." Translated by Susan de Muth. *Papers of Surrealism* 1 (2003): 1–15.

Asprem, Egil. "Aren't We Living in a Disenchanted World?" In *Hermes Explains: Thirty Questions about Western Esotericism*, edited by Marco Pasi, Peter Forshaw, and Wouter Hanegraaff, 13–20. Amsterdam: Amsterdam University Press, 2019.

Asprem, Egil. *The Problem of Disenchantment: Scientific Naturalism and Esoteric Discourse, 1900–1939*. Amsterdam: Brill, 2014.

Audinet, Gérard, Alexandra Bacopoulos-Viau, Jérôme Godeau, Renaud Évrard, and Bertrand Méheust. *Entrée des médiums: Spiritisme et art de Hugo à Breton*. Paris: Paris Musées, 2012.

Bacopoulos-Viau, Alexandra. "Automatism, Surrealism and the Making of French Psychopathology: The Case of Pierre Janet." *History of Psychiatry* 23, no. 3 (2012): 259–276.

Barrow, Logie. *Independent Spirits: Spiritualism and English Plebeians, 1850–1910*. New York: Routledge & Kegan Paul, 1986.

Bauduin, Tessel M. "Surely Modern Art Is Not Occult? It Is Modern!" In *Hermes Explains: Thirty Questions about Western Esotericism*, edited by Marco Pasi, Peter Forshaw, and Wouter Hanegraaff, 13–20. Amsterdam: Amsterdam University Press, 2019.

Bauduin, Tessel M. *Surrealism and the Occult: Occultism and Western Esotericism in the Work and Movement of André Breton*. Amsterdam: Amsterdam University Press, 2014.

Bauduin, Tessel, and Henrik Johnsson, eds. *The Occult in Modernist Art, Literature, and Cinema*. London: Palgrave Macmillan, 2018.

Bennett, Jessica. "When Did Everybody Become a Witch?" *New York Times*, October 24, 2019. https://www.nytimes.com/2019/10/24/books/peak-witch.html.

Bernheimer, Charles, and Claire Kahane, eds. *In Dora's Case: Freud–Hysteria–Feminism*. New York: Columbia University Press, 1990.

Bogdan, Henrik. *Western Esotericism and Rituals of Initiation*. New York: State University of New York Press, 2007.

Boivin, Patrice. "Preface." In Victor Hugo, *Le livre des tables: Les séances spirites de Jersey*, edited by Patrice Boivin, 7–47. Paris: Gallimard, 2014.

Bonnet, Marguerite. *André Breton: Naissance de l'aventure surréaliste*. Paris: José Corti, 1975.

Bosker, Bianca. "Why Witchcraft Is on the Rise." *The Atlantic*. March 2020. https://www.theatlantic.com/magazine/archive/2020/03/witchcraft-juliet-diaz/605518/.

Boyle, John. "Esoteric Traces in Contemporary Psychoanalysis." *American Imago* 73 (2016): 95–119.

Brabant Ernst, Falzeder Eva, and Giampieri-Deutsch, Patrizia, eds. *The Correspondence of Sigmund Freud and Sándor Ferenczi*. Cambridge, MA: Belknap Press of Harvard University Press, 1992.

Brain, Robert Michael. "Materialising the Medium: Ectoplasm and the Quest for Supranormal Biology in Fin-de-Siècle Science and Art." In *Vibratory Modernism*, edited by Anthony Enns and Shelley Trower, 115–144. London: Palgrave Macmillan, 1993.

Bramble, John. *Modernism and the Occult*. London: Palgrave Macmillan, 2015.

Braude, Ann. *Radical Spirits: Spiritualism and Women's Rights in Nineteenth-Century America*. Bloomington: Indiana University Press, 1989.

Breger, Louis. *A Dream of Undying Fame: How Freud Betrayed His Mentor and Invented Psychoanalysis*. New York: Basic Books, 2009.

Breton, André. "The Automatic Message." In André Breton, Paul Eluard, and Philippe Soupault, *The Automatic Message, The Magnetic Fields, The Immaculate Conception*, translated by Antony Melville, 11–36. London: Atlas Press, 1997.

Breton, André. *Entretiens, 1913–1952*. Paris: Gallimard, 1952.

Breton, André. "For Dada." In *The Lost Steps*, translated by Mark Polizzotti, 51–56. Lincoln: University of Nebraska Press, 2010.

Breton, André. *Manifestoes of Surrealism*. Edited by R. Seaver and H. R. Lane. Ann Arbor: University of Michigan Press, 1969.

Breton, André. "The Mediums Enter." In *The Lost Steps*, translated by Mark Polizzotti, 89–95. Lincoln: University of Nebraska Press, 2010.

Breton, André. *Nadja*. Translated by Richard Howard. New York: Grove Press, 1960.

Breton, André. *Le surrealisme et la peinture, nouvelle édition revue et corrigée, 1928–1965*. Paris: Gallimard, 2002.

Breton, André. *Les vases communicants*. Paris: Gallimard, 1933.

Brockington, Horace. "Creative Occupation: Collaborative Artistic Practices in Europe, 1937–1943." In *Artistic Bedfellows: Histories, Theories and Conversations in Collaborative Art Practices*, edited by Holly Crawford, 27–59. Lanham. MD: University Press of America, 2009.

Brottman Mikita. *Phantoms of the clinic: From Thought-Transference to Projective Identification*. London: Karnac Books, 2011.

Brouardel, Paul. "Préface." In Gilles de la Tourette, *L'hypnotisme et les états analogues au point de vue médico-légal*, i–x. Paris: Librairie Plon, 1887.

Brower, Brady. "The Medium Is the Message: Enunciation and the Scriptural Economy of Scientific Psychology." *History of the Present* 6, no. 1 (2016): 32–62.

Brower, Brady. *Unruly Spirits: The Science of Psychic Phenomena in Modern France*. Urbana: University of Illinois Press, 2010.

Brown, Edward M. "Pierre Janet and *Félida Artificielle*: Multiple Personality in a Nineteenth-Century Guise." *Journal of the History of the Behavioral Sciences* 39, no. 3 (2003): 279–288.

Burlet, Philibert. *Du spiritisme considéré comme cause d'aliénation mentale.* Lyon: Richard, 1863.

Butler, Judith. *Gender Trouble: Feminism and the Subversion of Identity.* London: Routledge, 1990.

Cardinal, Roger, and Martine Lusardy, eds. *Art spirite, médiumnique, visionnaire: Messages d'outre-monde.* Exhibition catalog. Paris: La Halle Saint-Pierre, 1999.

Carroll, Brett E. *Spiritualism in Antebellum America.* Bloomington: Indiana University Press, 1997.

Castellan, Yvonne. *Le spiritisme.* Paris: Presses Universitaires de France, 1954.

Cerullo, John. *The Secularization of the Soul: Psychical Research in Modern Britain.* Philadelphia: Institute for the Study of Human Issues, 1982.

Charcot, Jean Martin. "Spiritisme et hystérie." In *Œuvres complètes de J.M. Charcot,* vol. 3, *Leçons sur les maladies du système nerveux,* edited by Désiré Magloire Bourneville, 226–234. Paris: Progrès Médical, Lecrosnier et Babé, 1890.

Charcot, Jean Martin. "Sur deux cas de monoplégie brachiale hystérique de nature traumatique chez l'homme (suite)—monoplégies hystérico-traumatiques." In *Œuvres complètes de J.M. Charcot,* edited by Désiré Magloire Bourneville, vol. 3, *Leçons sur les maladies du système nerveux,* 315–343. Paris: Progrès Médical, Lecrosnier et Babé, 1890.

Charet, Francis Xavier. *Spiritualism and the Foundations of C. G. Jung's Psychology.* Albany: State University of New York Press, 1993.

Choucha, Nadia. *Surrealism and the Occult: Shamanism, Magic, Alchemy and the Birth of an Artistic Movement.* Rochester: Destiny Books, 1992.

Cifali, Mireille. "A propos de la glossolalie d'Élise Müller, et des linguistes, psychologues, qui s'y intéressèrent." In *Linguistique et partages disciplinaires à la charnière des XIXe et XXe siècles: Victor Henry (1850-1907),* edited by Christian Puech, 321–334. Leuven: Peeters, 2004.

Cifali, Mireille. "Appendix One." In Théodore Flournoy, *From India to the Planet Mars: A Case of Multiple Personality with Imaginary Languages,* translated by Daniel B. Vermilye, edited by Sonu Shamdasani, 269–287. Princeton, NJ: Princeton University Press, 1994.

Cifali, Mireille. "La fabrication du martien: Genèse d'une langue imaginaire." *Langages* 91 (1988): 39–60.

Cifali, Mireille. "Introduction." In Théodore Flournoy, *Des Indes à la planète Mars,* 7–16. Paris: Le Seuil, 1983.

Cifali, Mireille. "Postface." In Théodore Flournoy, *Des Indes à la planète Mars,* 371–385. Paris: Le Seuil, 1983.

Clair, Jean. "Le surréalisme entre spiritisme et totalitarisme : Contribution à une histoire de l'insensé." *Mil neuf cent* 1, no. 21 (2003): 77–109.

Clair, Jean. *Du surréalisme considéré dans ses rapports au totalitarisme et aux tables tournantes.* Paris: Mille et une nuits, 2003.

Claretie, Jules. *Les amours d'un interne.* Paris: E. Dentu, 1881.

Clinton, Alan Ramon. *Mechanical Occult: Automatism, Modernism and the Specter of Politics.* New York: Peter Lang, 2004.

Conley, Katharine. *Automatic Woman: The Representation of Woman in Surrealism.* Lincoln: University of Nebraska Press, 1996.

Conley, Katharine. *Robert Desnos, Surrealism, and the Marvelous in Everyday Life.* Lincoln: University of Nebraska Press, 2003.

Coon, Deborah J. "Testing the Limits of Sense and Science: American Experimental Psychologists Combat Spiritualism." *American Psychologist* 47, no. 2 (1992): 143–151.

Cooper, Elliot. "Saussure and the Psychic." *Semiotica* 217 (2017): 243–261.

Courtine, Jean-Jacques. "Des faux en langues? (Remarques linguistiques à propos des glossolalies)." *Le discours psychanalytique* 6 (1983): 35–47.

Courtine, Jean-Jacques. "La quête de l'inconscient linguistique: Victor Henry et le cas d'Hélène Smith. " In *Linguistique et partages disciplinaires à la charnière des XIXe et XXe siècles: Victor Henry (1850–1907)*, edited by Christian Puechs, 309–319. Paris: Peeters, 2004.

Crossley, Robert. *Imagining Mars: A Literary History*. Middletown, CT: Wesleyan University Press, 2011.

Cuendet, Henri. *Les tableaux d'Hélène Smith: Peints à l'état de sommeil*. Geneva: Atar, 1908.

Davis, Andrew Jackson. *The Temple: Concerning Diseases of the Brain and Nerves; With Full Directions for Their Treatment and Cure*. Boston: Colby & Rich, 1871.

de Certeau, Michel. "Vocal Utopias: Glossolalias." *Representations* 56 (1996): 29–47.

de la Tourette, Gilles. "Clinique nerveuse: Étude sur une affectation nerveuse caractérisée par de l'incoordination motrice accompagnée d'écholalie et de coprolalie." *Archives de neurologie* 9 (1885): 158–200.

de la Tourette, Gilles. *L'hypnotisme et les états analogues au point de vue médico-légal*. Paris: Librairie Plon, 1887.

de la Tourette, Gilles, and Paul Richer. "Hypnotisme." In *Dictionnaire encyclopédique des sciences médicales*, edited by Amédée Dechambre andLeon Lereboullet, vol. 15, 67–132. Paris: G. Masson, 1889.

Deonna, Waldemar. *De la planète Mars en Terre Sainte. Art et subconscient, un médium peintre: Hélène Smith*. Paris: De Boccard, 1932.

de Peyer, Janine. "Telepathic Entanglements: Where Are We Today? Commentary on Paper by Claudie Massicotte." *Psychoanalytic Dialogues* 24, no. 1 (2014): 109–121.

de Peyer, Janine. "Traversing the Ineffable: Commentary on Sharon Farber's 'Becoming a Telepathic Tuning Fork.'" *Psychoanalytic Dialogues* 27 no. 1 (2017): 735–740.

de Peyer, Janine. "Uncanny Communication and the Porous Mind." *Psychoanalytic Dialogues* 26, no. 2 (2016): 156–174.

Devereux, George. *Psychoanalysis and the Occult*. New York: International Universities Press, 1953.

Didi-Huberman, Georges. "L'incarnation figurale de la sentence (note sur la peau 'autographique')." *Scalène* 2 (1984): 143–169.

Didi-Huberman, Georges. *Invention of Hysteria: Charcot and the Photographic Iconography of the Salpêtrière*. Translated by Alisa Hartz. Cambridge: MIT Press, 2003.

Doyle, Sady. "Monsters, Men and Magic: Why Feminists Turned to Witchcraft to Oppose Trump." *The Guardian*, August 7, 2019. https://www.theguardian.com/lifeandstyle/2019/aug/07/monsters-men-magic-trump-awoke-angry-feminist-witches.

du Preez, Amanda. *Gendered Bodies and New Technologies: Rethinking Embodiment in a Cyber-Era*. Newcastle: Cambridge Scholars Publishing, 2009.

Dujardin-Beaumetz, Georges. "Notes sur des troubles vaso-moteurs de la peau observés sur une hystérique (femme autographique)." In *Bulletins et Mémoires de la Société Médicale des hôpitaux de Paris*, vol. 16, 197–202. Paris: Asselin et Cie, 1879.

Dumont, Frank. *A History of Personality Psychology: Theory, Science, and Research from Hellenism to the Twenty-First Century*. Cambridge: Cambridge University Press, 2012.

Edelman, Nicole. "Spiritisme et Politique." *Revue d'histoire du XIXe siècle* 28 (2004): 149–161.

Edelman, Nicole. *Voyantes, guérisseuses et visionnaires en France, 1785–1914*. Paris: Albin Michel, 1995.

Eisenbud, Jule. *Paranormal Foreknowledge: Problems and Perplexities*. New York: Human Sciences Press, 1982.

Ellenberger, Henri F. *The Discovery of the Unconscious: The History and Evolution of Dynamic Psychiatry*. New York: Basic Books, 1970.

Ellenberger, Henri F. "Freud in Perspective: A Conversation with Henri F. Ellenberger." *Psychology Today*, March 1973, 50–60.

Ellenberger, Henri F. "The Story of 'Anna O.': A Critical Review with New Data." *Journal of the History of the Behavioral Sciences* 8 (1972): 267–279.

Enns, Anthony. "Psychic Radio: Sound Technologies, Ether Bodies and Spiritual Vibrations." *The Senses and Society* 3, no. 2 (2008): 137–152.

Eshel, Ofra. "A Beam of 'Chimeric' Darkness: Presence, Interconnectedness, and Transformation in the Psychoanalytic Treatment of a Patient Convicted of Sex Offenses." *Psychoanalytic Revue* 99, no. 2 (2012): 149–178.

Eshel, Ofra. *The Emergence of Analytic Oneness: Into the Heart of Psychoanalysis*. London: Routledge, 2019.

Eshel, Ofra. "Patient-Analyst 'Withness': On Analytic 'Presencing,' Passion, and Compassion in States of Breakdown, Despair, and Deadness." *Psychoanalytic Quarterly* 82 (2013): 925–963.

Eshel, Ofra. "Would Clinical Psychoanalysis Shy Away from Delving Further into the Unknown? On the Mystery of Telepathic Dreams." *International Journal of Psychoanalysis* 100 (2019): 608–610.

Evrard, Renaud, Claudie Massicotte, and Thomas Rabeyron. "Freud as a Psychical Researcher: The Impossible Freudian Legacy." *Imago Budapest* 6, no. 4 (2017): 9–32.

Evrard, Renaud, Erika Annabelle Pratte, and Etzel Cardeña. "Pierre Janet and the Enchanted Boundary of Psychical Research." *History of Psychology* 21, no. 2 (2018): 100–125.

Farber, Sharon K. "Becoming a Telepathic Tuning Fork: Anomalous Experience and the Relational Mind." *Psychoanalytic Dialogues* 27 (2017): 719–734.

Fehr, Johannes. "Le mécanisme de la langue. Entre linguistique et psychologie: Saussure et Flournoy." *Langages* 120 (1995): 91–105.

Féré, Charles, and Henri Lamy. "La dermographie." In *Nouvelle iconographie photographique de la Salpêtrière*, edited by Bourneville, Desiré Magloire and Paul Regnard, vol. 2, 283–289. Paris: Progrès Médical, Lecrosnier et Babé, 1889.

Ferenczi Sandor. "Spiritism." 1899. Translated by Nandor Fodor. *Psychoanalytic Revue* 50A (1963): 139–144.

Ferentinou, Victoria. "Surrealism, Occulture and Gender: Woman Artists, Power and Occultism." *Aries: Journal for the Study of Western Esotericism* 13, no. 1 (2013): 103–130.

Ferentinou, Victoria, Tessel M. Bauduin, and Daniel Zamani, eds. *Surrealism, Occultism and Politics: In Search of the Marvellous*. London: Routledge, 2017.

Ferguson, Christine. *Determined Spirits. Eugenics, Heredity and Racial Regeneration in Anglo-American Spiritualist Writing, 1848–1930*. Edinburgh: Edinburgh University Press, 2012.

Ferguson, Christine "Other Worlds: Alfred Russel Wallace and Cross-Cultural Spiritualism." *Victorian Review* 41, no. 2 (2015): 177–191.

Ferguson, Christine. "Recent Scholarship on Spiritualism and Science." In *The Ashgate Research Companion to Nineteenth-Century Spiritualism and the Occult*, edited by Tatiana Kontou, 19–24. New York: Routledge, 2016.

Ferguson, Christine. "Recent Studies in Nineteenth-Century Spiritualism." *Literature Compass* 9 no. 6 (2012): 431–440.

Ferguson, Christine, and Efram Sera-Shriar. "Spiritualism and Science Studies for the Twenty-First Century." *Aries: Journal for the Study of Western Esotericism* 22 (2022): 1–11.

Flammarion, Camille. *The Planet Mars*. Translated by Patrick Moore. Springer, 2015.

Flammarion, Camille. *La planète Mars et ses conditions d'habitabilité*. Paris: Gauthier-Villars et Fils, 1892.

Flournoy, Olivier. *Théodore et Léopold : De Théodore Flournoy a la psychanalyse*. Neuchâtel: A la Baconnière, 1986.

Flournoy, Théodore. *Des Indes à la planète Mars*. Geneva: Ch. Eggimann, 1900.

Flournoy, Théodore. *Esprits et médiums*. Geneva: Kundig Fischbacher, 1911.

Flournoy, Théodore. *From India to the Planet Mars: A Case of Multiple Personality with Imaginary Languages*. Translated by Daniel B. Vermilye. Edited by Sonu Shamdasani. Princeton, NJ: Princeton University Press, 1994.

Flournoy, Théodore. *Nouvelles observations sur un cas de somnambulisme avec glossolalie*. Geneva: Ch. Eggimann, 1902.

Flournoy, Théodore. *Spiritism and Psychology*. Translated by Hereward Carrington. New York: Harper & Brothers Publishers, 1911.

Flournoy, Théodore. *Une mystique modèrne: Documents pour la psychologie religieuse*. *Archives de Psychologie* 15 (1915): 1–224.

Fodor, Nandor. "Sándor Ferenczi's Psychic Adventures." *International Journal of Parapsychology* 3 (1961): 49–63.

Forrester, John. "The True Story of Anna O." *Social Research* 53 no. 2 (1986): 327–347.

Foucault, Michel. *The History of Sexuality*. Vol. 1, *An Introduction*. Translated by Robert Hurley. New York: Vintage Books, 1990.

Freud, Sigmund. "An Autobiographical Study." In *The Standard Edition of the Complete Psychological Works of Sigmund Freud*, vol. 20, *1925–1926*, edited and translated by James Strachey, 7–74. London: Hogarth Press, 1959.

Freud, Sigmund. *The Complete Letters of Sigmund Freud to Wilhelm Fliess, 1887–1904*. Edited and translated by Jeffrey Moussaieff Masson. Cambridge, MA: Harvard University Press: 1985.

Freud, Sigmund. "Dreams and the Occult." In *Psychoanalysis and the Occult*, edited by George Devereux, 91–109. London: International University Press, 1953.

Freud, Sigmund. *Letters of Sigmund Freud, 1873–1939*. Edited by Ernst L. Freud. London: Hogarth Press, 1961.

Freud, Sigmund. "A Note on the Unconscious in Psychoanalysis." In *The Standard Edition of the Complete Psychological Works of Sigmund Freud*, vol. 12, *1911–1913*, edited and translated by James Strachey, 257–266. London: Hogarth Press, 1958.

Freud Sigmund. "The Occult Significance of Dreams." In *Psychoanalysis and the Occult*, edited by George Devereux, 87–90. New York: International Universities Press, 1953.

Freud, Sigmund. "Psychoanalysis and Telepathy." In *Psychoanalysis and the Occult*, edited by George Devereux, 56–68. London: International University Press, 1953.

Freud, Sigmund. "Screen Memories." In *The Standard Edition of the Complete Psychological Works of Sigmund Freud*, vol. 3, *1893–1899*, edited and translated by James Strachey, 299–322. London: Hogarth Press, 1962.

Friedman, Susan Stanford. "Creativity and the Childbirth Metaphor: Gender Difference in Literary Discourse." *Feminist Studies* 13, no. 1 (1987): 49–82.

Galvan, Jill L. *The Sympathetic Medium: Feminine Channelling, the Occult, and Communication Technologies, 1859–1919*. Ithaca, NY: Cornell University Press, 2010.

Gauld, Alan. "Notes on the Career of the Somnambule Léonie." *Journal of the Society for Psychical Research* 61, no. 844 (1996): 141–151.

Gay, Peter. *Freud: A Life for Our Time*. New York: Norton, 1988.

Gilbert, Sandra M., and Susan Gubar. *The Madwoman in the Attic: The Woman Writer and the Nineteenth-Century Literary Imagination*. New Haven: Yale University Press, 2000.

Glenn, J. "Freud, Dora, and the Maid: A Study of Countertransference." *Journal of the American Psychoanalytic Association* 34, no. 3 (1986): 591–606.

Goldsmith, Barbara. *Other Powers: The Age of Suffrage, Spiritualism, and the Scandalous Victoria Woodhull*. New York: Alfred A. Knopf, 1998.

Golomb Hoffman, Anne. "Archival Bodies." *American Imago* 66, no. 1 (2009): 5–40.

Granoff, Wladimir, and Jean-Michel Rey. *L'occulte: Objet de la pensée freudienne*. Paris: Presses Universitaires de France, 1983.

Grasset, Joseph. *L'occultisme, hier et aujourd'hui: Le merveilleux préscientifique*. Montpellier: Coulet et Fils, 1907.

Grey Ellis, Emma. "Trump's Presidency Has Spawned a New Generation of Witches." *Wired*. October 30, 2019. https://www.wired.com/story/trump-witches/.

Gutierrez, Cathy. "From Electricity to Ectoplasm: Hysteria and American Spiritualism." *Aries* 3, no. 1 (2003): 55–81.

Guttmann, Melinda G. *The Enigma of Anna O.: A Biography of Bertha Pappenheim*. London: Moyer Bell, 2001.

Gyimesi, Júlia. "The Problem of Demarcation: Psychoanalysis and the Occult." *American Imago* 66 (2009): 457–470.

Gyimesi, Júlia. "Sandor Ferenczi and the Problem of Telepathy." *History of the Human Sciences* 25 (2012): 131–148.

Hammer, Olav. "Stages in the Development of an Occult Linguistic." In *The Occult Nineteenth Century: Roots, Developments, and Impact on the Modern World*, edited by Lukas Pokorny and Franz Winter, 139–158. London: Palgrave Macmillan, 2021.

Hammond, William A. *Spiritualism and Allied Causes of Nervous Derangement*. Whitefish: Kessinger Publishing, 1876.

Hamon, Romuald. "Une mystique moderne: Cécile Vé, l'autre femme de Flournoy." *Revue cliniques méditerranéennes* 91 (2015): 183–194.

Hanegraaff, Wouter J. *Esotericism and the Academy: Rejected Knowledge in Western Culture*. Cambridge: Cambridge University Press, 2012.

Hanegraaff, Wouter J. *Western Esotericism: A Guide for the Perplexed*. London: Continuum Press, 2013.

Hass, Marjorie. "The Style of the Speaking Subject: Irigaray's Empirical Studies of Language Production." *Hypathia* 15, no. 1 (2000): 64–89.

Hayward, Rhodri. *Resisting History. Religious Transcendence and the Invention of the Unconscious*. Manchester: Manchester University Press, 2007.

Hazelgrove, Jenny. *Spiritualism and British Society between the Wars*. Manchester: Manchester University Press, 2000.

Henry, Victor. *Le langage martien: Etude analytique de la genèse d'une langue dans un cas de glossolalie*. Paris: J. Maisonneuve, 1901.

Herndl, Diane P. "The Writing Cure: Charlotte Perkins Gilman, Anna O., and 'Hysterical' Writing." *National Women Studies Association Journal* 1 (1988): 52–74.

Hewitt, Marsha. *Legacies of the Occult: Psychoanalysis, Religion, and Unconscious Communication*. Sheffield: Equinox Publishing, 2020.

Houdebine, Jean-Louis. "Méconnaissance de la psychanalyse dans le discours surréaliste." *Tel Quel* 46 (1971): 67–82.

Hugo, Victor. *Les contemplations*. Paris: Folio, 2010.

Hugo, Victor. *Le livre des tables: Les séances spirites de Jersey*. Edited by Patrice Boivin. Paris: Gallimard, 2014.

Hunter, Diane. "Hysteria, Psychoanalysis, and Feminism: The Case of Anna O." *Feminist Studies* 9, no. 3 (1983): 464–488.

Hustvedt, Asti. *Medical Muses: Hysteria in Nineteenth-Century Paris*. New York: Norton. 2011.

Irigaray, Luce. *Speculum of the Other Woman*. Translated by Gillian C. Gill. Ithaca, NY: Cornell University Press, 1985.

Irigaray, Luce. *This Sex Which Is Not One*. Translated by Catherine Porter with Carolyn Burke. Ithaca, NJ: Cornell University Press, 1985.

Jackowitz, Ann H. "Anna O. / Bertha Pappenheim and Me." In *Between Women: Biographers, Novelists, Critics*, edited by C. Ascher, L. DeSalvo, and S. Ruddick, 252–273. New York: Beacon Press, 1984.

Jakobson, Roman. *Selected Writings*. Vol. 8, *Major Works, 1976–1980*. Berlin: Mouton de Gruyter, 1988.

James, William. "Frederic Myers's Service to Psychology." *Popular Science Monthly* 54, no. 22 (1901): 384.

Janet, Pierre. "Les actes inconscients et le dédoublement de la personnalité pendant le somnambulisme provoqué." *Revue philosophique de la France et de l'étranger* 22 (1886): 577–592.

Janet, Pierre. "L'anesthésie systématisée et la dissociation des phénomènes psychiques." *Revue philosophique de la France et de l'étranger* 23 (1887): 449–472.

Janet, Pierre. *L'automatisme psychologique: Psychologie expérimentale sur les formes inférieures de l'activité humaine*, Paris: Felix Alcan Editeur, 1889.

Janet, Pierre. "Deuxième note sur le sommeil provoqué à distance et la suggestion mentale pendant l'état somnambulique (séance du 31 mai 1886)." *Bulletins de la Société de Psychologie physiologique* 2 (1886): 70–80.

Janet, Pierre. *L'état mental des hystériques: Les accidents mentaux*. Paris: Rueff et Cie, 1894.

Janet, Pierre. "Note sur quelques phénomènes de somnambulisme (séance du 30 novembre 1885." *Bulletins de la Société de Psychologie physiologique* 1 (1885): 24–32.

Janet, Pierre. "Les phases intermédiaires de l'hypnotisme." *Revue scientifique* 37 (1886): 577–587.

Janet, Pierre. "Le Spiritisme contemporain." *Revue philosophique* 33 (1892): 413–442.

Jasen, Patricia. "Mind, Medicine, and the Christian Science Controversy in Canada, 1888–1910." *Journal of Canadian Studies* 32, no. 4 (1998): 5–22.

Jenkins, Richard. "Disenchantment, Enchantment and Re-enchantment: Max Weber at the Millennium." *Max Weber Studies* 1, no. 1 (2000): 11–32.

Jones, Ernest. *The Life and Work of Sigmund Freud.* 3 vols. New York: Basic Books, 1953–57.

Josephson-Storm, Jason A. *The Myth of Disenchantment: Magic, Modernity, and the Birth of the Human Sciences.* Chicago: University of Chicago Press, 2017.

Jung, Carl Gustav. *Memories, Dreams, Reflections.* Translated by Clara Winston and Richard Winston. London: Fontana, 1961.

Jung, Carl Gustav. "On the Psychology and Pathology of So-Called Occult Phenomena." In *Psychology and the Occult,* 6–91. Princeton, NJ: Princeton University Press, 1977.

Juranville, Anne. *Figures de la possession: Actualité psychanalytique du démoniaque.* Grenoble: Presses Universitaires de Grenoble, 2001.

Kardec, Allan. *Le livre des médiums. Ou guide des médiums et des évocateurs.* Treizième Edition. Paris: Librairie de la Revue Spirite, 1873.

Keeley James P. "Subliminal Promptings: Psychoanalytic Theory and the Society for Psychical Research." *American Imago* 58 (2001): 767–791.

Keep, Christopher. "Hélène Smith, Clairvoyance, and Occult Media." *Journal of Victorian Culture* 25, no. 4 (2020): 537–552.

Laborde-Nottale, Élisabeth. *La voyance et l'inconscient.* Paris: Seuil, 1990.

Lacan, Jacques. "The Instance of the Letter in the Unconscious." In *Ecrits,* edited and translated by Bruce Fink, 412–441. New York: Norton, 1966.

Lacan, Jacques. *Séminaire XV: L'acte psychanalytique, 1967–1968.* Internal document of the Association freudienne internationale for its members.

Lachapelle, Sofie. "Attempting Science: The Creation and Early Development of the Institut Métapsychique International in Paris, 1919–1931." *Journal of the History of the Behavioral Sciences* 41, no. 1 (2005): 1–24.

Lachapelle, Sophie. *Investigating the Supernatural: From Spiritism and Occultism to Psychical Research and Metapsychics in France, 1853–1931.* Baltimore: Johns Hopkins University Press, 2011.

Le Clair, Robert C., ed. *The Letters of William James and Théodore Flournoy.* Madison: University of Wisconsin Press, 1966.

Leloup, Jean Michel. "Pierre Janet et l'hypnose à distance." Doctoral thesis, Faculté de médecine François Rabelais, Tours, 1978.

Lemaitre, Auguste. "Compte-rendu des séances psychiques du 28 octobre 1894 au 2 juillet 1899, et d'événements paranormaux survenus du 4 mars 1900 au 18 mai 1901." Papiers Auguste Micaël Lemaitre. Bibliothèque de Genève. Ms.Fr.6771.

Lemaitre, Auguste. "Un nouveau cycle somnambulique de Mlle Smith: Ses peintures religieuses." *Archives de psychologie* 7 (1907): 63–83.

Le Maléfan, Pascal. "L'hallucination télépathique ou véridique dans la psychopathologie de la fin du XIXe siècle et du début du XXe siècle." *L'évolution psychiatrique* 73, no. 1 (2008): 15–39.

Leonard, Maurice. *People from the Other Side: The Enigmatic Fox Sisters and the History of Victorian Spiritualism.* Stroud: History Press, 2011.

Lepschy, Giulio. "European Linguistics in the Twentieth Century." In *Studies in the History of Western Linguistics,* edited by Theodora Bynon and F. R. Palmer, 189–201. Cambridge: Cambridge University Press, 1986.

Levack, Brian. P. *The Devil Within: Possession & Exorcism in the Christian West.* New Haven: Yale University Press, 2013.

Loentz, Elizabeth. *Let Me Continue to Speak the Truth: Bertha Pappenheim as Author and Activist.* Jerusalem: Hebrew Union College Press, 2007.

Lomas, David. *The Haunted Self: Surrealism, Psychoanalysis, Subjectivity*. New Haven: Yale University Press, 2000.

Lorin, Claude. "Sandor et les fantômes." *Nouvelle revue d'ethnopsychiatrie* 13 (1989): 229–236.

Lowry, Elizabeth Schleber. *Invisible Hosts: Performing the Nineteenth-Century Spirit Medium's Autobiography*. Albany: State University of New York Press 2017.

Luckhurst, Roger. *The Invention of Telepathy, 1870–1901*. Oxford: Oxford University Press, 2002.

Marcus, Steven. "Freud and Dora: Story, History, Case History." In *Essential Papers on Literature and Psychoanalysis*, edited by Emanuel Berman, 36–80. New York: New York University Press, 1993.

Marvin, R. Frederic. *The Philosophy of Spiritualism and the Pathology and Treatment of Mediomania*. New York: Asa K. Butts & Co, 1874.

Massicotte, Claudie. "Psychical Transmissions: Freud, Spiritualism and the Occult." *Psychoanalytic Dialogue* 24 (2014): 88–102.

Massicotte, Claudie. *Trance Speakers: Femininity and Authorship in Spiritual Séances, 1850–1930*. Montreal: McGill-Queen's University Press, 2017.

Materer, Timothy. *Modernist Alchemy: Poetry and the Occult*. Ithaca, NY: Cornell University Press, 1995.

McCorristine, Shane. *Spiritualism, Mesmerism and the Occult, 1800–1920*. London: Routledge, 2012.

McGarry, Molly. *Ghosts of Futures Past: Spiritualism and the Cultural Politics of Nineteenth-Century America*. Berkeley: University of California Press, 2012.

McGuire, William, ed. *The Freud/Jung Letters: The Correspondence between Sigmund Freud and C. G. Jung*. Princeton, NJ: Princeton University Press, 1974.

Méheust, Bertrand. "Annexes." In *Art spirite, médiumnique, visionnaire: Messages d'outre-monde*, edited by Halle Saint Pierre and Hoëbeke, 149–161. Exhibition catalog. Paris: La Halle Saint-Pierre, 1999.

Méheust, Bertrand. *Somnambulisme et médiumnité*. 2 vols. Paris: Les Empêcheurs de Penser en Rond, 1999.

Meltzer, Francoise. *For Fear of the Fire: Joan of Arc and the Limits of Subjectivity*. Chicago: University of Chicago Press, 2001.

Mesch, Claudia. "Serious Play: Games in Early Twentieth-Century Modernism." In *Diversion to Subversion: Games, Play, and Twentieth-Century Art*, edited by David Getsy, 60–72. University Park: Pennsylvania State University Press, 2011.

Mitchell, Juliet. *Psychoanalysis and Feminism: Freud, Reich, Laing, and Women*. New York: Pantheon Books, 1974.

Monroe, John Wayne. *Laboratories of Faith: Mesmerism, Spiritism, and Occultism in Modern France*. Ithaca, NY: Cornell University Press, 2008.

Monroe, John Wayne. "The Way We Believe Now: Modernity and the Occult." *Magic, Ritual, and Witchcraft* 2, no. 1 (2007): 68–78.

Moore, Robert Lawrence. *In Search of White Crows: Spiritualism, Parapsychology, and American Culture*. Oxford: Oxford University Press, 1977.

Moreau, Christian. *Freud et l'occultisme*. Paris: Privat, 1976.

Morehead Allison. "Le legs et l'exposition des tableaux d'Elise Catherine Müller, dite Helene Smith, au Musée d'art et d'histoire de Genève, 1929–1937." *Genava* 49 (2001): 99–136.

Morehead, Allison. "Symbolism, Mediumship, and the 'Study of the Soul That Has Constituted Itself as a Positivist Science.'" *RACAR* 34, no. 1 (2009): 77–85.

Muslin, Hyman, and Merton, Gill. "Transference in the Dora Case." *Journal of the American Psychoanalysis Association* 26, no. 2 (1978): 311–329.

Neely, Leslie, et al. "Treatment of Echolalia in Individuals with Autism Spectrum Disorder: A Systematic Review." *Review Journal of Autism and Developmental Disorders* 3, no. 1 (2016): 82–91.

Noakes, Richard. *Physics and Psychics: The Occult and the Sciences in Modern Britain.* Cambridge: Cambridge University Press, 2019.

Oppenheim Janet. *The Oher World: Spiritualism and Psychical Research in England, 1850–1914.* Cambridge: Cambridge University Press, 1985.

Ovid. *Metamorphoses.* Translated by David Raeburn. London: Penguin Books, 2004.

Owen, Alex. *The Darkened Room: Women, Power and Spiritualism in Late Victorian England.* Chicago: University of Chicago Press, 1989.

Owen, Alex. *The Place of Enchantment: British Occultism and the Culture of the Modern.* Chicago: University of Chicago Press, 2004.

Parot, Françoise. "Le bannissement des esprits: Naissance d'une frontière institutionnelle entre spiritisme et psychologie." *Revue de synthèse* 3–4 (1994): 417–443.

Parot, Françoise. "Psychology Experiments: Spiritism at the Sorbonne. *Journal of the History of Behavioral Sciences* 29 (1993): 22–28.

Partridge, Christopher. *The Re-enchantment of the West: Alternative Spiritualities, Sacralization, Popular Culture and Occulture.* Vol. 1. London: Bloomsbury, 2004.

Partridge, Christopher. "Occulture and Everyday Enchantment." In *The Oxford Handbook of New Religious Movements*, vol. 2, edited by James R. Lewis and Inga Tøllefsen, 315–332. London: Oxford Handbooks, 2016.

Pierri, Maria. *Occultism and the Origins of Psychoanalysis: Freud, Ferenczi and the Challenge of Thought Transference.* London: Routledge, 2022.

Piot-Mayol, Geneviève. "Il était une fois Hélène Smith, Genève 1895." *Essaim* 18 (2007): 133–146.

Plas, Régine. *Naissance d'une science humaine, la psychologie: Les psychologues et le "merveilleux psychique".* Rennes: Presses Universitaires de Rennes, 2000.

Plas, Régine. "Psychology and Psychical Research in France around the End of the 19th Century." *History of the Human Sciences* 25, no. 2 (2012): 91–107.

Puech, Christian, ed. *Linguistique et partages disciplinaires à la charnière des XIXe et XXe siècles: Victor Henry (1850–1907),* Leuven: Peeters, 2004.

Rabeyron, Thomas, and Renaud Evrard. "Perspectives historiques et contemporaines sur l'occulte dans la correspondance Freud-Ferenczi." *Recherches en psychanalyse* 1, no. 13 (2012): 97–111.

Rabeyron, Thomas, Renaud Evrard, and Claudie Massicotte. "*Es gibt Gedankenübertragung*: Transfert de pensée et processus télépathiques en analyse." *Revue française de psychanalyse* 83, no. 4 (2019): 1239–1252.

Rabeyron, Thomas, Renaud Evrard, and Claudie Massicotte. "Psychoanalysis and the Sour Apple: Thought-Transference in Historical and Contemporary Psychoanalysis." *Contemporary Psychoanalysis* 56 (2020): 612–652.

Rabinovitch, Celia. *Surrealism and the Sacred: Power, Eros, and the Occult in Modern Art.* New York: Basic Books, 2002.

Raia, Courtenay. "From Ether Theory to Ether Theology: Oliver Lodge and the Physics of Immortality." *Journal of the History of the Behavioral Sciences* 43, no. 1 (2007): 18–43.

Raia, Courtenay. *The New Prometheans: Faith, Science, and the Supernatural Mind in the Victorian Fin de Siècle.* Chicago: University of Chicago Press, 2019.

Reichbart, Richard. *The Paranormal Surrounds Us: Psychic Phenomena in Literature, Culture and Psychoanalysis.* Jefferson, NC: McFarland, 2019.

Rhys, Jean. *Jean Rhys Letters, 1931–1966.* Edited by Francis Wyndham and Diana Melly. London: André Deutsch, 1984.

Robertson, Beth A. *Science of the Seance: Transnational Networks and Gendered Bodies in the Study of Psychic Phenomena, 1918–1940.* Vancouver: University of British Colombia Press, 2016.

Rosenbaum, Max, and Melvin Muroff, eds. *Anna O.: Fourteen Contemporary Reinterpretations.* New York: Free Press, 1984.

Rosenberg, Daniel. "Speaking Martian." *Cabinet* 1 (Winter 2000–2001). https://www.cabi netmagazine.org/issues/1/rosenberg.php.

Roudinesco, Élisabeth. "Des Martiens dans la tête." *Matin*, October 11, 1983, 26.

Roudinesco, Élisabeth. *Jacques Lacan & Co: A History of psychoanalysis in France, 1925–1985.* Translated by Jeffrey Mehlman. Chicago: University of Chicago Press, 1990.

Saussure, Ferdinand de. *Course in General Linguistics.* Translated by Wade Baskin. Edited by Charles Bally and Albert Sechehaye in collaboration with Albert Reidlinger. New York: McGraw-Hill, 1959.

Shamdasani, Sonu. "Automatic Writing and the Discovery of the Unconscious." *Spring: Journal of Archetype and Culture* 54 (1993): 100–131.

Shamdasani, Sonu. "Encountering Hélène: Théodore Flournoy and the Genesis of Subliminal Psychology." In Théodore Flournoy, *From India to the Planet Mars: A Case of Multiple Personality with Imaginary Languages*, edited by Sonu Shamdasani, translated by Daniel B. Vermilye, edited by Sonu Shamdasani, xi–li. Princeton, NJ: Princeton University Press, 1994.

Shamdasani, Sonu. "Misunderstanding Jung: The Afterlife of Legends." *Journal of Analytical Psychology* 45 (2000): 459–472.

Sharp, Lynn L. *Secular Spirituality: Reincarnation and Spiritism in Nineteenth-Century France.* Lanham, md: Lexington Books, 2006.

Shelley, Mary. *Frankenstein; or The Modern Prometheus.* London: Penguin Books, 2003.

Skues, Richard. *Sigmund Freud and the History of Anna O.: Reopening a Closed Case.* New York : Palgrave Macmillan, 2006.

Société d'études psychiques de Genève. *Autour "Des Indes à la Planète Mars".* Paris: Librairie Spirite, 1901.

Starobinski, Jean. "Freud, Breton, Myers." *L'arc* 34 (1968): 87–96.

Stead, William T. *Real Ghost Stories.* New York: George H. Doran Company, 1921.

Sterponi, Laura, and Jennifer Shankey. "Rethinking Echolalia: Repetition as Interactional Resource in the Communication of a Child with Autism." *Journal of Child Language* 41, no. 2 (2014): 275–304.

Strachey, James. "Editor's Introduction." In *The Interpretation of Dreams. The Standard Edition of the Complete Psychological Works of Sigmund Freud*, vol. 4, edited by James Strachey, xi–xxii. London: Hogarth Press, 1953.

Stuart, Nancy Rubin. *The Reluctant Spiritualist: The Life of Maggie Fox.* Orlando: Harcourt, 2005.

Sylvain, R. "Quand les tables dansaient et parlaient: Les débuts du spiritisme au dix-neuvième siècle." In *Mémoires de la Société royale du Canada*, edited by Royal Society of Canada, 4th series, 221–235. Toronto: University of Toronto Press, 1963.

Taylor, Eugene. "William James and C. G. Jung." *Spring* 39 (1980): 157–169.

Thompson, Rachel Leah. "The Automatic Hand: Spiritualism, Psychoanalysis, Surrealism." *Invisible Culture: An Electronic Journal for Visual Culture* 7 (2004): 1–14.

Thurschwell Pamela. "Ferenczi's Dangerous Proximities: Telepathy, Psychosis and the Real Event." *Differences: Journal of Feminist Cultural Studies* 11 (1999): 150–178.

Ticktin, Hillel. "Anna O.'s Other Story." *Moment* 23, no. 4 (1998): 40–45.

Todorov, Tzvetan. "L'étrange cas de Mlle Hélène Smith (pseudonyme)." *Romanic Review* 63, no. 2 (1972): 83–91.

Todorov, Tzvetan. *Theories of the Symbol*. Translated by Catherine Porter. Ithaca, NY: Cornell University Press, 1982.

Totton, Nick. *Psychoanalysis and the Paranormal: Lands of Darkness*. New York: Karnac Press, 2003.

Treitel, Corinna. *A Science for the Soul: Occultism and the Genesis of the German Modern*. Baltimore: Johns Hopkins University Press, 2004.

Tromp, Marlene. *Altered States: Sex, Nation, Drugs, and Self-Transformation in Victorian Spiritualism*. Albany: State University of New York Press, 2006.

Turnheim, Michael. "Freud le médium (notes sur l'affaire de la télépathie)." *Psychanalyse* 12 (2008): 41–53.

Walker, Josh. "TikTok Has Become the Home of Modern Witchcraft (yes, really)." *Wired*. January 11, 2020. https://www.wired.co.uk/article/witchcraft-tiktok.

Walkowitz, Judith. "Science and the Séance: Transgressions of Gender and Genre in Late Victorian London." *Representations* 22 (1988): 3–29.

Warner, Marina. *Phantasmagoria: Spirit Visions, Metaphors and Media into the Twenty-First Century*. Oxford: Oxford University Press, 2006.

Weisberg, Barbara. *Talking to the Dead: Kate and Maggie Fox and the Rise of Spiritualism*. New York: HarperCollins, 2005.

Weiss, Edoardo. *Sigmund Freud as a Consultant: Reflections of a Pioneer in Psychoanalysis*. London: Transaction, 1991.

Widlöcher Daniel. "The Third in Mind." *Psychoanalytic Quarterly* 73 (2004): 197–221.

Wilson, Leigh. *Modernism and Magic: Experiments with Spiritualism, Theosophy and the Occult*. Edinburgh: Edinburgh University Press, 2012.

"Witches Cast 'Mass Spell' against Donald Trump." *BBC News*. February 25, 2017. https://www.bbc.com/news/world-us-canada-39090334.

Wooffitt, Robin. "Relational Psychoanalysis and Anomalous Communication: Continuities and Discontinuities in Psychoanalysis and Telepathy." *History of the Human Sciences* 30, no. 1 (2017): 118–137.

Yaguello, Marina. *Lunatic Lovers of Language: Imaginary Languages and Their Inventors*. Translated by C. Slater. London: Athlone, 1991.

Index